JOURNAL FOR THE STUDY OF THE NEW TESTAMENT
SUPPLEMENT SERIES
140

Sheffield Academic Press

‘Put on the Armour of God’

The Divine Warrior from Isaiah to Ephesians

Thomas R. Yoder Neufeld

Journal for the Study of the New Testament
Supplement Series 140

Published by Sheffield Academic Press Ltd
Mansion House
19 Kingfield Road
Sheffield S11 9AS
England

Printed on acid-free paper in Great Britain
by Bookcraft Ltd
Midsomer Norton, Bath

British Library Cataloguing in Publication Data

A catalogue record for this book is available
from the British Library

ISBN 1-85075-655-4

CONTENTS

ACKNOWLEDGMENTS

I take pleasure in acknowledging my debt to the many teachers, students and colleagues who have accompanied me in this endeavour: Professors George McRae, SJ, and Helmut Koester, advisors of my doctoral thesis at the Harvard University Divinity School, the earlier version of this present work; Professors John Strugnell and Theodore Hiebert, readers of that first version; Professor Dieter Georgi, whose influence on my thinking reaches back to my MDiv studies at Harvard Divinity School in the early 1970s; fellow students, companions, and friends Barbara Bowe and Sze-Kar Wan, whose friendship will last a lifetime; and my colleagues and friends at Conrad Grebel College and the University of Waterloo. All scholarship is by its very nature collaborative. I give thanks for this collaborative community.

I owe an even greater debt of gratitude to my immediate and extended family for their prayerful and constant support, most especially to my almost always patient children David and Miriam and always encouraging spouse Rebecca, to whom this book is dedicated with much love.

My deepest gratitude belongs to God, whose sustaining and prodding presence has accompanied me throughout this process, and who has seen to it that the toil of scholarship has more often than not brought the pleasure of encounter with divine Wisdom.

Lastly, I gratefully acknowledge the support of the University of Waterloo/Social Sciences and Humanities Research Council in providing me with a grant for computer equipment and software that enabled me to prepare this manuscript for publication, and to my academic home, Conrad Grebel College, which aided generously in the costs of publication.

ABBREVIATIONS

AB	Anchor Bible
AGJU	Arbeiten zur Geschichte des antiken Judentums und des Urchristentums
AnBib	Analecta Biblica
ANET	J.B. Pritchard (ed.), *Ancient Near Eastern Texts*
BAGD	W. Bauer, W.F. Arndt, F.W. Gingrich and F.W. Danker, *Greek-English Lexicon of the New Testament*
BBB	Bonner biblische Beiträge
BDB	F. Brown, S.R. Driver and C.A. Briggs, *Hebrew and English Lexicon of the Old Testament*
BDF	F. Blass, A. Debrunner and R.W. Funk, *A Greek Grammar of the New Testament*
BHT	Beiträge zur historischen Theologie
Bib	*Biblica*
BNTC	Black's New Testament Commentaries
BWANT	Beiträge zur Wissenschaft vom Alten und Neuen Testament
CBQ	*Catholic Biblical Quarterly*
CBQMS	*Catholic Biblical Quarterly*, Monograph Series
EBib	Etudes bibliques
EKKNT	Evangelisch-Katholischer Kommentar zum Neuen Testament
FRLANT	Forschungen zur Religion und Literatur des Alten und Neuen Testaments
HAT	Handbuch zum Alten Testament
HNT	Handbuch zum Neuen Testament
HR	*History of Religions*
HSM	Harvard Semitic Monographs
HTR	*Harvard Theological Review*
ICC	International Critical Commentary
IDB	G.A. Buttrick (ed.), *Interpreter's Dictionary of the Bible*
IDBSup	*IDB*, Supplementary Volume
Int	*Interpretation*
IRT	Issues in Religion and Theology
ITC	International Theological Commentary
JAAR	*Journal of the American Academy of Religion*
JBL	*Journal of Biblical Literature*
JETS	*Journal of the Evangelical Theological Society*
JNES	*Journal of Near Eastern Studies*
JSJ	*Journal for the Study of Judaism in the Persian, Hellenistic and Roman Period*

JSNT	*Journal for the Study of the New Testament*
JSOTSup	*Journal for the Study of the Old Testament*, Supplement Series
LBS	Library of Biblical Studies
LCL	Loeb Classical Library
NCBC	New Century Bible Commentary
NHC	Nag Hammadi Codices
NovT	*Novum Testamentum*
NovTSup	*Novum Testamentum* Supplements
NTD	Das Neue Testament Deutsch
NTS	*New Testament Studies*
OTL	Old Testament Library
OTM	Old Testament Message
RB	*Revue biblique*
RevExp	*Review and Expositor*
SBLMS	SBL Monograph Series
SBS	Stuttgarter Bibelstudien
SBT	Studies in Biblical Theology
SHCT	Studies in the History of Christian Thought
SNTSMS	Society for New Testament Studies Monograph Series
SOTSMS	Society for Old Testament Study Monograph Series
ST	*Studia Theologica*
TBT	*The Bible Today*
TDNT	G. Kittel and G. Friedrich (eds.), *Theological Dictionary of the New Testament*
THKNT	Theologischer Handkommentar zum Neuen Testament
TLZ	*Theologische Literaturzeitung*
VC	*Vigiliae christianae*
VT	*Vetus Testamentum*
VTSup	*Vetus Testamentum*, Supplements
WUNT	Wissenschaftliche Untersuchungen zum Neuen Testament
ZAW	*Zeitschrift für die alttestamentliche Wissenschaft*
ZWT	*Zeitschrift für wissenschaftliche Theologie*

INTRODUCTION

The impetus for this study of the Divine Warrior in full armour was provided by the Harvard Divinity School New Testament Graduate Seminar in 1984 under the direction of the late George MacRae, SJ. The focus of the seminar was on Roman Christianity, one facet of which was an examination of the Letter to the Ephesians as a possible exemplar of Christianity centred in Rome. It fell to me and a few of my fellow students to explore that document for the term. While the question of its Roman provenance remained purely exploratory, and in the end unresolved, this did not inhibit a full and wide-ranging exploration of Ephesians. Indeed, the study of this central work within the Pauline corpus became and has remained a major focus of study for me over the past years, motivated by scholarly as well as theological and pastoral interests.

I remember well how on one long week-end in the basement of the Harvard Divinity School library (surely not the first or the last work conceived in that fruitful womb) I was struck by the importance of power and empowerment in Ephesians. My attention fixed quickly on chapters 1 and 3, but especially on the motif in chapter 6 of believers in the armour of God, at war with the powers in the heavens. I came to recognize in that image not only the author's dramatic concluding exhortation, but the climax of and the integrating motif for the whole of Ephesians and its vision of the church and its task. This encounter with the core vision of Ephesians gripped me to the degree that I engaged in a lengthy study of Eph. 6.10-20 and the tradition of the Divine Warrior which informs it. While the study of Ephesians 6 occasioned the quest, then, the following study was motivated not only by interest in the (canonical) end point of the tradition, but in the preceding stages of development as well—Isaiah 59, Wisdom of Solomon 5, and 1 Thessalonians 5.

Early aspirations to scratch the very edges of the cosmos in pursuit of the meaning of the Divine Warrior in full armour in Ephesians 6 eventually met up with reality and gave way to the more modest objective of understanding the pre-history of the motif of the Divine Warrior so as to assess more carefully the unique contribution of the author of Ephesians to that tradition. I set out to answer one small set of questions, which in turn became a window on an ever-widening horizon: what is behind the use of the motif of God's armour in Ephesians? from where did the author draw such imagery? and what happened to the tradition in the process?

Several issues attended this study from the very beginning: agency, status, the function of mythological and/or metaphorical terminology, and finally the relationship of the human to the divine. These issues have shown themselves to have been important whenever the motif was taken up, not only in Isaiah 59, but even when the tradition was turned on its head, as the analysis of 1 Thessalonians and Ephesians will show.

The phenomenon of taking up traditions and transforming them in order to address new circumstances and in conformity to new *Weltanschauungen* is of course by no means unique to the history of this particular motif. This study has, however, restricted itself to the single trajectory of how the Divine Warrior in full armour, appearing first in Isaiah 59, is taken up in the tradition. I have thus undertaken to examine each of the biblical texts that take up the very particular *topos* of the Divine Warrior dressed in the panoply of symbolic and metaphorical armour, beginning with Isaiah 59 and ending with Ephesians 6. Each of the texts has been given thorough attention, first, because they are each a creation in their own right, and secondly, because such attention allows for a greater appreciation of the creative and innovative intertextuality at work in the tradition of this specific *topos*. In this way the creative genius of each of the tradents emerges in its own right. The fact that this dissertation began as an attempt to understand the meaning and role of the tradition of the Divine Warrior in armour in Ephesians explains why Ephesians has received a disproportionate share of attention.

This study can be read, then, from a number of different yet overlapping vantage points. First, it represents careful exegetical attention to each of the texts which take up the motif of the armed deity—Isaiah 59, Wisdom of Solomon 5, 1 Thessalonians 5, and Ephesians 6. I have provided a commentary on each of these texts, guided albeit by the specific goal of illuminating the meaning of the central motif of the armed Divine Warrior.

Secondly, as a tradition-historical study of the motif of the Divine Warrior in full armour the study illumines the scriptural tradition which the author of Ephesians appropriates and in which the letter stands. In the process the study sheds light on how tradents within early Christianity used Scripture, and also on how the second generation—in this case the author of Ephesians—was both indebted to the apostolic generation—in this case Paul—and emulated the courage and creativity of that first generation of Christian prophets in its appropriation of the apostolic legacy.

Finally, this study can also be read from the other end as a *Wirkungsgeschichte* of Isaiah 59, a history that could well and fruitfully have been pursued beyond the New Testament. As such, the study can be viewed as a microscopic examination by means of one narrow tradition of how a *traditum*—to borrow terminology from Michael Fishbane—is affected, sometimes radically, by *traditio*, the act of tradition.

The present study is in essence unchanged from the dissertation accepted at the Harvard Divinity School in 1989 for the degree of Doctor of Theology in New Testament and Christian Origins. The original title was 'God and Saints at War: The Transformation and Democratization of the Divine Warrior in Isaiah 59, Wisdom of Solomon 5, 1 Thessalonians 5, and Ephesians 6'. It has been edited for purposes of style and accuracy, but the essential elements of analysis and argumentation have not been revisited and altered. The wisdom of leaving well enough alone lies in the careful attention the thesis received at the hands of advisor Professor Helmut Koester, who graciously took over the task of advising the project after the untimely death of my original thesis advisor, Father George MacRae, SJ, and readers Professors John Strugnell and Theodore Hiebert. The debt I owe Professor Dieter Georgi is evident throughout the study. They will be relieved to know that I take full responsibility for both listening to their wisdom and on occasion persisting in going my own way. The limitations of leaving things largely as they were are obvious. The river of scholarship never stops flowing. At the same time I remain convinced about the findings that constitute the core of this study and am delighted to contribute this small tributary to that river.

To conclude, the following quest is not unrelated to the vexing issues of ethics and theology, most particularly for one who stands quite consciously and unrepentantly within the so-called Historic Peace Church tradition, more specifically within the Mennonite community of faith. These connections and their implications will of necessity need to remain unexplored within the parameters of this particular study. Even so, the passion which has driven this project from the outset is rooted in the present quest of the church to find its way as a community of peace in a world marked by violence and oppression. It is my fundamental conviction that, whatever the difficulties and however ironically, the tradition of divine warfare is related to the concerns of peace in a salutary way.

Chapter 1

THE DIVINE WARRIOR IN ISAIAH 59

Isaiah 59 is a discrete unit of tradition within Third Isaiah. It constitutes a poetic response to a lament or an accusation that Yahweh is not capable of responding to a society run amok. After describing in striking and creative ways the nature of social disintegration, the poem concludes with a description of Yahweh arising as Divine Warrior, armed and clothed for battle. In the process a tradition is born which will be taken up in the texts studied in following chapters. Here we will explore both the traditions upon which and by means of which this poem is constructed and the innovations it introduces into the stream of tradition.

1. *The Context of Isaiah 59*

The historical context of Isaiah 59 is difficult to establish. This is not least the case because the poem is quite clearly a collage of various forms, containing elements of prophetic accusation, lament and theophany, elaborated with allegory-like metaphors (v. 14) and lists of vices (vv. 4-8, 13). This artful combination of once discrete forms need not indicate that Isaiah 59 itself emerged bit by bit over a long period of time in different contexts. Indeed, it is characteristic of postexilic prophecy to combine and alter once distinct forms and traditions in order to unleash the prophetic word into new contexts.[1]

While the nature of the material makes a specific determination of place and time difficult, there is no reason to debate the scholarly consensus that it is a postexilic text, part of the tradition labelled 'Third

1. P.D. Hanson, *The Dawn of Apocalyptic* (Philadelphia: Fortress Press, 1975), p. 113; Hanson believes the author of Isa. 59 to have generated a new form out of the mix, dubbing it the 'salvation-judgment oracle' (pp. 119-20). N.K. Gottwald suggests that this phenomenon characterizes prophecy generally (*The Hebrew Bible: A Socio-Literary Introduction* [Philadelphia: Fortress Press, 1985], p. 306).

Isaiah'. Much more than that is impossible to establish. While Paul Hanson recognizes this about Isaiah 59,[2] he has nevertheless furnished the most extensive proposal regarding the historical, religious, and social context of Third Isaiah, and reads Isaiah 59 in light of that larger picture.[3]

Hanson proposes that Isaiah 56–66 reflects a major change in the Palestinian community after the return of the exiles to Palestine. A serious rift developed between returning Zadokites who believed themselves to be the legitimate custodians of the cult, on the one hand, and Levites who had remained in Palestine as well as visionary followers of Second Isaiah, on the other. The coalition of Levites and visionaries was effectively barred from access to the cult. The literature identified as Third Isaiah expresses their early hopes (chs. 60–62), but also their increasing bitterness and hostility, one expression of which is Isaiah 59. In keeping with their inherited prophetic tradition, Third Isaiah visionaries identified themselves as a communal Suffering Servant (65.1-7). Their tactic was to call down oracles of judgment (ch. 59), and to disbar in their own way the majority party from the true cult (58.6; 66.1-3). But in discontinuity with that prophetic tradition, this visionary group reclaimed prophetic hope and expectation in a way indifferent to 'plain history' and thus quite separate from the dynamics of human instrumentality. Judgment and salvation were now conceived of in wider cosmic terms, but also in terms of a sectarian narrowness Hanson believes betrayed the universalism of Second Isaiah's vision of *shalom*. It is this which, according to Hanson, constitutes the matrix of apocalyptic eschatology.

In this scenario Isaiah 59 represents an important landmark on the road to apocalyptic, in that it employs the familiar motif of the Divine Warrior, but now in an unabashedly cosmic and mythological way adumbrative of later more fully-developed apocalyptic imagery and eschatology. The motif of the Divine Warrior is severed from Yahweh's

2. Hanson, *Dawn of Apocalyptic,* p.118.

3. Hanson, *Dawn of Apocalyptic,* pp. 25-31, 209-28, 280-86. Hanson has reiterated his thesis with little modification in *The People Called: The Growth of Community in the Bible* (San Francisco: Harper & Row, 1986), pp. 254-90; cf. also the earlier 'Jewish Apocalyptic against its Near Eastern Environment', *RB* 78 (1971), pp. 31-58; 'Old Testament Apocalyptic Reexamined', *Int* 25 (1971), pp. 454-79; repr. in P.D. Hanson (ed.), *Visionaries and their Apocalypses* (IRT, 4; Philadelphia: Fortress Press; London: SPCK, 1983), pp. 37-60).

acting in the 'real history' of real historical communities, that is, within 'the harsh realities of the mundane world'.[4] Hanson finds here the well-springs of the sectarianism and chiliasm characteristic of those communities that would for the next centuries be producing apocalyptic literature.[5]

There is little reason to doubt that Isaiah 59 emerged within an increasingly polarized Palestinian community. However, given that chapter's discrete nature within the corpus of Third Isaiah and the non-specific character of its contents, it is not necessary or even suitable to read the text solely in the light of specifically identifiable intracommunal factionalism. A more likely polarization is that of prophet (or prophetic circle) over against the people. Such a polarity fits quite well into virtually any postexilic situation.[6]

2. *An Analysis of Isaiah 59*

Isaiah 59 begins with a response to an implied lament like that found in Isa. 58.3, but now modelled specifically on Isa. 50.2, to the effect that Yahweh is too weak to liberate the suffering people. The prophetic poet responds that it is not the shortness of Yahweh's hand that accounts for the people's difficulties. It is their iniquities that have alienated them from Yahweh, or vice versa. Although somewhat muted, the prophetic

4. Hanson, *Visionaries*, pp. 50-51.

5. Cf. scholars who with some variation approach Third Isaiah similarly: J. Blenkinsopp, *A History of Prophecy in Israel* (Philadelphia: Westminster Press, 1983), pp. 242-51, but especially p. 249; *idem*, 'Interpretation and the Tendency to Sectarianism: An Aspect of the Second Temple History', in E.P. Sanders, A.I. Baumgarten and A. Mendelson (eds.), *Jewish and Christian Self-Definition*. II. *Aspects of Judaism in the Graeco-Roman Period* (Philadelphia: Fortress Press, 1981), p. 13; R.P. Carroll, *When Prophecy Failed: Reactions and Responses to Failure in the Old Testament Prophetic Traditions* (London: SCM Press, 1979), p. 205; O. Eissfeldt, *The Old Testament: An Introduction* (trans. P.R. Ackroyd; New York: Harper & Row, 1965), p. 344; J. Muilenburg, 'The Book of Isaiah, Chapters 40–66', in G.A. Buttrick (ed.), *The Interpreter's Bible* (New York/Nashville: Abingdon Press, 1956), V, p. 414; C. Westermann, *Isaiah 40–66: A Commentary* (trans. D.M.G. Stalker; Philadelphia: Westminster Press, 1969), pp. 295-96; Gottwald, *Hebrew Bible*, pp. 507, 509.

6. The lack of specific signals, and the presence of a collage of forms and traditions, led P. Volz (*Jesaia II* [KAT, Leipzig: Scholl, 1932; Hildesheim: Georg Olms, 1974], pp. 197-202) to date various portions from pre-exilic to Hellenistic times, illustrating the ubiquitously timely nature of the material.

condemnatory response in vv. 2 and 3 serves not only to condemn the people but to explain Yahweh's withdrawal of help.

Their iniquities are various. The polluting (גאל) of the hands with blood in v. 3 has been taken to refer to abuse of the cult, especially when read in light of the concerns of ch. 58.[7] However, the use of defilement language to describe violent behaviour does not necessarily imply cultic critique *per se*. Cultic behaviour is identified as the practice of social solidarity and justice in Isa. 58.6-7, 66.3, and earlier (or later?) in 1.10-17. And the issues under criticism in ch. 59 are quite generally socio-ethical, and not specifically related to the cult.[8] Indeed, the sins listed in v. 3 are so general as to serve as an 'all-purpose' characterization of social and ethical disintegration.

Verses 4-8 elaborate upon v. 3 in a tone less personal and more formally condemning, and with a change from the second to the third person plural.[9] Various images of adders, spiders' webs, and snakes, and general descriptions of people who have turned from peace, truth, and justice to violence and destruction are used to depict the disintegration of

7. E. Achtemeier, *The Community and Message of Isaiah 56–66* (Minneapolis: Augsburg, 1982), p. 64. Hanson (*Dawn of Apocalyptic*, pp. 120-21) sees also in פנים (v. 3) a *terminus technicus* of the 'normative cult', and translates it as 'presence'; cf. Muilenburg, 'Book of Isaiah', p. 687; J.D. Smart, *History and Theology in Second Isaiah: A Commentary on Isaiah 35, 40–66* (Philadelphia: Westminster Press, 1965), p. 253. Nothing else in this chapter implies an identifiable institutional setting, however. Cf. incidentally hand, arm, and countenance (פנה) as means of divine deliverance in Ps. 44.4.

8. This is not to deny the relationship between cultic and ethical performance: Isa. 58.6-7, 66.3, and 1.10-17 presuppose it. However, controversy over the cult is not the issue in Isaiah 59 (*contra* Hanson, *Dawn of Apocalyptic*, pp. 119-22).

9. K. Pauritsch, *Die neue Gemeinde: Gott sammelt Ausgestoßene und Arme (Jesaia 56–66)* (AnBib, 47; Rome: Biblical Institute Press, 1971), p. 96: the third person plural 'verweist [...] auf die Anklagenden vor Gericht', that is, the tone is typical of judicial accusation. Hanson (*Dawn of Apocalyptic*, p. 119) sees all of vv. 1-8 closely resembling 'the indictment section of the classical judgment oracle.' Pauritsch (*Die Neue Gemeinde*, p. 95) sees in v. 4 already a shift to a general state of apostasy. 'Die Lage ist festgefahren, die Gottesbeziehung gestört'. Westermann (*Isaiah 40–66*, pp. 344-46) suggests that vv. 1-8 represent a weakened form of the prophetic charge ('prophetic torah'—Achtemeier; 'Bußpredigt'—Volz). He sees it as a response to the implicit charge against God expressed in a lament—'weakened' in the sense that there is no clear relationship between the prophetic accusation and imminent judgment, only a desire to inform of transgression in order to 'mend' the present.

social solidarity.[10] Such 'generalized scolding'[11] is summarized in v. 8 with the twice-repeated phrase, 'The way of peace (דרך שׁלום) they know not'.

Verse 9 introduces another shift in perspective. The first person plural now ostensibly replaces the accuser. Whether or not this shift is modelled on a liturgical scenario of accusation–confession–promise,[12] the 'we' now own up to and lament the characterization of apostasy described in the first eight verses. Perhaps the 'we' includes the prophet or preacher who identifies himself rhetorically with the community he has been accusing. In that way the state of affairs is now not only identified but identified with.[13] Nothing changes thereby regarding the identity of the 'we'; they are the accused of vv. 3-8.[14] Once again the desperate state of affairs is described by means of a mixture of general moralisms and animal imagery (vv. 11-13). Rather than snakes and spiders who attempt to catch the innocent in their snares, we now find bears and doves hungrily bemoaning the absence of justice.[15]

10. M. Fishbane (*Biblical Interpretation in Ancient Israel* [Oxford: Clarendon Press, 1985], p. 498 n. 103) suggests that vv. 4-5 take up the language of 1.21, 24, 27. Cf. on this also especially H. Odeberg, who sees specifically vv. 5-8 as reflective of Hos. 10, Second Isaiah, and Job 15, belonging to 'a time when writings of so different ages already formed part of a treasure of holy or venerated books, which were read and meditated upon and which influenced, in unison, the language of religious authors' (*Trito-Isaiah: A Literary and Linguistic Analysis* [Uppsala: Lundeqvist, 1931], p. 181). Whether or not the recognition of dependency and reappropriation of tradition constitues a basis for denying these verses to the author of the rest of the chapter (denied by Hanson, *Dawn of Apocalyptic*, p. 119, Westermann, *Isaiah 40–66*, p. 347), it does suggest that traditional images and language are chosen to signal more than to describe the nature of apostasy.

11. W. Brueggemann, 'Unity and Dynamic in the Isaiah Tradition', *JSOT* 29 (1984), pp. 89-107 (p. 92).

12. Muilenburg ('Book of Isaiah', pp. 687, 690) refers to this section as the *Confiteor* of the liturgy; less explicitly liturgical is Pauritsch (*Neue Gemeinde*, p. 96), who sees the original matrix to have possibly been the *Bußfeier*, but he considers that context as no longer immediate.

13. J. Fischer, *Das Buch Isaias* (Bonn: Peter Hanstein, 1939), p. 167; Smart, *History and Theology*, p. 254; C.C. Torrey, *The Second Isaiah* (New York: Charles Scribner's Sons, 1928), p. 441; Westermann's position combines elements of the last two suggestions (*Isaiah 40–66*, pp. 348-49).

14. *Contra* those who see 'we' and 'they' reflecting two hostile camps.

15. Westermann (*Isaiah 40–66*, p. 347), among others, suggests that at least the doves are an allusion to the sounds of mourning. But given the difficulties he has with the bears making mourning sounds, perhaps the image of hunger is not too

Verse 12 explicitly transforms the lament of vv. 9-11 into a confession before Yahweh. Verse 13 then elaborates, much as do vv. 4-8 *vis-à-vis* v. 3, the sins admitted to in v. 12.[16] The absence of justice is identified as the result of the confessers' own sin, characterized as in vv. 3-8 as dishonesty and violence.[17]

Verses 14 and 15a continue the elaboration of the state of apostasy with a brief allegory on the fate of the virtues, already anticipated in the personification of משפט in v. 9 and perhaps even in v. 8:[18] Justice (משפט) is driven back, Righteousness (צדקה) stands at a distance, Truth (אמת) has stumbled in the squares, Uprightness (נכחה) cannot enter; Truth (אמת) is absent and the one who turns from evil (סר מרע) is victimized.[19] Verse 15a does not easily fit the allegory or 'story', but in its present location it does continue the story of the victimization of the good virtues.

Hereupon follows a dramatic scene change.[20] 'And Yahweh looked

farfetched. Fischer (*Buch Isaias*, p. 168) comes closest to this suggestion by having the bears grumble at the absence of justice ('Der brummende Bär symbolisiert den Unwillen der Gemeindeglieder über...') and the doves moan in anticipation of it ('...seufzen nach...'). To hunger for justice does not, however, mean that the hungry are not responsible for its absence (cf. Isa. 58.1-3).

16. Achtemeier refers to vv. 13-15a as a 'chilling catalogue of rebellion' (*Community and Message*, p. 64). She mistakes the generalized nature of this text, however, when she sees these verses as 'getting down to specifics' (p. 66).

17. The conceptual if not the linguistic parallelism to vv. 3-8 is too great not to be a deliberate allusion to the sins and sinners described there (*contra* Hanson [*Dawn of Apocalyptic*, p. 123] who sees this as a usual part of the genre of lament, and therefore in no way identifying the 'we' with the 'they' described earlier; but cf. the protestations of innocence in, e.g., Ps. 44.17-22).

18. Pauritsch, *Neue Gemeinde*, p. 96.

19. These terms have been purposely capitalized since within the 'allegory' they function as personified representatives of Yahweh. Perhaps 'the one who turns' should be capitalized too as the idealized righteous or repentant one.

20. Contrary to the position taken here, Fischer (*Buch Isaias*, p. 169) disagrees with most scholars and sees vv. 15b-20(21) as a later addition. The conclusion to the *Bußklage* has been suppressed in order to allow for a smooth transition by means of a *Stichwort* (משפט) to the theophany in vv. 15b-20, which in turn actually belongs immediately before Isa. 63.1-6, identifying it clearly with Yahweh's war against Gentiles; cf. here similarly J. Vella's reordering of the text in terms of a prophetic ריב ('court proceeding') pattern (*La giustizia di Dio nelle confessioni dei peccati* [1964], pp. 101-102; cited in D. Kendall, SJ, 'The Use of Mispat in Isaiah 59', *ZAW* 96 [1984], pp. 391-92) where Isa. 59.15b-21 also immediately precedes 63.1-6 and is thus clearly focussed on Yahweh's war against outside enemies. Thus Muilenburg's *Absolutio* (his liturgical characterization of vv. 15b-20, 'Book of Isaiah', p. 687)

and it was evil in his eyes that משׁפט was absent. And he saw that there was no man, no intervenor' (אין איש...אין מפגיע, vv. 15b, 16). Therefore Yahweh himself becomes a warrior. 'His own arm brought him victory, and his righteousness supported him' (v. 16b). The Divine Warrior is then depicted as arming and clothing himself for battle. He has put on an armour of righteousness (צדקה) and salvation (ישׁועה), but has clothed himself also in garments of vengeance (נקם) and jealousy (קנאה, v. 17). This is often read as Yahweh's response to the lament in vv. 9-15a, as his intervention on behalf of the victimized. The use of the past tense, however, suggests that these verses are intended to depict Yahweh's *past* response to the sins of the people, thereby explaining the present distress, and warning at the same time of future judgment.[21]

The introduction of the Divine Warrior thus continues the explanation begun at the outset of the chapter as to why things have been so bad. Only now the people themselves give voice to that recognition. The implied lament in v. 1 that Yahweh's help is absent gives way here to the recognition that Yahweh has indeed been present, but as enemy. In vv. 18 and 19 the Divine Warrior comes to repay, to frighten, and to overwhelm: Yahweh (will) bring(s)[22] requital (שׁלם) upon his enemies for their deeds.[23] They (will) fear Yahweh's name and glory, for he (will)

takes the form of suppression of 'Israel's' enemies, rather than punishment of intra-community enemies.

21. So also Pauritsch, *Neue Gemeinde*, p. 92: the image of the Divine Warrior in full armour describes 'verallgemeinernd das Gerichtshandeln Jahwes an den Gottlosen schlechthin…'

22. It is usual to translate the imperfect as a future tense. But it is possible to translate the imperfect as having the meaning of habitual action. Given the general nature of the factors which bring out the warrior in Yahweh (vv. 3-8, 12-15a), it may be fitting to translate this as a habitual present, 'According to their deeds does he requite…'

23. With most critics, Hanson (*Dawn of Apocalyptic*, p. 117 n. 1) sees 'to the coastlands he will render requital' as a gloss due to the secondary influence of Second Isaiah (40.15; 41.1, 5 [where the coastlands/islands are afraid of the Divine Warrior], 42.4, 10; 49.1; 51.5; cf. also 23.2, 6 and 60.9; 66.19). It may represent a glossator's attempt to universalize the Divine Warrior's activity, or perhaps to redirect his activity toward the Gentiles. Fischer (*Buch Isaias*, p. 170) agrees that this is likely a gloss, but he agrees with the glossator's understanding that the Divine Warrior's warfare is directed at the Gentiles. Cf. discussion in Odeberg, *Trito-Isaiah*, pp. 193-95. It is worth noting that the line is absent from the LXX (ὡς ἀνταποδώσων ἀνταπόδοσιν ὄνειδος τοῖς ὑπεναντίοις), which thus likely retains the better reading.

come(s) like a raging river driven by his wind. Both wind and river are traditional images of divine warfare.

Verse 20 introduces an almost dissonant note of redemption. Yahweh (will) come(s) to Zion as redeemer and avenger (גואל), specifically for those in Jacob who turn from the transgressions described earlier.[24] For whom is Yahweh גואל? Clearly for those in Jacob who turn from iniquity (v. 20; cf. 15a). Had the author wanted the audience to identify itself as victims at the hands of the evil doers described in vv. 1-8, they would take Yahweh's arming of himself with צדקה and ישועה as divine intervention *on their behalf*. This would be to read the text as reflecting a deep rift within the postexilic community. The chapter does not, however, allow room for any such innocent party. All are implicated in the description of this apostate society. To repent is to have been a part of that which falls under the wrath of Yahweh. His coming to Zion as גואל clearly represents promise for the repentant. But the text need not intend to say more than that those who persist in transgressions fall into the category of enemies who can expect the full wrath of the Divine Warrior; those who turn from these ways can expect that warfare to represent their vindication. This language does not emerge out of an existing rift within the community so much as it uses the motif of the Divine Warrior to warn urgently of the consequences of violence and corruption.

Finally, v. 21 represents Yahweh's covenantal promise or oracle of assurance to Jacob (v. 20b). While there is thematic continuity with the shift from requital to redemption in v. 20, and while it can function as a bridge to the invitation for Zion to rise to the light of Yahweh's glory (60.1), the vast majority of scholars see v. 21 as a redactional addition to Isaiah 59.

The structure of Isaiah 59 can thus be summarized as follows: The chapter begins with an accusatory and explanatory response to an implied lament by means of a general description of apostasy (vv. 1-8); an explicit lament follows (vv. 9-11), giving way to a confession (v. 12), which in turn includes further characterization of apostasy. The description of the (past) appearance of the Divine Warrior at this point functions as the further explanation of the full consequences of apostasy, as a warning of judgment and as a promise of vindication for the repentant.

24. The ו in ולשבי is epexegetical (so also Hanson, *Dawn of Apocalyptic*, p. 117).

3. *The Divine Warrior*

The figure of the Divine Warrior in Isaiah 59 owes much to the tradition of the Divine Warrior in Israel, and is thus a familiar figure to both author and audience.[25] Indeed, the striking modifications to which the author subjects the motif presuppose such familiarity.

The Divine Warrior is celebrated in the great war hymns of Israel such as Exodus 15, Deuteronomy 32, 33, Judges 5, 2 Samuel 22//Psalm 18,

25. The literature on the tradition of divine warfare is extensive. For example, B. Albrektson, *History and the Gods: An Essay on the Idea of Historical Events as Divine Manifestations in the Ancient Near East and in Israel* (Lund: Gleerup, 1967); F.M. Cross, 'The Divine Warrior in Israel's Early Cult', in A. Altmann (ed.), *Biblical Motifs: Origins and Transformations* (Studies and Texts, 3; Cambridge, MA: Harvard University Press, 1966), pp. 11-30; *idem*, 'The Song of the Sea and Canaanite Myth', *JTC* 5 (1968), pp. 1-25; both in his *Canaanite Myth and Hebrew Epic: Essays in the History of the Religion of Israel* (Cambridge, MA: Harvard University Press, 1973), pp. 79-144; H. Fredriksson, *Jahwe als Krieger: Studien zum alttestamentlichen Gottesbild* (Lund: Gleerup, 1945); R.M. Good, 'The Just War in Ancient Israel', *JBL* 104 (1985), pp. 385-400; N.K. Gottwald, *The Tribes of YHWH: A Sociology of the Religion of Liberated Israel 1250–1050 BCE* (Maryknoll, NY: Orbis Books, 1979); *idem*, 'War, Holy', *IDBSup* (1976), pp. 942-44; T. Hiebert, *God of my Victory: The Ancient Hymn in Habakkuk 3* (HSM, 38; Atlanta: Scholars Press, 1986); M.C. Lind, *YHWH is a Warrior: The Theology of Warfare in Ancient Israel* (Scottdale, PA: Herald Press, 1980); P.D. Miller, *The Divine Warrior in Early Israel* (HSM, 5; Cambridge, MA: Harvard University Press, 1973); *idem*, 'El the Warrior', *HTR* 60 (1967), pp. 411-31; *idem*, 'God the Warrior: A Problem in Biblical Interpretation and Apologetics', *Int* 19 (1965), pp. 39-46; G. von Rad, *Der heilige Krieg im alten Israel* (Göttingen: Vandenhoeck & Ruprecht, 5th edn, 1969 [1951]); H.H. Schmid, 'Heiliger Krieg und Gottesfrieden im Alten Testament', in *Altorientalische Welt in der alttestamentlichen Theologie: Sechs Aufsätze* (Zürich: Theologischer Verlag, 1974); F. Schwally, *Semitische Kriegsaltertümer, Erstes Heft: Der heilige Krieg im alten Israel* (Leipzig: Dieterich'sche Verlagsbuchhandlung, Theodor Weicher, 1901); R. Smend, *Jahwekrieg und Stämmebund: Erwägungen zur ältesten Geschichte Israels* (Göttingen: Vandenhoeck & Ruprecht, 1963); F. Stolz, *Jahwes und Israels Kriege: Kriegstheorien und Kriegserfahrungen im Glauben des alten Israels* (Zürich: Theologischer Verlag, 1972); L.E. Toombs, 'War, ideas of', *IDB*, IV, pp. 796-801; M. Weinfeld, 'Divine Intervention in War in Ancient Israel and in the Ancient Near East', in H. Tadmor and M. Weinfeld (eds.), *History, Historiography and Interpretation: Studies in Biblical and Cuneiform Literatures* (Jerusalem: Magnes, 1983), pp. 121-47; M. Weippert, '"Heiliger Krieg" in Israel und Assyrien: Kritische Anmerkungen zu Gerhard von Rads Konzept des "Heiligen Krieges im alten Israel"', *ZAW* 84 (1972), pp. 460-93.

Psalms 68, 77, and Habakkuk 3.[26] The Isaianic corpus also contains references to Yahweh as an איש מלחמות (Isa. 42.13; cf. Exod. 15.3). In Isaiah of Jerusalem the most characteristic feature of the Divine Warrior is that of Yahweh warring against his own people.[27] To be sure, there are also a number of instances where Yahweh makes war against foreign nations.[28] In Second Isaiah most striking is the way the Divine Warrior fights mostly as גואל on behalf of his people[29] against the nations (איים, 'coastlands' or 'islands').[30] Particularly illustrative is ch. 51, where Yahweh comforts Zion with assurances of justice, deliverance, his mighty arm, and salvation (vv. 4-6). This is followed by the fusion of the cosmogonic myth of the destruction of the sea monster Rahab and allusion to the Exodus as a plea for Yahweh to rise once again to lead the way to a second Exodus (vv. 9-11).

26. An inventory of divine weaponry in these texts indicates the provenance of some of the imagery in Isa. 59. Exod. 15: floods, right hand, fury as fire, breath, wind; Deut. 32: arrows, hunger, heat, pestilence, sword, vengeance and requital (נקם ושלם); Deut. 33.1, 2 (a fragment of one of the oldest war hymns): flaming fire; 2 Sam. 22.9-16//Ps. 18.8-15: smoke, fire, darkness, brightness, cherub, wind (spirit), arrows, lightning, breath; Ps. 68.17: mighty chariotry by the thousands; Ps. 77.16-18: thunder, lightning, whirlwind; Hab. 3: pestilence, plague, horses, chariots, bow and arrows, and spear.

27. For example, 1.24-26 (wrath, hand, smelter's fire); 5.25 (following woes against Israel; note the 'hand' as representative of Yahweh's might and the sentence, 'For all this his anger is not turned away and his hand is stretched out still'); 9.8–10.11 (note the refrain in 9.12, 17, 21; 10.4: 'For all this his anger is not turned away...'); cf. the reference to Assyria as Yahweh's means of judgment against Ephraim in 28.2 (hail, tempest, storm of waters, violence); Yahweh puts Jerusalem under siege in 29.3-10 (thunder, earthquake, great noise, whirlwind, tempest, flame, multitude of nations, deep sleep).

28. For example, 13.3-5; 19.1-5; 30.27-28 (name, burning with anger, smoke, lips and tongue of fire, breath like a raging river); cf. especially ch. 34, where Yahweh's rage extends to all peoples, and to the host of heaven itself; see prominent role of the sword (vv. 5, 6) and the representative role of Bozrah and Edom (v. 6b; cf. 63.1); there is a strong likelihood that ch. 34 may derive from the same general postexilic period as Third Isaiah (cf. R.E. Clements, *Isaiah 1–39* [NCBC; Grand Rapids: Eerdmans, 1980], p. 271, for literature and arguments); cf. here also Isa. 66.15, 16 (chariots like the stormwind, anger and fury, flames of fire, sword).

29. For example, 40.9-10 (might and arm, reward and recompense); 41.1-4 (trampling under foot, sword, bow). גואל is particularly characteristic of Second Isaiah (e.g., 41.14; 43.1, 14; 44.6, 22, 24; 49.26; 52.9; 54.8).

30. איים, 40.15; 41.1, 5; there is also a usage that is not hostile: 42.4, 10; 51.5 (here the coastlands in fact await צדקה and ישועה), 60.9.

Present in most if not all of these texts is a mixture of general metaphors of strength in combat, attendant emotions attributed to Yahweh, occasional references to weapons such as sword or bow, and more often references to phenomena such as storm, flood, or plague. Having their origin within ancient Near Eastern mythologies, in which many were once war deities in their own right,[31] they function now as symbols of the comprehensiveness and the overwhelming vehemence of Yahweh's warfare. The mythological language serves to leave the precise nature of Yahweh's means undefined yet suggested. No essential distinction is made between such images when they refer to Assyrians (cf. Isa. 10.3) or when they refer to the calamities of disease or famine.

With all of the rich prehistory of the imagery employed in Isa. 59.15b-19, there is an immediate *Vorlage*, namely, Isa. 63.1-6.[32] In that poem, Yahweh returns as warrior from defeating Bozrah and Edom, his battle garments still dripping with blood. In response to the sentry's query Yahweh announces צדקה, and identifies himself as one mighty to save (רב להושיע). This vocabulary is picked up in 59.16b and 17a, as are other words and phrases: Yahweh regrets having had to fight alone (אין־איש, 63.3; Yahweh had 'no helper'—אין עזר and 'no supporter'—אין סומך, v. 5; cf. 59.16a), and thus his own arm brought him victory (63.5b; cf. 59.16b); his disposition is one of anger (אף) and wrath (חמה; vv. 3, 5, 6; cf. 59.18); this is the day of vengeance (יום נקם, v. 4; cf. 59.17b) and the year of redemption (שנת גאולי, v. 4; cf. 59.20). Fundamentally different from 59.15b-20 is the slaughter of foreign enemies rather than of the unfaithful within the community. Apart from the feet that have done the trampling, as in 59.15b-20, there is no mention of weaponry such as sword or bow. Unlike 59.17, however, there is no armour imagery either. The garments (לבוש and בגד 63.1-3; cf. 59.17) have no symbolic value other than as a visual image of the effects of slaughter. If it is correct to posit a dependency of Isaiah 59 on Isaiah 63, then the armour of

31. Weinfeld, 'Divine Intervention', pp. 121-30.

32. R.N. Whybray, *Isaiah 40–66* (NCBC; Grand Rapids: Eerdmans, 1981 [1975]), p. 226; cf. also Westermann, *Isaiah 40–66*, p. 350. Volz, *Jesaia II*, p. 263, on the other hand, sees 63.1-6 as a poem directly dependent on 59.15b-20, and a *Vorlage* rather for 34.5-7. The following discussion assumes 59.15-20 to be dependent on 63.1-6. It would not be affected were both texts to be dependent on a common tradition. The position taken here would nevertheless see 59.15b-20 as the more innovative appropriation of that tradition.

the Divine Warrior in Isaiah 59 represents a significant expansion of the motif of the Divine Warrior.

More common, as we have shown, is the tradition of listing weapons and allies at Yahweh's disposal, as is the case in Isaiah 59 as well. Verse 16 refers to Yahweh's arm (זרוע),[33] which brings him victory, a familiar anthropomorphism for Yahweh's prowess as warrior in performing mighty acts of deliverance in the past. Here it represents the vindication of those for whom there was 'no man'.[34] The parallel to the victorious arm is צדקה, Yahweh's supportive ally in battle.[35] Verse 18[36] takes up the language of retributive violence already familiar in part from 63.5 (חמה; גמול and שלם, Isa. 35.4; 66.6; Jer 51.6, 56 [כי אל גמלות יהוה שלם]). Verse 19b contains the images of an enemy river (נהר צר)[37] driven by the breath, wind, or spirit of Yahweh (רוח יהוה).[38] As in Isa. 30.27 even 'the name of Yahweh' (שם־יהוה) signifies the active engagement in battle of the Divine Warrior. While Yahweh's glory (כבוד) is less directly

33. Cf. here especially its relation to mythified exodus and cosmogonic war (Rahab) in Isa. 51.9,10.

34. Cf. the texts in Deut. in which the parallelism of hand and arm function as shorthand for recollecting the Exodus event (4.34; 5.15; 7.19; 11.2; cf. Exod. 15.16!). Cf. also Jer. 32.21, and a striking inversion in Jer. 21.5, where it is the arm and the hand, combined with anger, fury, and wrath which now are forecast as coming against Zedekiah and Jerusalem. Cf. also Pss. 44.4 (3); 77.16 (15); 89.14 (13); 98.2 (1) which closely resembles Isa. 59.16, and finally Ps. 136.12. In the Isaianic corpus the image is concentrated in late texts: 30.30,32 (may be Hellenistic), 33.2 (also likely late), 40.10; 51.5, 9; 52.10; 62.8, and the parallel to 59.16 in 63.5b.

35. Cf. Isa. 63.5, where it is rage (חמה) that parallels the victorious arm. חמה appears in 59.18. Cf. also Ps. 89.14, 15 (13, 14); note there especially that arm, hand, and right hand are followed immediately by a listing of righteousness, justice, loyalty, and truth as supporting and going before the great warrior.

36. See n. 23 above for discussion of the textual problems of this verse.

37. Cf. nn. 26, 27 for river and flood images. Cf. also Ps. 93.3, 4, and within the Isaianic corpus 8.7, where Assyria is a flood overflowing its banks. In Isa. 11.15 and 19.5 the river is Yahweh's (primeval) enemy (reflective of the mythological origin of this motif). In 48.18 and 66.12 'river' becomes an image of Yahweh's blessing of his people, in contrast to images of desert and dryness. The singular combination of צר (enemy) with נהר (river) accentuates the warfare dimension of the river image (cf. also LXX: ἥξει γὰρ ὡς ποταμὸς βίαιος ἡ ὀργὴ παρὰ κυρίου, ἥξει μετὰ θυμοῦ). Note also 10.22, where צדקה overflows as destruction.

38. Cf. Isa. 40.7; Ps. 103.16, 17. More to the point is Ps. 104.3, 4.

an image of victorious warfare, one finds even there a number of striking associations.[39]

Thus while the images of weaponry and battle are not as numerous or as elaborate as in many other texts, the Divine Warrior is presented in language that clearly evokes the fearsome warrior of not only the Exodus, but of cosmogonic myth. Isaiah of Jerusalem's pre-exilic use of Divine Warrior imagery to warn of impending disaster ensures that for the postexilic audience the imagery is also evocative of the warrior's rage as experienced in the exile.

Distinctive of Isaiah 59 is attention to the Divine Warrior's taking up and clothing himself in armour in order to go into battle. Within the Isaianic corpus the only precedent for such an image is Isa. 11.5:[40] 'Righteousness (צדק) will be the girdle (אזור) or belt (אסור)[41] of his waist, and faithfulness (אמונה) the girdle (אזור) of his loins.' To be sure, this imagery refers less to armour than to the symbolic vestments of a king who judges justly. Isa. 11.4b, nevertheless, suggests a correlation between judge and victorious warrior, between judgment and warfare. Furthermore, this paean to the great warrior judge is not to God (at least not directly) but to the king, who is at best Yahweh's surrogate.[42] If the armour in Isaiah 59 is meant to allude to Isa. 11.5, then the point may well be that since there was 'no man' (i.e. a king), Yahweh himself took up the task to see to it that abuse was avenged and victims vindicated. In short, inasmuch as Isaiah 59 is read through the prism of Isaiah 11,

39. Cf. e.g. especially Exod. 15.11; Num. 14.21; Pss. 24.7-10; 29.1, 2; 97.1-6, and also Isa. 10.16, 17; 40.3-5; 58.8, and 62.2.

40. Clements, *Isaiah 1–39*, p. 122, sees this as a postexilic text, and thus not necessarily a precedent; see discussion also in O. Kaiser, *Isaiah 13–39: A Commentary* (trans. R.A. Wilson; Philadelphia: Westminster Press, 1974), p. 152-55, who takes the position that it originates with Isaiah (p.155); note the close similarity between v. 4 and Ps. 2.9.

41. Clements, *Isaiah 1–39*, p. 123.

42. The symbiotic connection between deity and king *qua* surrogate is well represented in the biblical tradition, and has its roots in Ancient Near Eastern royal ideology. (Cf. especially, Albrektson, *History and the Gods*, pp. 40-51; Weippert, '"Heiliger Krieg"', pp. 460-93.) Not surprisingly, the psalms express this relationship clearly (cf. Pss. 2, 20, 21, 72, 89, 110, 144). Psalm 18 is noteworthy in this regard for there it is Yahweh who 'girds' (מאזרני; v. 33 MT) the king with strength, and who provides him with a 'shield of (your) victory' (מגן ישעך; v. 36 MT). Cf. also Ps. 132.9, 16, 18, where Yahweh clothes his priests with צדק and ישע, and his enemies with shame (בשת).

Yahweh is pictured as exercising his functions as cosmic king and judge, smiting the earth (in particular his faithless people) with the breath of his lips.

The closest non-biblical parallel is the Akkadian *Enuma Elish,*[43] where Marduk equips himself for battle with Tiamat with weapons such as bow, arrow, mace, and net, which are then further identified as lightning, fire, wind, and flood-storm. But these are not identified symbolically as virtues, attributes, or strategic initiatives such as salvation, truth, or righteousness. Marduk is turbaned with a 'fearsome halo' and cloaked with an 'armour of terror', but there is no sign of wanting to give special symbolic significance to either cloak or halo other than as ways of speaking of his awe and power.

An important innovation in Isaiah 59 is, then, the metaphorical and symbolic dimension of the Divine Warrior's clothing and armour. The warrior's breastplate is צדקה, his helmet ישועה (welfare, deliverance, salvation, victory[44]); his garments are נקם (vengeance) and קנאה (ardour, zeal,[45] jealousy, anger). This way of describing the Divine Warrior is thoughtful and deliberate, and is thus shaped by the conviction that both the motif of the warrior and the various 'virtues,' however familiar, are capable of carrying great theological freight. The freight they carry is directly dependent on the allusive capacity they have for both author and audience.

4. *The Armour*

Comparison with the image of the warrior in Isa. 63.1-6 only accentuates the importance in ch. 59 of the warrior's armour. The focus on the warrior's appearance in 59.17 may have been given impetus by Yahweh's frightening appearance with clothes dripping with blood in 63.1-6. The focus of that poem is Yahweh's answer to the sentry's query. Yahweh boasts of his furious treading underfoot of his enemies. In Isaiah 59, however, the most memorable aspect of the theophany becomes Yahweh's armour and clothing.

This focus on armour should, nevertheless, not be taken as replacing active warfare with a static image of defence. A great deal in this

43. *ANET*, p. 66.

44. This is the preferred reading of BDB, p. 447.

45. This is the preferred reading of BDB, p. 888, understanding it as zeal for battle.

pericope evokes the active engagement of the Divine Warrior in battle. Ancient armour, it should also be remembered, served not only to protect but to impress and intimidate.[46] It represented the character and strength of the warrior, and symbolized his past and present actions.[47]

In addition to being one of the most frequent ways of speaking of Yahweh's will realized in community, as expressed in Torah and celebrated in the cult (cf. especially the psalms), צדקה (and the masculine צדק) expresses the interventions of the Divine Warrior,[48] not least in the Isaianic corpus.[49]

In Second and Third Isaiah צדקה is frequently found alongside ישועה (or variant forms of it), a term naturally often found within battle imagery, especially within contexts where Yahweh is celebrated as victorious liberator.[50] In Isa. 45.21 Yahweh introduces himself as אל־צדיק ומושיע. In 51.4-8 the terms are combined a number of times in an oracle of assurance to God's people, indeed to the nations (the coastlands eagerly await the צדקה and ישועה, the arm of God [אל־זרעי, v. 5]).[51] צדקה and ישועה thus represent the certainty and the comprehensiveness of the Divine Warrior's intervention. It is striking that in Isaiah 59 these terms appear within a context of judgment *against* Yahweh's own people. Apparently the dimension of vindication and deliverance has given way to its inverse—retributive vengeance.

Such a warrior is, not surprisingly, clothed in נקם and קנאה, symbol-

46. Cf. here again the connection of Marduk's halo and armour with terror and fright. Cf. also Homer, *Iliad* 3.319-39; 11.15-46 for examples of imposing armour.

47. Cf. the representative character of the vestments in Isa. 11.5. This feature will be explored more fully in relation to younger texts such as Wis. 5, but also Wis. 18.24, 25, and not least Eph. 6.

48. Note here particularly Pss. 48.11; 89.15, and 94.15, where Yahweh the אל־נקמות promises that משפט will return to צדקה; cf. also 97.2.

49. E.g. Isa. 1.27; 10.22; 41.2, 10.

50. Cf. especially within the Isaianic tradition 26.1; cf. 60.18; note the metaphorical use of ישועה as wall; cf. here also Ps. 62. 3, 7 (2, 6) where ישועה is listed together with rock and fortress; also Isa. 49.8; 52.7, 10, and 51.6, where it is parallel with צדקתי. Cf. its presence in the great theophanic war hymns such as Exod. 15.2; Ps. 68.20; Hab. 3.18. We might note finally Ps. 65, where the God of ישועה answers the people with צדק (again RSV translates it as 'deliverance') in v. 6 (5), but the appeal is to the deity 'girded with power' (נאזר בגבורה; v. 7 [6]), fashioning the world out of chaos by means of his might, a clear allusion to the cosmogonic conflict myth, here as a source of confidence in a liberator God.

51. Cf. also Isa. 61.10 (where Yahweh clothes Zion as a bride with righteousness and salvation); cf. 62.1; 63.1.

izing more abstractly but no less unambiguously than Isaiah 63 the retributive dimension of Yahweh's warfare. נקם and קנאה play a significant role in the characterization of the Divine Warrior within the Divine War tradition, most particularly within the postexilic Isaiah tradition: the day of vengeance (יום נקם, Isa. 34.6; 61.2; 63.4) parallels the year of requitals (שנת שלמים), the year of favour (שנת רצון), and the year of (my) deliverance (שנת גאולי) respectively. A quite possibly contemporaneous instance is found in Deut. 32.35, 41, where נקם parallels שלם (requital; cf. Isa. 59.18). נקם thus signals unambiguously the destructive side of Yahweh's deliverance.[52]

קנאה also has strong allusive qualities, dramatically expressed in the story of Phineas (Num. 25.11), who is said to have stayed the קנאה of Yahweh ('plague'[53]) with his own קנאה. The suggestion that קנאה be translated as 'ardent love',[54] as jealousy for the object of love, undervalues the context of battle and vengeance within which קנאה functions in this instance. More to the point are Isaianic texts such as Isa. 9.7 (6), where the קנאה of 'Yahweh of the armies' (יהוה צבאות) will ensure the reign of a Davidic ruler marked by משפט and צדקה.[55] Isaiah 42.13 is the most forceful precedent, where Yahweh is represented as a mighty man of wars (יהוה כגבור...כאיש מלחמות; cf. Exod. 15.3) who stirs up his zeal (קנאה).[56]

Of special importance is that the elements of Yahweh's armour are already (with the exception of נקם and קנאה) familiar from what has preceded in ch. 59 itself. Before they appear as armour they are encountered as personifications of Yahweh's initiatives toward his covenant people, as Yahweh's messengers or surrogates. They are participants, albeit as victims, in the social dynamics that are the subject of prophetic

52. Cf. again Yahweh as אל־נקמות in Ps. 94.1.

53. Plague is an ancient mythological war image; cf. e.g., Deut. 32.24; Hab. 3.5.

54. BDB, p. 888; Volz (*Jesaia II*, p. 238) wants it both ways: 'Der Eifer ist Racheeifer und Liebeseifer'. Love as 'jealousy' or 'extreme partiality' would move it closer to the context of forceful intervention *on behalf of* the loved one; cf. here Isa. 26.11 and the more contemporaneous 63.15. The question still to be answered is who the loved ones are in Isa. 59.

55. This text is likely earlier than Isa. 59, and reflective of an accession oracle for either Hezekiah or Josiah. See Clements, *Isaiah 1-39*, pp. 103-104.

56. In Isa. 42 the rising of the warrior precedes the warnings against those doing wrong. Note the mix of 'you', 'we', 'they', and 'him' (vv. 23-25) referring to the same people whose faithlessness precipitates the warfare of Yahweh against them. This is not unlike the changes in person observed in Isa. 59.

critique. צדקה, for example, is encountered first in v. 9, where the people lament that she does not overtake them. She is met again in v. 14, where, along with her companions Justice (משפט), Truth (אמת), and Uprightness (נכחה), she is being persecuted by the people. She then makes her appearance in v. 16b, supporting (סמך) the Divine Warrior, and finally in v. 17 as Yahweh's breastplate (צדקה כשרין). Yahweh's helmet, ישועה, is also encountered in v. 11, where, along with משפט, she is vainly sought for by the people.

This same personification can be observed in the case of 'virtues' or 'messengers' not specifically taken up into the armour. משפט has been banished or, at least, cannot be found on 'their' (the evil doers') roads (v. 8). The absence or distance of משפט is again noticed in v. 9 and in v. 11 where 'we' look for him, but he remains at a great distance; in v. 14 משפט is 'driven back'.[57] It is, finally, the fact that Yahweh notices what has happened to his messenger משפט, and that there was no one to intervene on his behalf, which precipitates the theophany.

Personification appears to be present as well in the case of אמת ('truth', 'fidelity') and נכחה ('uprightness') in v. 14. Less certain is the personification of אור ('light') and נגהות ('brightness') or, for that matter, חשך ('darkness') in v. 9.[58] But even a conservative count presents us with a large coterie of personified divine attributes, virtues, or messengers.

The observation is frequently made that צדקה means quite different things in the various places in this chapter. A distinction is made between צדקה as the exercise of justice in social relationships and צדקה as

57. BDB, p. 691, reads a *hophal*, as does the MT, in contrast to Hanson (*Dawn of Apocalyptic*, p. 115) who evidently reads a *hiphil* ('justice has turned back').

58. BDB, p. 618, understands נגהות (lit. 'brightness') as figurative of prosperity. Here it would seem rather to be intentionally parallel to light, and marked by association with the appearing of the Divine Warrior. Cf. especially the older text Isa. 60.1-3, at which the complaint in v. 9 may have originally taken aim, if not to the text per se, then at least to the prophecy of Third Isaiah. On the other hand, נגה and חשך do play a role in one of the most dramatic of theophanies, the pre-exilic Royal Psalm found in slightly varied form in 2 Sam. 22.13//Ps. 18.12, where חשך is a cloak in which the Divine Warrior wraps himself, and where נגה precedes him, raining coals of fire upon his enemies. In that light both brightness and darkness can be seen retrospectively (that is, within the reading of this 'sermon') as varied parts of the arsenal (or as allies) of the Divine Warrior rather than as the state of despair (9.2). Already in vv. 9-11, then, the lamenters see themselves as under attack by the Divine Warrior.

the initiative of Yahweh.[59] Verse 14 indicates, however, that a mini-allegory is being employed by which the 'virtues' later taken up in the armour are here Yahweh's messengers who are being persecuted. Thus, the distinction should not be made between social justice and Yahweh's justice. Instead, it is the intention of the author to relate the intervention of Yahweh to the exercise of justice and righteousness in human relationships.

In other instances where צדקה is pictured as a personified initiative of Yahweh, the relationship between the human and the divine is evident, and indeed accentuated. Of particular interest in this regard is Ps. 85.11 (10), a 'prophetic psalm' with strong cultic associations.[60] The realms of nature and society are deeply interwoven, and the initiatives of Yahweh and the people are thus also deeply intermeshed. Here too there is personification of חסד ('steadfast love'), אמת ('truth, faithfulness'), צדק ('righteousness'), and שׁלום ('peace', 'wholeness', 'health', and 'security'), variously dubbed by commentators as 'covenantal virtues',[61] 'personifications of divine attributes',[62] 'mythologically personified spiritual powers...messengers and servants',[63] or 'attendants of God'.[64]

If צדק together with the other characters can be said to smooth the way for Yahweh in Ps. 85.13, or, as Ps. 89.14b puts it, to go before Yahweh as his attendants, then it is not farfetched to read Isaiah 59 in this light. This reflects a growing propensity to speak of 'covenantal

59. Cf., e.g., Westermann, *Isaiah 40–66*, p. 349; Kendall, 'Use of Mispat', p. 397.

60. S. Mowinckel, *The Psalms in Israel's Worship* (trans. D.R. Ap-Thomas; 2 vols.; New York/Nashville: Abingdon Press, 1962), I, pp. 185, 191; II, pp. 61, 63.

61. C. Stuhlmueller, *Psalms*, II *(Psalms 73–150)* (OTM, 22: Wilmington, DE: Glazier, 1983), p. 51.

62. A.A. Anderson, *The Book of Psalms*. II. *(Psalms 73–150)* (NCBC; Grand Rapids: Eerdmans, 1972), p. 612.

63. A. Weiser, *The Psalms: A Commentary* (OTL; Philadelphia: Westminster Press, 1962), p. 574.

64. M. Dahood, SJ, *Psalms* (AB, 17; Garden City, NY: Doubleday, 1968), II, p. 289. With respect to Ps. 89.14, Anderson (*Psalms*, II, pp. 612, 638) disagrees with Ahlström's suggestion (*VT* 8 [1958], pp. 426ff.) that this should be seen as hypostatization. To speak of hypostatization in Isa. 59 may be to overinterpret what is still more playfully metaphorical in its personification. Cf. here also Isa. 60.17b, where Yahweh will appoint שׁלום and צדקה as overseers and taskmasters. The metaphorical nature of this is shown in the next verse, where walls are named ישׁועה (salvation, victory). Cf. also the possibly postexilic Isa. 32.16, where משׁפט and צדקה take up their dwelling in the desert and the fruitful field.

virtues' as exercised by the people and as the initiatives of Yahweh in anthropomorphic, metaphorical, even allegorical terms. To the degree that this reflects a cultic context, examples such as Psalm 85 may also indicate the origin of this representation. The audience of Isaiah 59 will thus have been familiar with personification of this kind.

Such personification aids the sermonic or confrontative purpose of the rise of the Divine Warrior. Within the 'story' of Isaiah 59, v. 15b represents a moment of suspense when Yahweh notices what has been going on. Yahweh is said to have 'seen' (ירא) and to have been 'displeased' (ירע)[65] 'that there was no justice' (כי אין משפט), 'that there was no man' (כי אין איש), and 'that there was no intervener' (כי אין מפגיע).[66] While this happens in the past tense, and thus initially as reminiscence, the triple refrain ('that there was no...') heightens the sense of gravity over Yahweh's growing awareness of the situation. Here lies the occasion for the theophany. Yahweh's fury (קנאה) is aroused by the fate of the victims, of his messengers, and he now rises to wreak vengeance upon his and their enemies.

Several interpretations offer themselves. One can read this brief litany as depicting the fate of *human* victims at the hands of the violent and corrupt. If משפט is understood correctly as representative of the exercise of justice within the covenant community, then Yahweh's intervention is a response to human victimization, that is, on behalf of those who have been denied access to משפט and צדקה (vv. 4-8). אין איש can then be read as a lament that there is no longer anyone left, i.e., as an image of human devastation. Along with the demise of משפט and צדקה, the sounds of human life have been extinguished.

More likely is that אין איש is parallel to 'no intervener' (אין מפגיע) that is, no one takes note of and intervenes on behalf of the victims of the oppressors. Here too it can be said that 'there is no משפט'. Support for

65. Hanson prefers 'realized' (וידע) and suggests that there has been significant disruption to the meter and parallel structure of 15b, and that 'balance and good sense are restored by merely supposing that an original וידע from the second stichos has been misplaced, and under the force of its new context, the ד has been changed to ר' (*Dawn of Apocalyptic*, p. 117 n. j).

66. BDB, p. 803, suggests the more general 'interposing' or 'intervening'. But as Isa. 53.12 illustrates, one might also translate מפגיע as 'intercessor.' The effect would be to accentuate the role of Yahweh as intervenor, moving the understanding close to the construct of passivity and intervention in Wis. 2–5. I sense a note of lament or accusation in this text, however, that Yahweh is forced to intervene directly in the absence of human initiatives.

this can be found in several ריב texts in Second Isaiah (41.28; 50.2) where Yahweh notices that there is 'no man' (אין איש) איש refers to a defence lawyer or advocate.[67] In short, in the personification of משפט rests the function of advocacy and intervention. With the banishing of משפט has also come the removal of the advocate of victims. Justicc has himself fallen victim. More broadly, one would read this as corresponding to the absence of a helper in the task of liberation and judgment (cf. 63.3, 5). The lament over the absent man may be allusive of the high hopes previously placed in Yahweh's prime vicar, his anointed one, here specifically as judge, advocate, and intervener. Echoes of Isaiah 11 hint at that. The terseness and generalizing tendency of this text nevertheless make that a possibility only on the level of allusion.

More likely still, however, is that the victims on whose behalf the Divine Warrior arises are not those who growl like bears and moan like doves for the food of משפט and ישועה (v. 11). For them the Divine Warrior comes cloaked in vengeance and furious zeal. Human victims may be cryptically present in 'the one who turns from evil,' whose turning brings about greater hostility yet on the part of those controlling the marketplace and the highways (v. 15a). More importantly, human victims are hidden in the personified משפט and צדקה, who are themselves driven off the highways and out of town. There are no innocent human victims who are addressed here with words of assurance, other than at the very end of the poem, and even then only the newly innocent, that is, those who repent. A fitting interpretation, then, is that Yahweh notices the disappearance of (personified) משפט, who is thus himself in need of an advocate and intervener. And since no one is there to see to the welfare of Yahweh's messenger משפט, Yahweh himself puts on the armour to act as avenger and vindicator.[68]

The scenario in Isaiah 59 is thus very much like the ubiquitous sapiential motif of the persecuted messenger of Yahweh, underlying the motif of the fate of the Just One in Wisdom, and of Jesus, Sophia, and Logos

67. Cf. here also Ezek. 22.30, where Yahweh is looking for a 'wall building man' (איש גדר גדר) who can 'stand in the breach' as an advocate for the 'people of the land' (עם הארץ) who have been treating the sojourners without justice (משפט בלא, v. 29).

68. Isa. 5.7 may be a precedent for this way of speaking about justice and righteousness within the Isaianic context. In the sapiential allegory of the Song of the Vineyard in Isa. 5.1-7 (cf. Clements, *Isaiah 1-39*, p. 57) Yahweh comes to seek out his messengers only to find the signs of murder and torture. This is then immediately followed by woes against Yahweh's enemies within Israel (cf. v. 25).

in Matthew, John, and Paul. Indeed, it appears that the author of Isaiah 59 has adapted the scenario of the faithful servant who is abused by faithless people to the fate of Yahweh's virtues at the hands of those who have turned against their God.

The human community is thus present in Isaiah 59 principally not as victim but as victimizer. The foes and enemies of Yahweh are human, more specifically members of Yahweh's own covenant community. There are no symbols of enmity such as 'the deep' (צולה; Isa. 44.27), Rahab (Isa. 51.9; cf. Ps. 89.8, 9 [9, 10]), or Leviathan (Isa. 27.1).[69] Instead, violence, falsehood, and legal corruption (vv. 3-7,13) are pictured as a direct attack on the *vicarii dei*—משפט, צדקה, אמת, and נכחה. What is to be noted here is not that Yahweh has human enemies. That is endemic to the traditions of Yahweh as a judge who enters lawsuits with his own people and who goes to war against them.[70] What is noteworthy, rather, is that even though the people's sin is pictured as against the personified virtues of Yahweh, the representation of the enemies remains solely human. This reflects clearly the sermonic emphasis on the breach between the people and Yahweh.

The response of the Divine Warrior to the outrage against his messengers happens in a number of ways. To summarize the discussion earlier, Yahweh's response is painted in the colors of mythology (arm, flood, wind, name, and glory), in order to signify that an affront against Yahweh's representatives provokes his wrath on a scale best expressed in the fearsome images of cosmogonic warfare. These are more than metaphors of violent destruction. They are evocative of Yahweh's great battles of the past and those anticipated in the future, battles both of liberation and great punishment.

A further dimension of Yahweh's response to the abuse of his messengers is to elevate them to the status of participants in the war of vindication. צדקה and ישועה, once victims, now become part of the arsenal and armour of the avenger. The audience will not miss that here it is not faithful people (whether king or the suffering righteous ones) but personified virtues whose status changes. Again, the sermonic intention of this scenario is to leave the human community little role other than that of persecutor—even if ultimately to provoke repentance within that same community (v. 20).

69. The 'coastlands' are not to be considered here as a symbol of enmity, since 59.18c is a gloss. Cf. n. 23.

70. See n. 27 for instances of this within the Isaianic corpus.

5. *Observations*

A number of features of the treatment of the Divine Warrior have been explored in this study of Isaiah 59. First of all, the author appropriates familiar traditions, both in the imagery with which the picture of the Divine Warrior is painted, and in the role the warrior plays as judge and vindicator. Yahweh is a fearsome and jealous warrior whose warfare has cosmic scope. All of these features are traditional and familiar.

For all its familiarity, a considerable degree of modification appears in the traditional motif of the Divine Warrior, specifically in the introduction of the highly metaphorical armour. Familiarity with the war poem in 63.1-6 ensures that the armour in Isaiah 59 which incorporates central virtues of Yahweh takes on central importance. Yahweh appears enveloped in those virtues which assure the survival of the covenant community, צדקה and ישועה. The fact that he is further clothed in the frightening impulses of נקם and קנאה, and that they cloak צדקה and ישועה, only accentuates the terrifying aspect of this motif. That these are nouns rather than verbs heightens their representative value as abstractions, thus forcing the audience to deal with these as representative of 'the way Yahweh is'.

The use of the motif of the Divine Warrior as response to the 'story' or allegory of the fate of Yahweh's messengers at the hands of God's people adds yet another level of adaptation and modification. צדקה and ישועה, as representatives of the other messengers, are taken up into the centre of the warfare and indeed into the very representation of the Divine Warrior. Thus the abstraction in the armour combines with personification in the story to produce a forceful indictment of the people as the enemies of Yahweh. The Divine Warrior becomes in the first instance the saviour not of his people[71] but of his own messengers or virtues.

Such a complex interweaving of familiar traditions with novel associations witnesses not to oracular activity so much as to the creative reuse of past traditions. Such a highly sapiential rearticulation of the familiar traditions of divine warfare serves precisely to surprise and confront.[72] The intent of the preacher is thus to use the tradition of the fearsome

71. To be sure, hope is held out to those who repent.

72. That dynamic is observable in Isa. 58 very clearly, as Fishbane's discussion of this phenomenon in relation to that text shows (*Biblical Interpretation*, pp. 408-40).

warrior in order to explain past experience, the people's present distress, and to warn of judgment for those who do not turn from their wicked ways.

Secondly, the gathering up of צדקה and ישועה into Yahweh's armour implies that his intervention may take the form of the forcible reestablishment of the rule of justice in the covenant community. How this is to be done is left undefined. The use of the past tense in introducing the warrior suggests to the hearers that Yahweh's warfare can take the form of natural and national disaster known from the past, that is, in ways often celebrated when directed at Israel's enemies. It also leaves open the inference that when צדקה and ישועה are practised, accompanied by whatever disruption and conflict their appearance provokes, Yahweh is active as Divine Warrior. This suggests that minimally the so-called 'recrudescence' of mythology[73] this text is sometimes seen to illustrate is indeed deeply interested in 'plain history'.[74] Mythology or at least mythologizing language in this case serves the interests of social critique. There is a certain ethicizing (and thus historicizing) of what is celebrated in the cult and in hymnody in supra-earthly terms. Apocalyptic and mythology generally calls for more or less equal enemies—for example, sons of light fighting sons of darkness, angels fighting angels, God fighting Belial.[75] Human beings fade increasingly from the centre of the action, becoming in the end little more than the field of battle between supernatural forces. In Isaiah 59 that has not happened. There are no supernatural mythological enemies. The impression is left, nevertheless, that the nature of human enmity against Yahweh as reflected in the abuse of Yahweh's initiatives is more than simply faithless and unethical living. It is participation, albeit as enemies of Yahweh, in the battle of the gods.

That is illustrated uniquely in the way the poet juxtaposes the story of the abuse of Yahweh's messengers with the appearance of the Divine Warrior, an appearance in which the once abused messengers reappear as his allies and armour, as vindicated victims, or better, as victims participating in their own vindication. This is a clever sermonic device which uses the theme of the vindication of the innocent in order to instil in the

73. Hanson, *Dawn of Apocalyptic*, p. 300.

74. *Contra* Hanson, *Dawn of Apocalyptic*, p. 292.

75. Cf. e.g. the complimentarity of various levels in 1QM, especially in chs. 15–19.

hearers a sense of how grave it is to rebel against Yahweh's will and initiative.

The basic content of this poem is then that Yahweh looks after his own, in this case to see that righteousness and justice receive their due. That means that when they are flagrantly abused or their demands ignored, Yahweh can be counted on to punish his enemies and to vindicate the victims, as he is recognized and remembered to have done so often in the past. It is an essential strategy of this sermon to leave no room for the readers other than to identify themselves with Yahweh's foes. But the strategy serves the basic goal of cajoling to repentance, to 'turning'. That, in the end, is the *raison d'être* of the sermonic poem.

Whether these tendencies should be characterized as sapiential, as suggested earlier, is open to debate.[76] Present in this text are, however, such sapiential or at least sapientializing elements as the appropriation of oracles and traditions of the past through collection, edition, addition, and restatement. This is shaped by the conviction that past oracles are eminently contemporary and that the demands of the present necessitate their adaptation and even transformation.[77] The act of collection, edition, transmission, and finally of the inclusion of interpretation into the *traditum* itself,[78] suggests that the charismatic and the prophetic are not at

76. On the difficulties of establishing the parameters of wisdom, see R.E. Murphy, 'Wisdom—Theses and Hypotheses', in J.G. Gammie, *et al.* (eds.), *Israelite Wisdom: Theological and Literary Essays in Honor of Samuel Terrien* (Missoula, MT: Scholars Press, 1978), pp. 35-42; cf. R.N. Whybray, 'Prophecy and Wisdom', in R. Coggins, A. Phillips and M. Knibb (eds.), *Israel's Prophetic Tradition: Essays in Honour of Peter R. Ackroyd* (Cambridge: Cambridge University Press, 1982), pp. 181-89.

For the relationship between the Isaianic tradition and wisdom, see Johannes Fichtner, 'Jesaja unter den Weisen', *TLZ* 74 (1949), pp. 75-80; repr. as 'Isaiah among the Wise', trans. B.W. Kovacs, in J.L. Crenshaw (ed.), *Studies in Ancient Israelite Wisdom* (LBS; New York: Ktav, 1976), pp. 429-38; J. Jensen, OSB, *The Use of tôrâ by Isaiah: His Debate with the Wisdom Tradition* (CBQMS, 3; Washington, DC: Catholic Biblical Association, 1973); W. McKane, *Prophets and Wise Men* (SBT, 44; London: SCM Press, 1965); J.M. Ward, 'The Servant's Knowledge in Isaiah 40–50', in Gammie, *et al.* (eds.), *Israelite Wisdom*, pp. 121-36.

77. See discussion in J. Barton, *Oracles of God: Perceptions of Ancient Prophecy in Israel after the Exile* (London: Darton, Longman and Todd, 1986), *passim;* his approach is anticipated by G. von Rad, *Old Testament Theology*. II. *The Theology of Israel's Prophetic Tradtions* (trans. D.M.G. Stalker; New York/ Evanston: Harper & Row, 1965), pp. 33-49.

78. Cf. Fishbane, *Biblical Interpretation*, pp. 495-99.

war with the oral or literary act of tradition. Indeed, the redactional and interpretive activity is evidence of schoolish[79] or even 'bookish'[80] activity. That is to say, the way traditions such as those encountered in Isaiah 59 are digested, utilized, and transmitted is essentially communal.[81]

In this sermonic poem, then, sapiential and prophetic interests and strategies converge. The author is concerned to lay bare the socio-ethical disintegration of the postexilic community. This is done not with specific descriptions but with generalized lists of vices. It is also done by means of metaphor and allegorical allusions to the fate of Yahweh's messengers. This may as yet be no more than a sophisticated preaching device, intended in parable-like fashion to accuse the readers and hearers of their sin and to cajole them to repentance.[82] But it is done in a mode anticipatory of future sapiential developments, namely, personification and hypostatization.

All this happens with at most allusions and generalizations—albeit allusions and generalizations which beg for application. The impulse underlying this text is not disinterest in history. The sapiential nature of the text may mute the specific historical signals, or better, may indeed want to be supra-specific in the interests of generalizability and repeatability. But the interest is directed precisely to the historical experience of a people's rebellion and conversion, and more narrowly, a person's rebellion and conversion,[83] and thus to the history of salvation and judgment—however often repeated, on whatever scale. In short, this chapter

79. Most recently, Achtemeier, *Community and Message*, p. 15; Gottwald, *Hebrew Bible*, p. 378; J. Eaton speaks instead of an 'Isaiah tradition' ('The Isaiah Tradition', in Coggins, *et al.* (eds.), *Israel's Prophetic Tradition,* pp. 58-76).

80. D. Petersen, *Late Israelite Prophecy: Studies in Deutero-Prophetic Literature and in Chronicles* (SBLMS, 23; Missoula, MT: Scholars Press, 1977), p. 26.

81. Hence correctly Hanson's positing of multiple authorship (*Dawn of Apocalyptic*, 41). The use of the singular in this study ('author' instead of 'author[s]') is for convenience; it does not assume single authorship. Nothing can be said about the size of the community participating in the production of this text, however.

82. Cf. Clements on Isa. 5.1-7 in *Isaiah 1–39*, n. 65.

83. The degree of individualization is debatable. There is the reference to the one who turns from evil in v. 15a, and the lament at the absence of the 'man' in v. 16. See the discussion above. The separating of the repentant ones from the rest as is implied by the restriction of the recipients of redemption in v. 20 does not imply individualization any more than conversionist groups generally are individualistic. On the other hand, the focus on repentance as the moment of separation within a nation does raise to new levels of importance the experience and the integrity of the individual.

may reflect the proposed conditions of early postexilic Palestine; it will fit just as well, indeed by intention, into most any context marked by social oppression and the absence of human defenders of משפט. And while that concern has profound roots in the prophetic movement, it is an agenda the wisdom tradition picks up with great interest in the motif of the righteous sufferer.

On the basis of this analysis it is unlikely that Isaiah 59, including the use of the motif of the Divine Warrior, is in any *exclusive* sense eschatological, let alone apocalyptic.[84] As indicated in the introductory discussion of Isaiah 59, several tenses are used in vv. 15b-20. Verse 15 begins with a converted imperfect. This tense is essentially maintained until v. 18, where a simple imperfect suggests a future orientation. It is possible that the past tense intends to signify as completed the future intervention of Yahweh; hence the easy transition to the future tense in v. 18.[85] There are, however, a number of reasons for not reading the appearance of the Divine Warrior in purely eschatological terms.

First of all, war hymns (e.g., Exod. 15; Judg. 5; 2 Sam. 20//Ps. 18; Ps. 68; Deut. 32, 33; Hab. 3) are intended to recall the *past* exploits of the Divine Warrior in order to cajole the Warrior into yet another foray, and/or to create and then to bolster in believers a sense of confidence and trust in the Lord's strong arm. But as Ps. 68.19 illustrates, the recital of the past and the anticipation of the future intervention of Yahweh does not necessitate an exclusively eschatological reading.[86] Indeed, inasmuch as the motif of the Divine Warrior is rooted in cosmogonic myth, one is speaking of a past occurrence repeatedly celebrated in the cult as

84. While D. Georgi understands apocalyptic to be a species of wisdom, taking issue with the Cross/Hanson school ('Das Wesen der Weisheit nach der "Weisheit Salomos"', in J. Taubes (ed.), *Gnosis und Politik* [Religionstheorie und Politische Theologie, 2; Munich: Fink; Paderborn: Schöningh, 1984], p. 72 n. 14), which roots it in prophecy, he nevertheless understands Isa. 59.15b-20 to be an apocalyptic hymn about the divine eschatological warrior. The interpretation offered here goes in a decidedly different direction.

85. Muilenburg, 'Book of Isaiah', p. 694.

86. That point can be made whether or not v. 19 was originally part of the theophanic hymn. In fact, the point is made more strongly if the redactor did not read it as eschatological. Even the individualized poems celebrating the arising of the Divine Warrior such as 2 Sam. 22//Ps. 18, etc., are premised upon past experience of deliverance. In that sense the praise hymn functions as a lever on Yahweh to act again. This feature is ubiquitous within the psalms.

assurance of the ongoing and thus also future sustaining power of the deity.

Furthermore, the evocation of past experiences of Yahweh's power can be used inversely, as it is in our text, as a warning to those among the covenant people who have become Yahweh's enemies. The quite possibly contemporaneous[87] Song of Moses (Deut. 32) illustrates this.[88] It initiates the theophany of the Divine Warrior in the same way as does Isa. 59.15b: 'And Yahweh saw...' (וירא יהוה, 32.19). As in Isaiah 59, this phrase follows a description of past faithlessness on the part of the people of Yahweh and precedes the promise of divine warfare. In Deuteronomy 32 Yahweh's warfare against his people is difficult to specify historically, but it is no doubt an allusion to past calamities. This is suggested also by its redactional location as part of the final testamentary utterances of Moses.[89] The pseudepigraphic device of the testament illustrates that the recital in theophanic fashion of past disaster is meant to function as warning and promise for the future. As in Isaiah 59, there is the promise of vengeance and requital against God's enemies, in particular those in Israel who have been faithless. Such prediction and description of judgment does not prevent the Song from ending on a note of assurance that God will deliver his own people, his own servants (vv. 36, 43). But it is not at all clear that the Song should be read in an eschatological light for it to function as warning and promise. Its redactional location prior to the story of entry into the land means that it was not read in that way by the redactor.

That there is a view to the future in Isaiah 59 has clearly been recognized in this study. It is precisely the intention of this text to warn and call to repentance. That call is motivated by the understanding that as Yahweh has acted in the past so he can be counted on to act in the future. But that the future act is envisioned as a final, conclusive, and comprehensive judgment is not the view of the author(s) of Isaiah 59.

87. G. von Rad, *Deuteronomy: A Commentary* (trans. D. Barton; OTL; Philadelphia: Westminster Press, 1966), p. 200.

88. G.A.F. Knight (*Isaiah 56–66* [ITC; Grand Rapids: Eerdmans, 1985], p. 35) refers to Deut. 32 as Third Isaiah's 'source book.' There are many affinities with Isa. 59 in particular.

89. As von Rad has indicated (*Deuteronomy*), this text is quite likely an exilic piece, reflecting, as does Isa. 59, characteristic fusing of various literary forms and genres into a new literary whole, here likely of a testamentary nature. Von Rad suggests that for this reason it should be located within the Wisdom tradition.

6. *The Septuagint Translation of Isaiah 59*

The Greek translation of Isaiah 59 in the Septuagint represents a bridge of sorts to the reappropriation of the motif of the Divine Warrior in full armour in the subsequent texts Wisdom of Solomon 5, 1 Thessalonians 5, and Ephesians 6. Generally dated around the middle of the second century BCE,[90] it provides a window on how second century (BCE) translators and interpreters understand the motif of the Divine Warrior as seen in Isaiah 59.

The Septuagint version of Isaiah is anything but slavish, since apart from the reality that all translations are unavoidably interpretations, the translator[91] quite consciously edits the text as well. The translator is thus an active participant in the shaping of tradition. The following section will briefly identify ways the Divine Warrior in Isaiah 59 has been received and modified in this act of tradition.

There are a number of textual differences between the Septuagint (LXX) and the Masoretic Hebrew text (MT) of Isaiah 59, most notably in vv. 6 and 18, where the metre is disrupted. Beyond that, there are differences which may be rooted in a different Hebrew *Vorlage* than the one reflected in the MT, but just as easily or more likely may reflect the tendencies of the translator.

Overall the sermonic and didactic intentions discerned in the MT continue to control the translation, this being sharply noticeable in the depiction of the people as rebellious candidates for divine judgment. This is illustrated in various ways. First, whereas the Hebrew begins with an implied lament or challenge, the LXX begins with questions that bait the accusing people.

Second, the characterization of the people is more uniformly negative in Isaiah 59 LXX than in the MT. In vv. 9-11a the first person is changed to the third, and the past tense is changed into a future tense, with the result that what can be read as a lament in the MT is changed into a

90. E. Bickermann, *Studies in Jewish and Christian History* Part 1 (AGJU, 9; Leiden: Brill, 1976), p. 147 and p. 147 n.42; Bickermann cites also I.L. Seligmann, *The Septuagint Version of Isaiah* (Voraziatisch-Egyptisch Genootschap, 9; Mededelingen, 1948), p. 90; the *terminus post quem* is Isa. 9.11 and 23.1 the *terminus ante quem*.

91. As in the case of 'author' in the first chapter, no claim is hereby made that one translator alone is responsible. The tradition of the translation of the LXX itself suggests the opposite.

prediction of judgment for the same people whose wickedness is described earlier. No room for doubt is left that the sufferers of vv. 9-11a are the ἄνομοι of vv. 4-8. Verses 11b-15a thus constitute the acknowledgment of the sins described in vv. 3-8, but hardly an act of repentance.[92] Not surprisingly, while repentance is not beyond the ultimate purpose of the translator, the recurring phrase in 59.15 and 20 MT regarding those who turn from evil is absent from LXX. Replacing 'the one who, turns from evil' in v. 15 is, instead, another virtue, namely Διάνοια, who along with Ἀλήθεια falls victim to the violence and abuse of the people.[93] The epexegetical narrowing in v. 20 of the category of those for whom the Divine Warrior comes as גואל as 'those in Jacob who turn from transgression' (MT) is replaced in the LXX by the more abstract assertion that the deliverer (ῥυόμενος) will come to remove the ἀσέβεια from Jacob 'for the sake of Zion' (ἕνεκεν Σιων). While that wording *can* include the basic sense of the MT, the people themselves are more removed, leaving the impression that in the mind of the translator the people have essentially one role to play in this text, that of opponents (ὑπεναντίοι, v. 18) of the Κύριος. From this perspective οὐκ ἦν ἀνήρ in v. 16 must surely mean that the Κύριος saw that there was no one among the people who practiced solidarity (οὐκ ἦν ὁ ἀντιλημψόμενος). At the cost of overstatement, readers are not allowed to find refuge in some faithful, even repentant, remnant.

The antipathy between God and people is accentuated in Isaiah 59 LXX by the contrasting of the polluted hands of the people (χεῖρὲς ὑμῶν; v. 3) with the hand of the Lord (ἡ χεὶρ κυρίου; v. 1). Further, the miserable web the ἄνομοι weave as a garment (ἱμάτιον), or the works of ἀνομία which presumably are meant to serve as cloak (περιβάλωνται; v. 6) stand in stark contrast to the ἱμάτιον ἐκδικήσεως and the περιβόλαιον ὡς ἀνταποδώσων ἀνταπόδοσιν of the Κύριος (v. 17b).

The people's apostasy and rebellion is chiefly characterized as ἀνομία, which renders שקר ('iniquity') in v. 3, און ('vanity' or 'wickedness') in vv. 4 and 6, and פשע ('fault,' 'rebellion,' or 'transgression') in v. 12.

92. Note Wis. 5.3, where the μετάνοια of the wicked amounts to insight into the reasons for their judgment; it comes too late to avert it.

93. Odeberg (*Trito-Isaiah*, p. 188), among others, has suggested that the text of v. 15 is corrupt, and that LXX may be dependent on an alternative text. It is more likely, in my view, that this is a case of harmonizing around the motif of the fate of the virtues, and thus also rendering the people more uniformly the enemies of God.

Within the Isaianic corpus at large ἀνομία also renders a variety of terms. It is concentrated heavily in Isaiah 53, where it translates פשׁע, עון, and חמם, transgressions for which the Servant suffers, suggesting an identification between the oppressors of the Servant in Isaiah 53 and those criticized in Isaiah 59. The rebellion of the people can thus best be summarized as lawlessness, accentuating the legal and covenantal nature of their apostasy.

The people's lawlessness is further described as trust in μάταιοι and as the speaking of κενά (v. 4). Virtual synonyms, they are on the fringes of the semantic field of ἀνομία.[94] Such vocabulary is at home in sapiential literature. In fact, the sapiential flavour is increased by the description of the people as ἄφρονοι (v. 7), and by the addition of διάνοια to the list of abused virtues in v. 15a.

The brief allegory of people's victimization of divine virtues as discussed at length above is obviously appreciated by the translator. The shift from the first to the third person in vv. 9-11 puts the antipathy of the people toward the representatives of God into even greater relief. Thereby, indeed, the narration of the abuse of the Lord's representatives begins in v. 8, and extends to the end of v. 15a: Εἰρήνη (v. 8)[95], Κρίσις (vv. 8, 9, 11, 14, 15), Δικαιοσύνη (vv. 9, 14, [17]), Φῶς (v. 9), Σωτηρία (vv. 11, [17]), Ἀλήθεια (vv. 14, 15), and Διάνοια (v. 15) all fall victim to the abuse of lawless people.

In Isaiah 59 LXX the mythological elements are generally muted in favor of abstraction and metaphor. But that does not lessen the sermonic power of the scenario of the victimization of the Lord's virtues or messengers at the hands of the Lord's own people. In fact, it is the presence of these virtues as victims and the characterization of the people as their abusers which, given the conviction that the Divine Warrior goes to war on behalf of victims, necessarily ushers in the Divine Warrior at this point, although against his own people, and not on their behalf.

First of all, the Κύριος 'saw' what was going on (v. 15b). The Lord was displeased because Κρίσις was not; Κρίσις had been driven off and banished (vv. 8, 9, 11, 14). And the Lord noticed that there was no

94. μάταιος translates און in Isa. 31.2 and 32.6, whereas און is translated as ἀνομία in 59.4, 6. The translation of און as ἀνομία is, apart from the two instances in Isa. 59.4, 6 and Job 31.3, exclusive to the Psalms.

95. I have intentionally capitalized the virtues in order to accentuate the personification that marks this text.

ἀνήρ, no ἀντιλημψόμενος. The various forms of ἀντιλαμβάνω frequently describe the intervening and protective loyalty of the Κύριος, also in Isaiah. It expresses the certainty of divine 'help' to the Servant in 41.9 and 42.1. Further, in Isa. 51.18 Jerusalem is described as a mother without sons to 'uphold' or defend her, whose plight the Lord then addresses. The king as surrogate of the Κύριος is said in 9.6 to 'uphold' the people with δικαιοσύνη and κρίματα. Most striking is the late text Isa. 26.2,3, where the gates are to be opened for a people (λάος) which guards and protects (φυλάσσων) δικαιοσύνη and ἀλήθεια, and which 'upholds' or 'defends' (ἀντιλαμβανόμενος) ἀλήθεια and εἰρήνη. Notably, the people as a whole are rewarded with exaltation to royal status for their solidarity and protectiveness of precisely those virtues found also in Isaiah 59 (cf. Ps. 24.7-10). In Isaiah 59, however, God takes notice that no-one (among the people) has been willing to take on the role of upholder and defender.

The Κύριος must himself now act as ἀντιλημψόμενος: with his own arm he now comes to the assistance[96] of the virtues, taking a firm stand (ἐστηρίσατο) with (or for[97]) mercy or pity (ἐλεημοσύνη). 'Ελεημοσύνη should perhaps have been listed earlier among the virtues, since one of the features of the rising of the warrior is the taking up of the virtues either as allies or as part of his armour. Thus, after characterizing the firmness of battle position as that of pity for victims, the Divine Warrior now puts on δικαιοσύνη as a shield and the crown or helmet of σωτήρια on his head; then he throws on garments of ἐκδίκησις and ἀνταπόδοσις so as to repay the opponents for their insult (ὄνειδος).

A difference from the panoply as described in the MT comes at the end of vv. 17 and 18. קנאה, which is always translated as ζῆλος, is not in the inventory of garments. Instead, נקם/ἐκδίκησις is retained and the περιβόλαιον ὡς ἀνταποδώσων ἀνταπόδοσιν takes the place of the מעיל קנאה, which would have been translated as ζῆλος ὡς περιβόλαιον. Ζῆλος appears a number of times within the Isaianic corpus, specifically within texts in which the warfare or the intervention of God is pictured

96. BAGD, p. 47, suggests that ἀμύνομαι should be translated here as 'coming to the assistance of'.

97. If τῇ ἐλεημοσύνῃ is a Dative of Advantage (Smyth §1481) then ἐλεημοσύνη is not the means of or the nature of the Lord's firmness, but the recipient of the Lord's vindication. In this case ἐλεημοσύνη would be one of the virtues, and in that manner one of the ways the mighty Lord intervenes (cf. 59.2b; cf. also Wis. 16.10—τὸ ἔλεος). Both meanings fit quite nicely into the same scenario.

as *on behalf of* his people.[98] That is clearly not within the redactional interests of the translator.

It was noted in the discussion of v. 18 MT that the text is seriously disturbed. However, not only does Isaiah 59 LXX not contain the reference to the coastlands, that is, to the Gentile nations as the recipients of the warrior's wrath, but it also does not contain a reference to חמה, which, if Isa. 34.2, 42.25, and 63.6 are any indication, would have been translated as ὀργή. Ὀργή does appear in the next verse, so it is best not to consider this a deliberate attempt to mute the force of the passage. The doubling of terms (ὡς ἀνταποδώσων ἀνταπόδοσιν) is familiar (even if ἀνταπόδομα is the more frequent term in the doubling[99]). This is the vocabulary of retaliation. The Lord's appearance as Divine Warrior is thus chiefly punitive. Appropriately, as in Deut. 32.35, ἐκδίκησις, ἀνταπόδοσις, and ὀργή are in immediate proximity to each other.

Mythological elements are present, to be sure, but only to the degree to which they are endemic to the motif of the Divine Warrior to begin with. As mentioned, they are muted in favour of abstract metaphor, where the values of the covenantal community, pictured previously as the messengers or virtues of the Κύριος, now make up the armour of the Divine Warrior. Whereas, then, the MT is still close to the mythological origins of the language by having Yahweh himself come like a violent river driven by the רוח יהוה, in Isaiah 59 LXX it is ὀργή which emanates from God (παρὰ κυρίου) like a violent river (ὡς ποταμὸς βίαιος). The רוח יהוה, ambiguous as to whether what is meant is Yahweh's spirit or his storm wind, has been replaced by μετὰ θυμοῦ.

Finally, the Κύριος comes as ῥυόμενος, not 'to Zion', but 'for the sake of Zion' (ἕνεκεν Σιων; v. 20). This may not be a significant distinction, but since Zion functions as a symbol of the Lord's throne, of his status as king, his rising as warrior becomes a defending of his own honour, and thus liberation and defence of his own virtues. Isaiah 59 LXX mutes the connection between the ῥυόμενος and the people, precisely because they have thus far had the sole role as the ὑπεναντίοι of the Κύριος. Thus there is also no mention here of the repentant ones for whose sake the Lord comes as deliverer. Rather, it is said very abstractly that the deliverer will drive away the ἀσέβεια from Jacob. In

98. E.g. Isa. 11.11; 42.13; 63.15.

99. E.g. Gen. 50.15; Judg. 7.15; 16.28; Pss. 27.4; 93.2; Sir. 17.23; Joel 3.4; Isa. 66.6; Jer. 28.6, 57.

short, he will root out the ἀνομία.[100] That this comes as good news for Zion and Jacob is clear. It is even possible to see in this the radical removal of the proclivity to rebellion. It is equally allusive, however, of the kind of judgment which will remove the people along with the ἀσέβεια. The degree of abstraction shrouds the nature of the Lord's judicial warfare in mystery.

One can summarize the findings of this analysis of Isaiah 59 LXX as follows. First, criticism of the people is accentuated in this translation. The aspect of lament has been heavily muted. The only role accorded the people is that of enemies of the Lord and of his virtues.

Secondly, the Lord as Divine Warrior is presented almost exclusively in his historic role as avenging and punitive judge. There is nothing specifically apocalyptic or exclusively futuristic about the way the Divine Warrior is described in this passage. This impression is aided by the fact that throughout Isaiah 59 LXX there is a constant shifting of tenses. In part this is due to the translation from the Hebrew. But the switching back and forth also serves to diffuse the precise historical location of divine warfare. This serves the need to explain past and present distress, the need to warn about the future, and the need for hope for those who wonder whether God's enterprise will lose out in the end.

Third, whereas the passage serves to explain and warn, that is, to state the 'why' of the Lord's warring against his own poeple and on behalf of his own virtues, the 'how' and the 'what' remain at the level of suggestion. Given the ubiquity of the motif of the Divine Warrior within biblical traditions, the theme of the theophany and the allusions to the forces of nature (albeit less prominent in Isaiah 59 LXX than in the MT) serve to evoke the varied manifestations of divine warfare familiar to the people. But this evocation of the Lord's warring gives primacy to the assurance that God's initiatives at bringing about a covenant community will not finally be thwarted. The Lord himself will make certain that in the absence of a man or a people who will 'uphold' or 'defend' his virtues and messengers, he himself will see to their vindication and make sure that the impiousness of the people will be expunged.

100. 'Ασέβεια and ἀνομία function very much as synomyms in Isa. 59; in v. 20 ἀσέβεια translates פשׁע, which in v. 12 is translated as ἀνομία.

Chapter 2

THE DIVINE WARRIOR IN WISDOM OF SOLOMON 5

The first fully creative appropriation of Isaiah's motif of the Divine Warrior in armour appears in the Wisdom of Solomon. The nature of this pseudepigraphic document, most particularly its deliberate smudging of all temporal and geographical indicators (with the one exception of the Red Sea in 10.18), allows for little certainty as to authorship, date, and provenance other than that it was written within a highly hellenized context by a hellenized Jewish author some time between the last part of the second century BCE and the early part of the first century CE.[1] Dieter Georgi has suggested that the nature of the assimilation and digestion of diverse wisdom traditions points to multiple or collective authorship such as that of a school, the present form of Wisdom being

1. See discussions of this in J.J. Collins, *Between Athens and Jerusalem: Jewish Identity in the Hellenistic Diaspora* (New York: Crossroad, 1983), p. 182; D. Georgi, *Weisheit Salomos: Jüdische Schriften aus hellenistisch-römischer Zeit*. III. *Unterweisung in lehrhafter Form* (Gütersloh: Gütersloher Verlagshaus/Gerd Mohn, 1980). pp. 394-97; cf. *idem*, 'Wesen der Weisheit', pp. 66-68, and the earlier 'Der Vorpaulinische Hymnus, Phil 2, 6-11', in E. Dinkler (ed.), *Zeit und Geschichte: Dankesgabe an Rudolf Bultmann zum 80. Geburtstag* (Tübingen: Mohr, 1964), p. 269 n. 30; M. Gilbert, 'Wisdom Literature', in M.E. Stone (ed.), *Jewish Writings of the Second Temple Period* (Philadelphia: Fortress Press, 1984), pp. 301-13, especially p. 312; J.M. Reese, OSFB, *Hellenistic Influence on the Book of Wisdom and its Consequences* (Rome: Biblical Institute Press, 1970); G.W.E. Nickelsburg, *Jewish Literature Between the Bible and the Mishnah: A Historical and Literary Introduction* (Philadelphia: Fortress Press, 1981), p. 184; A. Schmitt, *Das Buch der Weisheit: Ein Kommentar* (Würzburg: Echter Verlag, 1986), pp. 8-9; D. Winston, *The* Wisdom of Solomon*: A New Translation with Introduction and Commentary* (AB, 43; Garden City, NY: Doubleday, 1979), pp. 12-14, 20-25. Most take the Hellenistic character of the document to signal an Alexandrian provenance, but Georgi opts for a Syrian context (*Weisheit*, p. 396). The pervasiveness of Hellenism makes any determination difficult if not impossible (*Weisheit*, p. 395).

the contribution of what might be called a final redactor.[2] This has the effect of moving precise date and provenance even further beyond the reach of the scholar. It is sufficient for this study to note that whichever date is finally chosen, Wisdom of Solomon clearly falls between the taking up of the Divine Warrior in Isaiah 59 LXX and Paul's appropriation of that motif in 1 Thessalonians 5. It thus represents a point in the trajectory from Isaiah 59 to Ephesians 6.[3]

The motif of the Divine Warrior in full armour appears at or near the end of what is generally identified as the first major section of Wisdom of Solomon, sometimes seen as concluding with ch. 6[4] and at other

2. Georgi, *Weisheit*, pp. 393-94; *idem*, 'Wesen der Weisheit', p. 67-8.

3. 'Trajectory' does not imply a clear line of dependency between the texts that chronologically take up the motif as it first appears in Isa. 59. C. Larcher (*Études sur le Livre de la Sagesse* [Paris: Librairie Lecoffre, 1969], pp. 85-91) has shown that the author of Wisdom of Solomon is chiefly dependent on LXX for scriptural usage (e.g., Isa. 3.10 LXX and Wis. 2.12; Isa. 44.20 LXX and Wis. 15.10; and Job 9.12, 19 LXX and Wis. 12.12; see also P.W. Skehan, 'Isaias and the Teaching of the Book of Wisdom', *CBQ* 2 [1940], p. 299; Winston, *Wisdom*, p. 17). But Larcher suggests that the sage is also familiar with the Hebrew, and on occasion, as is the case in our text, can reach back to the Hebrew, or at least to a Greek text much like the MT (*Études*, p. 85). Further, there is no evidence that Paul and the author of Ephesians were dependent on Wisdom of Solomon for their appropriation of the Divine Warrior motif (see discussion in Larcher, *Études*, pp. 14-20, and *Le Livre de la Sagesse ou la Sagesse de Solomon* [3 vols.; Paris: Librairie Lecoffre, 1984], p. 392). That Wisdom of Solomon's appropriation of the motif likely played a role in their reflections, especially in those of the author of Eph. 6, is not thereby denied. What should be kept in mind is that critical appropriation of past traditions, including scriptural traditions, increasingly characterized the writings of the Second Temple period for purposes of updating and restatement in the light of new circumstances and insights (cf. Georgi, 'Wesen der Weisheit', p. 67; cf. also Fishbane, *Biblical Interpretation*, pp. 465-99). This use of the familiar to estrange and reacquaint in the interests of critical appropriation is what marks Wisdom of Solomon in particular. What Isa. 59, Wis. 5, 1 Thess. 5, and Eph. 6 share, in addition to likely 'conversation' with each other either directly or indirectly by participating in the larger written and unwritten flow and act of tradition, is a desire to rearticulate the motif of the Divine Warrior in full armour first encountered in Isa. 59. 'Trajectory' will thus necessarily have to include this dynamic of critical restatement. I am employing the term in a more restricted sense than do Koester and Robinson (J.M. Robinson and H. Koester, *Trajectories through Early Christianity* [Philadelphia: Fortress Press, 1971]).

4. E.g., Winston, *Wisdom*, p. 4, where the call to monarchs to seek wisdom in chs. 1 and 6 represents an *inclusio*. Cf. also Gilbert, 'Wisdom', pp. 301-302;

times with ch. 5.[5] This section has been characterized as focussing on wisdom's offer of immortality as reward for faithfulness,[6] or as affording a clear glimpse at the author's eschatology, in particular the last judgment. Indeed, it has been referred to as the 'Book of Eschatology'.[7] Neither characterization is in my view quite a propos. But the specifics of the debate over the structure and unity of Wisdom of Solomon need not preoccupy us. Nor is it necessary or even fitting to establish under which precise conceptual heading the first five chapters of Wisdom are to be read.[8] However, in order to appreciate the significance and purpose of the theophany of the Divine Warrior in the Wisdom of Solomon, brief attention to the present structure and content of the first part of Wisdom is in order.

1. *The Context of the Theophany of the Divine Warrior*

Wisdom of Solomon begins with an appeal to those who judge the earth (οἱ κρίνοντες τὴν γῆν) to love righteousness and to seek the Lord (1.1). While this appeal is ostensibly directed at monarchs,[9] it is clear that the general nature of these comments signals a larger intended audience.

Nickelsburg, *Jewish Literature*, p. 175; Reese, *Hellenistic Influence*, p. 109; Schmitt, *Buch der Weisheit*, p. 15.

5. Georgi, *Weisheit*, p. 393, Larcher, *Études*, p. 86. The exact division is not significant for the study of our pericope.

6. Winston, *Wisdom*, p. 10.

7. See discussion and literature in Reese, *Hellenistic Influence*, pp. 109-110. Recently also Collins, *Between Athens and Jerusalem*, p. 183, and Nickelsburg, *Jewish Literature*, p. 175.

8. Georgi has made it a *Leitmotiv* of his study of Wisdom of Solomon to show the extent to which Wisdom of Solomon is marked by discontinuities, contradictions, and repetitions, with no apparent desire on part of the author (or, as he prefers, redactor) to resolve them (see previously cited literature). It is Georgi's conviction that these peculiarities of the document are, in fact, central to its strategy (*Weisheit*, pp. 393-94; cf. the whole of 'Wesen der Weisheit'). The present study is indebted to Georgi's reading of Wisdom of Solomon.

9. The intended audience is here broader than royalty, and those who practise justice are friends of wisdom generally and not simply good kings (note not least the first reference to the δίκαιος as a poor day labourer [πένης δίκαιος; 2.10]); conversely, the godless are not simply bad monarchs but more broadly those who ignore the call of wisdom and instruction. However, the politically critical element suggested by Wisdom of Solomon's juxtaposing of the reference to the kings with the immediately following speech of the godless should not be missed.

All who are concerned with wisdom are addressed, teased, as it were, into identifying themselves as those with potential royal status by their alignment with wisdom, co-terminous here with the practice of δικαιοσύνη (1.1, 4, 5). The exhortation is buttressed with observations that wisdom (σοφία) and spirit (πνεῦμα) separate and distance themselves from those who do not love and practise justice and truth (vv. 4,5). The exhortation concludes with warning and admonition not to seek death (θάνατος; 1.12), for there is no reality to be found there. Whatever reality or force θάνατος might have has nothing to do with God's creation. 'Hades has no kingdom on earth' (οὔτε ᾅδου βασίλειον ἐπὶ γῆς; 1.14). God has not created death (1.13); what God has created serves salvation (1.14). Thus, finally, righteousness stands in complete contradiction to death (δικαιοσύνη ἀθάνατος ἐστιν; 1.15).

Coming to the fore in this initial section is the unresolvable contradiction between the reality of righteousness, spirit, and wisdom, on the one hand, and the counter-reality, or unreality, of injustice, distorted and perverse thought and words, on the other.[10] Injustice has the effect of ignorance, and, more importantly, communion with death and exclusion from God's reality, from creation itself. If creation is experienced at all by the impious (ἀσεβεῖς), it is in the ironical sense, as will be seen, of judgment and divine warfare, not as salvation. Living in contradiction to God's creation, then, does not happen with impunity; word reaches the zealous ear of God, and judgment follows (1.10). This *quid pro quo* is thus rooted in the eager attentiveness of God, and not in an inexorable cause-and-effect mechanism built into the fabric of the cosmos.

Hereupon follow the deliberations of the impious (2.1-20). First, they mimic the familiar scepticism of the wise regarding the meaninglessness of human life, but then infer two things: one, full enjoyment of creation, and two, impunity. The decision is then explicitly taken to oppress the impoverished δίκαιος, the widow and the aged (v. 10). The δίκαιος is accused of resisting and exposing the ways of the ἀσεβεῖς, even if only through his non-conformity, of claiming to have knowledge of God, and finally of claiming to be a παῖς θεοῦ (vv. 13-16). The decision is taken to torture and kill the δίκαιος in order to test whether the claim to sonship implies salvation (vv. 19-20).

Such reasoning grows out of ignorance and blindness—ignorance of

10. Cf. Georgi, 'Vorpaulinischer Hymnus', p. 270.

the mysteries of God (v. 22), namely that ἄνθρωπος[11] is created for incorruptibility and resides in the hand of God (2.23-3.1). The death of the δίκαιοι is only apparent (3.2). And whatever real suffering they experience is finally a testing by God, one they pass with flying colours (3.5, 6). Indeed, they go on to the royal task of judging the nations and ruling the peoples, in effect to being co-regents with God (3.7, 8).[12] The impious, on the other hand, are punished commensurate with their misdeeds (3.10), in keeping with who they are as members of Death's party (2.24; cf. 1.16).

This ultimate reversal of fortunes is in some sense only an apparent reversal, in that the ironies of the present life already anticipate that reversal. This is illustrated with a discussion of childlessness and brevity of life among the just (3.10-4.9). The brief life of the δίκαιος outlasts the long life of the unrighteous, in that the just who have completed this life will judge those still living (4.16). Once again, as in 3.8, the condemnation of the ἀσεβεῖς by the δίκαιος in 4.16 is paralleled by the judgment of the κύριος in 4.18,19.

The reversal is subsequently described as one in which the δίκαιος stands facing the tormenters with the confidence of king and judge (παρρησία; 5.1).[13] This elicits a speech of recognition on the part of the ἀσεβεῖς (5.4-13).[14] Ignorance gives way to insight into the true reality the ἀσεβεῖς have in fact been living, a reality which in the end has boomeranged on them, as it were. Their life shows itself to have been a chimera.

In contrast, the δίκαιοι live on into eternity (5.15), and their welfare rests with the Most High, whose right hand and arm covers and shields

11. I take this to be coterminous with δίκαιος; so also Georgi, 'Vorpaulinischer Hymnus', p. 272.

12. I read 3.8 as a parallelism, and the αὐτῶν in v. 8b as referring to the nations and the peoples.

13. Georgi (*Weisheit*, p. 416) translates παρρησία as the *souveräne Freiheit* of heavenly beings. I see here first and foremost the confidence and freedom accorded monarchs in their function as judges (so also Georgi earlier in 'Vorpaulinischer Hymnus', p. 274, especially n. 39). The salvation of 5.2 is thus also the exaltation to the status of royal judge over the tormenters.

14. Μετάνοια in v. 3 should not be read as conversion or repentance, but as denoting a new level of insight brought on by the encounter with the confident, standing δίκαιος. It amounts to an admission of the rightness of judgment brought against the ἀσεβεῖς, the correctness of their fate, and thus essentially to self-condemnation.

them. For that reason (διὰ τοῦτο; v. 16) they will experience exaltation and enthronement. This shielding and covering, exaltation and enthronement, as well as judgment on tormenters, is now elaborated by means of the image of the Divine Warrior in full armour, dressed in the virtues, and employing all creation in his warfare of judgment.[15]

This brief overview of these chapters leading up to the rise of the Divine Warrior strongly suggests contact with the Fourth Servant Song in Isa. 52.13–53.12.[16] The deliberations of the ἀσεβεῖς in 2.10-20 and 5.4-13 in particular indicate reliance on the Servant Song. However, there are some notable differences between the way the δίκαιος *qua* παῖς is pictured here and the way the παῖς is represented in Isa 52.13–53.12.[17] For one, there is no hint that Wisdom's δίκαιος is ever 'numbered among the transgressors' (ἐν τοῖς ἀνόμοις ἐλογίσθη; Isa. 53.12). Nor is there even a suggestion of vicarious salvific suffering for the sins of others, as is the case with the Servant (53. 4-6, 10-12).[18] Instead, here

15. As the subsequent discussion of the Divine Warrior will show, neither a 'scientifically' perceived cosmos (J.J. Collins, 'Cosmos and Salvation: Jewish Wisdom and Apocalyptic in the Hellenistic Age', *HR* 17 [1977], p. 131) nor a thoroughgoing ontological (gnostic) dualism (Georgi, 'Vorpaulinischer Hymnus', p. 270) quite does justice to the way the 'realities' of the δίκαιοι and the ἀσεβεῖς intersect in Wisdom of Solomon. Both interpretations have the tendency to render the appearance of the Divine Warrior either unintelligible or as a cipher for the nature of consequence within creation as structured by God. The subsequent discussion understands the author of Wisdom of Solomon to posit a radically interventionist deity. That clearly places stress on such 'ontological' notions as immortality. But that kind of stress would correspond to the strategies of the author(s).

16. Cf. M.J. Suggs, 'Wisdom of Solomon 2:10-5: A Homily on the Fourth Servant Song', *JBL* 76 (1957), pp. 26-33; cf. earlier J. Fichtner, 'Der Alttestamentliche Text der Sapientia Salomonis', *ZAW* NS 16 (1939), p. 166 (see especially also n. 1); J. Jeremias, 'παῖς θεοῦ', *TDNT*, V, p. 684; also Georgi, 'Vorpaulinischer Hymnus', p. 266, *idem*, *Weisheit*, pp. 405-6, *idem*, 'Wesen der Weisheit', p. 73; G.W.E. Nickelsburg, *Resurrection, Immortality, and Eternal Life in Intertestamental Judaism* (HTS, 26; Cambridge: Harvard University Press, 1972), pp. 58-68; J. Shaberg, 'Major Midrashic Traditions in Wisdom 1.1-6, 25', *JSJ* 13 (1982), pp. 75-101. For a contrary view see Reese's criticism (*Hellenistic Influence*, p. 113) that while Isaiah traditions clearly play a role in these chapters of Wisdom of Solomon, this is not an interpretation (midrash) of Isa. 52, 53.

17. Larcher, *Études*, pp. 91-92; Shaberg, 'Midrashic Traditions', *passim*.

18. Georgi, among others, recognizes this (*Weisheit*, p. 407; 'Vorpaulinischer Hymnus', p. 271 n. 37). His rejoinder is that the fourth Servant Song was seldom interpreted with a view to vicarious suffering, but rather with an emphasis on the vindication of the δίκαιος. A sapiential interpretation would thus take its cue from

the scenario is a fairly simple one: the wicked oppress the just, thinking their oppressing has real effect. They are surprised not by their own salvation, which clearly does provide the element of surprise in Isaiah 53. Their surprise is at the salvation of the δίκαιος. For Wisdom of Solomon's royal ἀσεβεῖς there is only judgment and condemnation. Wisdom thus represents a reinterpretation of the Servant Song, a backing away from the generosity of the vision expressed there, and a return of sorts to the simpler calculus of retaliation, mixed now, however, with the more sophisticated assault on time and matter. The reflections on the Lord's mercy in 12.12-22 do not alter this basic disposition. One device by which that happens is the employment of another Isaianic text, namely, Isaiah 59.[19]

The similarities and points of contact between Isaiah 59 and Wisdom of Solomon 1–5 are numerous. Isaiah 59 begins with a characterization of the sins of the people as consisting of false words, unjust judgments, and violence (Isa. 59.3-7; cf. Wis. 1.6-11; 2.10-11). Moreover, this sinful mode of life is described by means of the image of road, path, or way (Isa 59.7,8; cf. Wis. 5.6, 7). It is this way of life which separates the people from God (Isa 59.2; cf. Wis. 1.3), and it is this which distances the virtues from the people (Isa. 59.8-15; cf. Wis. 1.4, 5). Most characteristic of Isaiah 59 is the representation of sin as abuse of the personified divine virtues such as משפט/κρίσις, צדקה/δικαιοσύνη, and אמת/ἀλήθεια, to name a few. While hypostasization is no stranger to Wisdom of Solomon, in chs. 1–5 it is the δίκαιος who takes the place of the virtues as the

Isa. 52.13-15. This may reflect not fidelity to the true concerns of Isa. 52–53, but retreat from the friendliness of the author(s) of the Servant Song toward the abusers of the righteous servant, a friendliness reflected in the meaning accorded the Servant's suffering. This retreat may already have happened within the Isaianic tradition. (See discussion of Hanson's thesis regarding Third Isaiah in the previous chapter.) In Wisdom of Solomon there is a deep gulf fixed between the δίκαιοι and the ἀσεβεῖς that the suffering of the δίκαιοι cannot and does not bridge.

19. This is not to deny that other texts also play a role in these chapters. See Fichtner, 'Alttestamentliche Text', pp. 155-92; also Shaberg's discussion of Ps. 2, Dan. 7–12, and suspected Enoch traditions, especially in Wis. 4.10-15 ('Major Midrashic Traditions', pp. 74-87). As Larcher observes (*Études*, p. 91), there is a predilection on the part of the author of Wis. for the latter part of Isaiah, including Isa. 59 (*Études*, p. 91, and especially also n. 6; this is not to claim for Wisdom's author a modern understanding of the composition of the Isaianic corpus). Cf. also Schmitt, *Buch der Weisheit*, p. 16, and Skehan, 'Isaias', pp. 89-99 (especially pp. 93-96).

one who suffers the abuse of the impious.

A closer examination of the δίκαιος shows that, much as with the virtues in Isaiah 59, he is at the same time extremely vulnerable and invulnerable.[20] He is vulnerable to the attack and abuse of the ἀσεβεῖς. They conspire against him because of his confrontation (ἐλέγχειν) of their lawless and violent ways[21] with sufficient success to think they have indeed killed him. The ἀσεβεῖς, moreover, do not encounter the δίκαιος as a royal person, but rather as someone who is poor and weak, to be grouped together with defenceless widows and old men. The δίκαιος, much as the victimized virtues in Isaiah 59, is thus a prime candidate for the engagement of the Divine Warrior on his behalf, as the ἀσεβεῖς themselves attest (2.17-20).[22]

Whereas in Isaiah 59 those who practise ἀσέβεια are unfaithful members of the covenant community (indeed, as shown, in Isaiah 59 LXX little if any room is left for anyone other than faithless members of the community), here the identity of the ἀσεβεῖς is more enigmatic. The introductory verses of Wisdom of Solomon might leave the impression that they are the unjust royal oppressors of the Jews, whose identity in turn is subsumed under the paradigmatic and representative figure of the δίκαιος. However, the almost immediate diffusing of identity suggests that the line between the δίκαιοι and the ἀσεβεῖς runs through the middle of the Jewish community, indeed of the human community as a whole. In any event, the δίκαιος is the prime target of the abuse of those whose 'wisdom' has led to the false conclusion of impunity, indeed to a false γνῶσις as to the nature of reality as such.

In Isaiah 59 the virtues are not only vulnerable to the violence and injustice of the human community, but are also 'invulnerable', as their being taken up as allies and weapons into the armour of the Divine Warrior indicates. In Wisdom of Solomon the δίκαιοι share in that invulnerability. The δίκαιος makes himself an apparently vulnerable target with his words, both by his preposterous claims of status (παῖς

20. 'Invulnerable' is not really adequate. Invulnerablility, it will be shown, rests in the certain intervention of the Divine Warrior on behalf of faithful victims.

21. This parallels the role both of the 'prophet' who speaks in Isa. 59 and the virtues whose very existence is an affront to the ἄνομοι, and who for that reason must be removed from the roads and the marketplaces.

22. See the many texts which illustrate the relationship between the Divine Warrior and the outnumbered, defenseless, and abused faithful. E.g. Exod. 14, 15; Judg. 5-9; Pss. 9, 10; Isa. 40.10-11, 27-31; 41.8-20; 42.10-13, and, in effect, much of the rest of Second Isaiah.

κυρίου, 2.13; υἱὸς θεοῦ, v. 18; cf. v. 16) and by his critique of the impious (vv. 12-14). The narrator, however, goes on to picture the δίκαιος as an extraordinary person: he is created for immortality (ἀθανασία) and incorruptibility (ἀφθαρσία), that is, as the image of God's eternity (εἰκὼν τῆς ἰδίας ἀϊδιότητος; 2.23, 3.4). The δίκαιος is the true ἄνθρωπος (2.23). Furthermore, while the impious are pictured as torturing and murdering the δίκαιος, the narrator assures the reader that ultimately no torment will ever touch the δίκαιος (3.1-3). Thus, just as δικαιοσύνη is ἀθάνατος (1.15), so finally is the δίκαιος, whose passing only seems (δοκεῖν) to be death (3.2).

With evident care, the writer avoids using a certain kind of death language for the δίκαιος, namely θνήσκω and θάνατος. Those terms are reserved for the kind of death the impious experience, indeed for the kind of life they live (1.16, 5.13). I am not convinced that it is correct to refer to their death as a *Straftod*, as does Schmitt.[23] That has the effect of undervaluing the allusions to the Genesis account of death's entry into creation. While the δίκαιοι clearly do pass from this scene, their passing is not death. This is illustrated by the taking up of the Enoch tradition in ch. 4. While the earthly life of 'the one who pleased God' came to an end of sorts, he 'was taken up,' 'caught up' while living in the midst of sinners (4.10, 11). That explains the careful use of τελευτάω for the passing of the δίκαιος (3.18; 4.7) with its overtones of completion and purpose, evidently meant to convey a sense of passing from one chapter or phase of life to the next.[24]

To analyse the conceptualization of death and immortality in Wisdom of Solomon goes beyond the focus of this investigation.[25] At issue, rather, is the way the δίκαιος is understood. First of all, there is the image of the δίκαιος as paradigmatic innocent victim, dependent in large measure on the Fourth Servant Song. One sees also a high degree of idealization, an identification of the δίκαιος with supra-terrestrial reality, at the same time with creation prior to and beyond its conflict with corruption and death. One might even say that the δίκαιοι and the ἀσεβεῖς live in different worlds within the same reality, or vice versa.[26]

23. *Buch der Weisheit*, p. 54.

24. Larcher (*Études*, p. 300) refers to the 'death' of the righteous as 'le changement de mode d'une vie'.

25. See discussion and literature in Larcher, *Études*, ch. 4, and Reese, *Hellenistic Influence*, pp. 62-71.

26. See the striking description of this in relation to light and darkness in 17.20–

One is thus tempted to read Wisdom of Solomon as providing a certain metaphysic of righteousness and the righteous one(s), of immortality and incorruptibility.[27]

The reader is tipped off, however, that this 'static' and apparently ontological language is in actuality related to the dynamics of struggle. It is the 'hope' of the δίκαιοι which is full of immortality (3.4). Their status as sons, to the degree to which it connotes kingship, is dependent on the act of exaltation and enthronement at the hand of God. Survival at the hands of the violent and oppressing ἀσεβεῖς is dependent on the hand and arm of the Divine Warrior. Even the ἀσεβεῖς know that. The δίκαιος is, as the ἀσεβεῖς recognize, God's son (2.18; 5.5). But he is God's son if and only if God will act as ἀντιλαμβανόμενος and ῥυόμενος (2.18; cf. Isa. 59.15). Indeed, the vocabulary placed in the mouth of the ἀσεβεῖς in 2.18 prepares the ground for the theophany of the Divine Warrior as known from Isaiah 59 (cf. especially Isa 59.16, 20). Thus, while the theophany is introduced in Wis. 5.15 with the assertion that the δίκαιοι live into eternity, it becomes immediately apparent that immortality does not reside inherently in their 'anthropology' (3.2 notwithstanding), but in the fact that there is a reward (μισθός) with the Lord (ἐν κυρίῳ), that their welfare is being looked after by the Most High (cf. 3.1). It is for that reason (διὰ τοῦτο) that they will be exalted to royal status, which is signalled by the bestowal of royal crown and diadem (τὸ βασίλειον τῆς εὐπρεπείας καὶ τὸ διάδημα τοῦ κάλλους; 5.16). This is grounded (ὅτι) on the Divine Warrior's defence and intervention, elaborated in the theophany which follows. Thus while the ἄνθρωπος *qua* δίκαιος was created for ἀφθαρσία (2.23), at present, or ever since death and devil made their appearance (2.24), ἀθανασία is a hope, however certain for δίκαιοι, which requires the vindicating intervention of the Divine Warrior. The theophany of the Divine Warrior functions as an elaboration of the basis and process of the exaltation of the δίκαιοι, albeit in familiar symbolic and mythological language. It is thus not too strong to say that the appearance of the Divine Warrior is

18.1. The 'deep gulf' referred to earlier between the δίκαιοι and the ἀσεβεῖς in Wisdom of Solomon comes to the fore quickly when comparing the way darkness and light function in the Isaianic corpus. For example, 9.2; 42.6, 7; 60.1-3. Interestingly, the interpretation given Isa. 59 by Wisdom of Solomon reads Isa. 59.9 very much in keeping with Wis. 17.20–18.1.

27. Cf. again Georgi, 'Vorpaulinischer Hymnus', p. 270.

necessary to complete the scenario as it unfolds in Wisdom of Solomon.[28]

2. *The Divine Warrior*

The first section of Wisdom of Solomon (chs. 1–5) ends with the rising of the Divine Warrior as found in Isaiah 59. But the appropriation of Isa. 59.15b-20 is by no means slavish, or even strict. In Isa 59.15-16 יהוה/κύριος sees the deplorable state of affairs, notices that there is no one who comes to the aid (ἀντιλημψόμενος) of the abused (cf. Wis. 2.18) and then steps in to right the wrong by acting as warring judge and liberator. In Isaiah 59 MT the vindication and deliverance is not only of the virtues, but secondarily also of those who turn from evil (vv. 15 and 20). They have largely disappeared from Isaiah 59 LXX. In Wisdom of Solomon too there is little obvious attention paid to repentance. The δίκαιοι have little or no need of repentance.[29] They have no need to change. They have need only of vindication. The μετάνοια of the ἀσεβεῖς (5.3) is not repentance, in the sense of turning from evil.[30] Instead, μετάνοια represents their belated recognition of the salvation of the δίκαιος and the futility of their own existence. As such it parallels the insight of the people in Isa 59.9-15a into the reasons for their own fate. Also, as in Isaiah 59, the Divine Warrior rises following the recognition on the part of the ἀσεβεῖς of their misdeeds and the gravity of them.[31]

28. This is not to suggest that the scenario unfolds in linear fashion. On the contrary. A linear unfolding of the process has led precisely to the misguided attempts to sort out a sequential eschatology. It also runs aground on the deliberately unresolved tension between docetic and radically interventionist vocabulary.

29. Even the attack of the serpents in ch. 16 is not a response to sin but a preventative measure, lest (ἵνα μή) the people fall into deep forgetfulness (βαθεῖα λήθη; 16.11; cf. in contrast Num. 21.6-9). Mitigating this, on the other hand, is the view that suffering is the merciful discipline of God meant to make room for repentance (cf. 12.10); but even there the sage reminds God that mercy is wasted on those who are by origin evil (12.11), implying, conversely, that discipline is only effective for those who are not really in need of repentance. Little attempt is made to resolve the inherent tension in this juxtaposition.

30. Cf. 18.13, where the enemies of the just come to recognize them as God's son (sg.!) *after* their own first-born are slaughtered, i.e., after punishment.

31. 'Following' in a structural sense. In Isa. 59 the rising of the warrior is initially in the past tense, and should thus be considered as part of the recognition of the sinful people, i.e., 'that is why the Lord rose against us; that is why we experienced the absence of light and salvation.' In Wisdom of Solomon the Divine Warrior's

In Isaiah 59 the impious recognize what they have done to the divine virtues, and that the Divine Warrior rose (note the tense!) to defend and vindicate those virtues, bringing punishment on their tormenters. In Wisdom of Solomon the coming to consciousness of the ἀσεβεῖς centers on the futility (unreality) of their own lives, on the true nature of what the impious have done to the δίκαιοι, and on the exaltation of the δίκαιοι to the status of sons, kings, and co-regents through the intervention of the Divine Warrior.

Wisdom of Solomon's dependency on Isaiah 59 is further illustrated by the mixture of virtue and nature imagery that characterizes the appearance and warfare of the Divine Warrior.[32] Both dimensions are summarily stated in Wis. 5.17 and then elaborated in the verses following.

קנאה/ζῆλος, absent from Isaiah 59 LXX but present in the MT as the cloak in which the Divine Warrior wraps himself, is reintroduced in Wis. 5.17, although in a stronger light even than in Isaiah 59 MT.[33] In

rising is from the outset in the future tense. However, as will be pointed out, it is his rising which results in the παρρησία of the δίκαιοι, which in turn is precisely what has provoked the μετάνοια of the ἀσεβεῖς. 'Temporally', if it is appropriate to speak in this way in the case of Wisdom of Solomon, the rising of the warrior *precedes* the recognition of the ἀσεβεῖς, as is the case in Isa. 59.

32. Georgi views this as an apocalyptic *Kriegslied* employed here for quite unapocalyptic purposes (*Weisheit*, p. 418; 'Wesen der Weisheit', pp. 72, 73). There is no doubt that these verses constitute a hymn or poem which would have found resonance within apocalyptic circles. That is, after all, the basis of Hanson's thesis regarding Isa. 59. But as Georgi himself rightly points out, the motif of the Divine Warrior appears in prophetic and narrative writings, and especially also in the hymnody of the Hebrew/Jewish tradition ('Wesen der Weisheit', p. 72 n.14). The discussion of Isa. 59 above shows that as well. Given the skill with which the author of Wisdom of Solomon is credited with both writing and employing traditions and biblical texts, it is more likely for the author to have creatively elaborated upon the motif as found initially in Isa. 59, especially given his predilection for the latter part of the Isaianic corpus. After all, while it is muted in the LXX, the Hebrew, with which the author was evidently also familiar (or at least with a Greek translation reflective of the MT), clearly uses wind and water imagery dramatically to suggest the scope and vehemence of the Divine Warrior's intervention. The fact that that imagery is expanded here need not be witness to more than the creativity of the sage/poet.

33. Larcher (*Livre de la Sagesse*, p. 387) suggests that originally ζῆλος represented not an attribute or disposition of the Lord, but a hypostasized force that stirs up the Lord to put on his virtues as armor. If that is the case, which in Larcher's mind would very early on have required a correction to make God the subject, it would represent a reversal of Isa. 42.13 (κύριος ὁ θεὸς τῶν δυνάμεων ἐξελεύσεται καὶ

Wisdom of Solomon ζῆλος characterizes the whole of the Lord's armour (λήμψεται πανοπλίαν τὸν ζῆλον αὐτοῦ, 5.17). The virtues identified in vv. 18-19 (and, if ὀργή is to be counted a divine virtue, then also 20a) are subsumed under the rubric ζῆλος.

Ζῆλος carries connotations of fierce love and jealous wrath. It is unlikely that קנאה in Isaiah 59 has overtones of ardent love for the object of love, especially given its being paired with נקם and its rootage in Isaiah 63. It represents rather the ferocity of the warrior. In Wisdom of Solomon, however, the meaning of ζῆλος is somewhat more ambiguous, most especially since the phrase λήμψεται πανοπλίαν τὸν ζῆλον αὐτοῦ follows immediately upon references to the Lord's covering and shielding his δίκαιοι with his right hand and his arm. There is no mistaking the strong punitive and vengeful tone towards the ἀσεβεῖς. In its present location it is difficult to exclude from the meaning of ζῆλος the fierce love of the Most High for the δίκαιοι, expressed through the overwhelming power of the Divine Warrior.[34] The two connotations are of course closely related, differing in their effect largely on whether one is victim or victimizer.

Strict correspondence to the armour of Isa 59.17 is restricted to δικαιοσύνη as θώραξ (Wis. 5.18a). Isaiah's περικεφαλαία σωτηρίου becomes κόρυς κρίσις ἀνυπόκριτος (v. 18b). More important than the switch to κόρυς, which Larcher calls 'an ancient and poetic word',[35] illustrating what Georgi and others have noted about the proclivity by the author of Wisdom of Solomon toward novel or unusual vocabulary, is the replacing of σωτήριος with κρίσις. This accentuates the role of the κύριος as true king and judge regarding victims of oppression. Ἀνυπόκριτος is a *paranomasia*,[36] and is only weakly translated as

συντρίψει πόλεμον, ἐπεγερεῖ ζῆλον καὶ βοήσεται ἐπὶ τοὺς ἐχθροὺς αὐτοῦ μετὰ ἰσχύος).

34. Isaiah itself furnishes the author of Wisdom of Solomon with a number of instances where the connotation of ζῆλος is closer to fierce commitment to the object of God's love; e.g. Isa. 11.11 (καὶ ἔσται τῇ ἡμέρᾳ ἐκείνῃ προσθήσει κύριος τοῦ δεῖξαι τὴν χεῖρα αὐτοῦ τοῦ ζηλῶσαι τὸ καταλειφθὲν ὑπόλοιπον τοῦ λαοῦ); 42.13 (κύριος ὁ θεὸς τῶν δυνάμεων ἐξελεύσεται καὶ συντρίψει πόλεμον, ἐπεγερεῖ ζῆλον καὶ βοήσεται ἐπὶ τοὺς ἐχθροὺς αὐτοῦ μετὰ ἰσχύος); 63.15 (ποῦ ἐστιν ὁ ζῆλός σου καὶ ἡ ἰσχύς σοὺ ποῦ ἐστιν τὸ πλῆθος τοῦ ἐλέους σου καὶ τῶν οἰκτιρμῶν σου, ὅτι ἀνέσχου ἡμῶν...).

35. Larcher, *Livre de la Sagesse*, p. 389 (my translation).

36. One of several within this passage. στενοχωρίαν...στενάξονται (5.3); ἀτραπὸν τρόπιος (5.10); ποταμοὶ...ἀποτόμως (5.22).

'impartial.' Its relationship to judicial warfare is seen in 18.15, where the λόγος as divine executioner carries the ξίφος ὀξὺ τὴν ἀνυπόκριτον ἐπιταγήν σου. The shift from σωτήριος (Isa. 59.17) to κρίσις (Wis. 5.18) also illustrates the adjustment of the elements of armour to the activity of the virtues in Wisdom of Solomon, much as happens in Isaiah 59. Κρίσις, like δίκη, functions as means of judicial warfare.[37] While these virtues are not characterized as victims (that role is reserved for the δίκαιος), they are active within the Divine Warrior's activity as judge.

Verse 19 adds a novel item to the armour, a shield (ἀσπίς) of invincible holiness, piety, or integrity (ἀκαταμάχητος ὁσιότης[38]). 'Integrity' is likely the best rendering, given that that is the preferred translation for the other occasions where it appears in Wisdom of Solomon.[39] The author of Wisdom of Solomon intends to contrast the Divine Warrior and his virtues with the lack of integrity of his opponents. In 2.22 the ἀσεβεῖς do not know that the wages of ὁσιότης are nothing less than divine existence (v. 23). Their 'hope' rests in a pact with the devil, in an alliance with death (v. 24). The introduction of the ἄσπις as ἀκαταμάχητος ὁσιότης shows the way in which the motif of the Divine Warrior taken from Isaiah 59 is being shaped in the light of that contrast.

Verse 20 draws the ὀργή of Isa. 59.19 into the equipment of the warrior. Here the warrior will sharpen wrath (ἀπότομος ὀργή) into a sword (ῥομφαία). There is in my view no great significance to this choice of vocabulary for sword. Isaiah 66.16 employs ῥομφαία, a *hapax legomenon* in the Isaianic corpus, which otherwise uses μάχαιρα.[40] This may be evidence for the Wisdom of Solomon's already observed predilection for the latter part of Isaiah. However, it is also ubiquitous in Ezekiel, and Larcher has suggested that Ezek. 21.8-22, 33-36 is influential

37. Κρίσις: 6.5; 12.25, 26; 16.18; δίκη: 1.8; 11.20; 14.31.

38. 'Ακαταμάχητος should go with ὁσιότης rather than with ἀσπίς, since in both the preceding and following instances the modifiers clearly apply to the virtue rather than to the elements of the armour. So also Schmitt, *Buch der Weisheit*, p. 70.

39. 2.22; 9.3; 14.30; 18.9 Symmachus; but cf. 6.10. Georgi (*Weisheit*, p. 419) translates it this way as well, although he wonders whether the apocalyptic flavour of this passage is such that one should translate ὁσιότης as 'holiness'. However, the word never appears elsewhere within a context of war or in descriptions of the Divine Warrior in LXX, and in each instance (Deut. 9.5, 1 Kgdms 14.41, 3 Kgdms 9.4, and Prov. 14.32) can be translated by 'integrity'.

40. Indeed, μάχαιρα is overwhelmingly the preferred term for sword in Divine War contexts: e.g., Isa. 34.1-15, especially vv. 2, 5, 6.

here.[41] On the other hand, in Wis. 18.15 the λόγος wields the ξίφος in the exercise of ὀργή (cf. also vv. 20, 23), illustrating that even in similar contexts the author likes to vary the vocabulary. What the author clearly intends is to heighten the aggressive imagery of the *topos* as found in Isaiah 59. Thus ὀργή becomes a sword which the Divine Warrior readies, a wrath which is described as ἀπότομος, no doubt a deliberate play on 'cutting'. ὀργή is thus likened to the severing blow of a sword.

Verse 20a completes the clothing and equipment of the warrior, adding the weapon of the sword to the armour as found in Isaiah 59. It also shifts the focus from the armour to the weaponry of the Lord. Much as ζῆλος introduced the virtues in v. 17, of which ὀργή can be considered the last listed, ὀργή now also introduces the traditional 'nature' weapons of the Divine Warrior. Indeed, apart from 10.3 and 10 where it characterizes the disposition of the ἄδικοι, ὀργή is shorthand in Wisdom of Solomon for the judging and punishing activity of the Divine Warrior, either of God himself or of his surrogate λόγος. Its close connection here to the cosmos fighting as an ally of the Divine Warrior anticipates precisely that usage in the rest of Wisdom of Solomon.[42]

Verse 17 has the Divine Warrior making creation (κτίσις) into a weapon (ὁπλοποιέω). That Isaiah 59 furnishes some of the vocabulary for this is shown by the use of ἀμύνω/ἀμύνομαι, which can mean both to retaliate and to defend. Again the creativity with which vocabulary is adapted becomes apparent. In Isa. 59.16 LXX ἀμύνομαι describes the action of the right arm of God in defending his virtues. In Wisdom of Solomon 5, by contrast, the right arm is described as shielding and protecting the δίκαιοι (v.16), whereas the κτίσις is used to 'ward off' (ἄμυναν), or, if something like the Lucianic recension of Isa. 59.18 LXX was available to the author,[43] to 'punish' the enemy.

In Isaiah 59 LXX ὀργή follows immediately after the description of the armour and clothing of the Divine Warrior, and is then described as analogous to a violent river (ὡς ποταμὸς βίαιος), thus identifying ὀργή with traditional divine warfare nature imagery. Correspondingly, in Wisdom of Solomon ὀργή is employed both to complete the image of the

41. Larcher, *Livre de la Sagesse*, p. 390.

42. 11.9—allusion to the Nile being turned to blood; 16.5—affliction by wild beasts; 18.20-25—affliction through plague, the instrument of personified ὀργή.

43. '..., ἀμύναν τοῖς ἐχθροῖς αὐτοῦ,...' See discussion of the textual problems of Isa. 59.18 above.

warrior and to introduce the range of weaponry at his disposal. Larcher[44] has suggested that much the way ζῆλος is a rubric for the virtues in v. 17, ὀργή subsumes the following list of ways the cosmos represents the weaponry of the Lord. One should not push this too far, since the phenomena which are now described all function more or less as hypostasized powers, the troops, as it were, of the cosmos which fights as God's ally (συνεκπολεμέω) against the madmen (παράφρονες, 5.20[45]).

These are clearly meant to signify ways God himself wars. But within this poem the cosmos 'comes to the aid of Yahweh', to borrow a phrase from the war song of Deborah and Barak (Judg. 5.20). As indicated earlier, these manifestations are familiar from Divine War songs: lightning as arrows from a well-strung bow of clouds, hailstones as from a giant slingshot or catapult, raging sea and river, and a powerful wind.[46] Water and wind/spirit are already familiar from Isa. 59.19. They follow the fearsome name (and glory [MT]) of the Lord. In Wisdom of Solomon Isaiah's ποταμὸς βίαιος has become 'rivers which flood relentlessly' (ποταμοὶ συγκλύσουσιν ἀποτόμως[47]), paired with the raging water of the sea (ὕδωρ θαλάσσης). Wisdom of Solomon follows water with wind imagery, now in imitation of Isaiah 59 MT.[48] The ἀσεβεῖς will be resisted by a πνεῦμα δυνάμεως[49] that will winnow them like a storm (λαῖλαψ). These are preceded by images of arrows and bow, hail and catapult/slingshot (once again possibly suggested by Ezek. 13.11, 13 LXX; 38.22), thus expanding the traditional nature war imagery, and

44. *Livre de la Sagesse*, p. 391.

45. Cf. the similar characterization of the lawless as ἄφρονες in Isa. 59.7.

46. See the inventory of nature phenomena as divine weaponry in Chapter 1, nn. 26-28, 37.

47. Note again the *paranomasia* ποταμοι...ἀποτόμως (Winston, *Wisdom*, p. 16 n. 12; Larcher, *Livre de la Sagesse*, p. 395).

48. Isaiah LXX either does not know of the רוח יהוה in 59.19 or 'interprets' it as θύμος.

49. 'Powerful blast' (Winston and similarly others) rather than 'spirit of power' is likely correct, most especially since it is paired with λαῖλαψ. However, there is resonance with the spirit referred to repeatedly in Wis. 1. There πνεῦμα *qua* σοφία flees deceit and foolishness (vv. 4-6), but nevertheless functions as the eyes and ears of justice (δίκη, v. 7). Πνεῦμα can be seen now as returning in ch. 5 to wreak vengeance. Notice also the way πνεῦμα δυνάμεως and δίκη are joined with creation in 11.20 in a description of judgment (cf. verses preceding 11.20; cf. also 14.31). It is misguided to exclude the resonance of either wind or spirit, regardless of which meaning is preferred.

replacing the name and glory of Isa. 59.19.

This use of nature imagery and the reference to the cosmos as ally draws not only on imagery suggested by Isaiah 59, but reaches back more broadly to the traditional ways of characterizing the power and intervention of Yahweh. The Song of Miriam and Moses in Exod. 15, the Song of Deborah and Barak in Judg. 5, the Song of Moses in Deut. 32, and numerous other Divine War texts illustrate that the author is on familiar ground. In Wisdom, however, the idea of the cosmos as warrior, or the use of creation as weapon, is repeatedly illustrated in the following chapters and constitutes a particularly important way in which the author of Wisdom of Solomon understands divine warfare. Chapter 11, for example, characterizes natural phenomena, whether water or beast, as part of the arsenal of the creator/warrior (v. 11), who can use the same elements as a means of meeting the need of his people and of meting out punishment and torment on their victimizers. The very creation that God has arranged by measure, number, and weight[50] is at the same time a malleable weapon in the hands of the Divine Warrior.[51] This theme is expanded upon within the critique of the worship of living creatures, as in the text just cited, and also in generalizing reflections on the experience of Israel in Egypt, specifically the plagues (16.17, 24; 18.8). Even the essential elements of creation such as water and fire can 'forget' their (usual) power when acting at the behest of the Divine Warrior (16.22, 23; cf. 19.18-21).[52] The subservience of creation to the active and responsive will of the Divine Warrior is made quite explicit in that in the end it is not creation *qua* creation which saves, but the all-healing word (ὁ λόγος ὁ πάντας ἰώμενος; 16.12; cf. ῥῆμα in v. 26); conversely it is not plague and flood as such which destroy, but the all-powerful word (ὁ παντοδύναμος λόγος; 18.15).

Creation is thus a moral phenomenon. On the one hand, it is well-ordered and solid, so much so that the ἀσεβεῖς think they can enjoy it

50. Cf. v. 20: ἀλλὰ πάντα μέτρῳ καὶ ἀριθμῷ καὶ σταθμῷ διέταξας.

51. God can create new hitherto unknown beasts (v. 17), even though creation is repeatedly celebrated as a well-ordered whole (v. 20; cf. 7.17-22). Georgi (*Weisheit*, p. 443) sees 11.20d as beginning a new section. Even if that is so, the ἀλλά presently juxtaposes the notion of order with God's intention as Divine Warrior, an emphasis immediately present again in v. 21.

52. Cf. the strikingly similar reflections on the role of the elements in the destruction of the Egyptians in Philo, *Vit. Mos.* 1.96. Note the stress that God can use the elements as means of destruction 'whenever he wishes' (ὁπότε βουληθείη).

(2.6). On the other hand, it is profoundly precarious.[53] It serves to punish and to save, by the very same means. While 'cause and effect' is too simple a way to state Wisdom of Solomon's understanding of the way reality boomerangs, as it were, there is a sense in which Wisdom plays on that theme. There is no impunity. Evil has its consequences. Only, the author of Wisdom of Solomon identifies the 'effect' of injustice as the deliberate and direct intervention of the Divine Warrior, whose direct action it is when evil deeds, whether the worship of animals, the fashioning of idols, or the practice of violence, return to haunt and bring down the ἀσεβεῖς (11.16; 12.23; 14.11 [31]; 16.1). Thus, if there is cause and effect, it is repeatedly initiated by God. It is not rooted in the structures of a cosmos located this side of God's activity. Creation makes war alongside of, or rather, in the hand of the Divine Warrior. Not surprisingly, as 11.15-20 shows clearly, to be pursued by δίκη is not of a different order than to be pursued by a hostile κόσμος.

Intimately related to this is the notion that the very means of doing evil become a weapon in the hands of the Divine Warrior. Not surprisingly then, the imagery of storm and raging water gives way to the warriors named ἀνομία and κακοπραγία in v. 23cd. 'Ανομία's effect is described in the imagery of natural disaster, while the effect of κακοπραγία has explicit political consequence. One might thus see this as a movement back to the political vocabulary of 1.1, preparing the way for the reintroduction of the kings or judges of the earth in 6.1.[54] This is no doubt the effect. But one should not thereby sever lawlessness and 'criminal action' (Winston) from the weaponry listed previously. There is biblical precedent for identifying the evil deeds of oppressors as the action of the Divine Warrior against them, not least in the Isaianic

53. 'Precarious' as 'depending on the will or pleasure of another' and 'characterized by a lack of security or stability that threatens with danger' (*Webster's New Collegiate Dictionary*, 1980). Collins ('Cosmos and Salvation') misreads, in my opinion, Wisdom of Solomon's understanding of creation. Collins's stress on wisdom as mediator of a well-structured, 'scientifically' predictable universe, thus rendering the experience of God as only indirect, undervalues the presence of the Divine Warrior motif within Wis. The presence of that tradition renders the universe as anything but 'fixed' (p. 128) or 'essentially impersonal' (p. 130). Instead of 'natural laws' (p. 131) one should speak of the constant alertness and vigilance of the Divine Warrior (e.g. 1.7-10), who, as is shown in the paradigmatic experience of Israel, is and will be quite prepared to unleash creation as weapon.

54. Schmitt refers to v. 23cd as a *kompositorische Gelenkstelle* (*Buch der Weisheit*, p. 73), Georgi as *redaktionelle Überleitung* (*Weisheit*, p. 418).

corpus.[55] In Wisdom of Solomon it is explicitly stated again in 11.16 and 12.23. Furthermore, the language of laying waste the land is familiar to the readers and hearers of Wisdom as the language of divine warfare.[56] Thus while the last part of v. 23 may indeed function as a bridge to the focus on kings in ch. 6, it should not be missed that ἀνομία and κακοπραγία are here described as warring hypostases, one way κτίσις and κόσμος fight alongside the Divine Warrior.

3. *Eschatology*

Much scholarly discussion of this text centres on the eschatology it implies or in which it participates. Wisdom of Solomon 5.15-23 has been seen as the culminating event of the 'Book of Eschatology'. It has been identified by Georgi as an apocalyptic war hymn, though one adapted by a redactor for quite unapocalyptic purposes.[57] As I have argued in Chapter 1, it is by no means necessary to view the introduction of the Divine Warrior in Isaiah 59 as eschatological in any exclusive or final sense. The writer(s) and the audience of Isaiah 59 had ample opportunity to identify their corporate suffering in the more or less recent exilic and postexilic past as the action of the Divine Warrior against them. Thus the introduction of the Divine Warrior in the past tense in Isa. 59.15b comes as no surprise. But then neither does the shift to the future tense in v. 18. After all, the intention of this literature is not only to explain the past and present, but to warn of judgment and to call to repentance, precisely by means of an appeal to the familiar figure of the Divine Warrior and his well-known past activity. There can be no doubt that the motif of the Divine Warrior coming as judge at the end of the present evil age plays a prominent role in apocalyptic literature. But the ubiquity of that motif within the narrative, poetic, and liturgical traditions of Israel and Judah, and, as we see here, in the sapiential tradition, suggests wide appropriation and use of the motif for eschatological and noneschatological purposes.[58]

55. Cf. especially the parallelism in Isa. 9.18, 19.

56. Cf. Isa. 13 and 24. Noteworthy is that specific judgments rather than final judgment, at least in the case of ch. 13, are described in the macro-language of the devastation of the whole earth. This form of exaggeration is endemic to the imagery of Divine War, as the war hymns of Israel amply attest.

57. Georgi, *Weisheit*, p. 418.

58. Georgi makes this point when arguing for a sapiential matrix of apocalyptic ('Wesen der Weisheit', p. 72 n.14).

Wisdom of Solomon is one important instance of this. What leads to an eschatological reading of the Divine Warrior motif in Wisdom is, first of all, the sole use of the future tense in 5.17-23. If, as here proposed, the author is directly dependent on Isaiah 59, then this represents an innovation. But it need not represent more than the intention to warn and frighten on the one hand, and to comfort on the other. That it plays on eschatological and apocalyptic fears and anticipations is not thereby denied.

The second factor leading to an eschatological reading of this text is the relationship of the rising of the Divine Warrior to the vindication of the just and the punishment of the impious. The theophany is immediately preceded by the exaltation and enthronement of the just (5.15-16), and earlier by the recognition of the impious that the just have survived their torture, and have been shown to be sons of God (5.4-5). This has led to various attempts to sort out what kind of an eschatological scenario the author of Wisdom of Solomon employs as he unfolds the drama of the first five chapters.[59]

Attempts at a clear eschatological scenario are, however, misguided.[60] The reference to the day of decision (ἡ ἡμέρα διαγνώσεως) in 3.18 suggests that the author may hold to some notion of a final vindication of the just. It may also be, however, that operating alongside is a parallel notion of an immediate vindication of the individual δίκαιος upon his passing. The nature of the document and the rhetorical and theological strategies are such that they render any attempt to establish a clear schema, as one might within an apocalyptic frame of reference, quite impossible. What tips the reader off that a linear scenario is not the point is, first of all, the combination of an anthropology of immortality and an eschatology of vindication. Secondly, the reader's sense of sequence is disrupted by a bewildering dislocation of events. While the impious come to recognize the vindication of the just, they do so *after* his passing but *before* the coming of the Divine Warrior which would bring about their own death. Their death is presumably subsumed under the destruction implied by the rising of the Divine Warrior (cf. 4.18, 19). On the other hand, it is the rising of the Divine Warrior which brings about the vindication and exaltation of the just (5.15-17). In short, the 'standing' of the δίκαιοι as confident judges in condemnation over the impious in 5.1

59. See especially discussion in Larcher, *Études*, pp. 301-305, and the comments throughout his discussion of Wis. 5.15-23 in *Livre de la Sagesse*, pp. 381-99.

60. Cf. Nickelsburg, *Resurrection*, pp. 88-89.

presupposes the *prior* intervention of the Divine Warrior. Furthermore, the fact that the activity of the δίκαιοι is at certain points described as that of kings and judges *vis-à-vis* the impious (e.g. 4.16) forces the unavoidable conclusion that the just participate in some way in the judicial warfare of the Divine Warrior. Finally, much of the rest of Wisdom of Solomon elaborates not only on the evil practices of the ἀσεβεῖς and the suffering of the δίκαιοι, but on the intervention of the Divine Warrior on their behalf, and finally also on the δίκαιος as warrior.[61] This is done with allusions to recognizable but unnamed past events—the plagues of Egypt—which, precisely because of their paradigmatic character, have clear implications about the present and future. Here lies in large measure the reason for the systematic deletion of the names from persons and places that are nevertheless immediately familiar to the audience. It becomes abundantly clear, then, that the author does not intend to describe a uniquely future event, but rather an oft-repeated one, moreover one which is certain to repeat itself in the face of future victimization and injustice by past, present, and future pharaohs and their ilk (note 6.1). My reticence to read Isaiah 59 as solely or even primarily eschatological is thus pertinent to Wisdom of Solomon 5 as well.

4. *Observations*

To summarize, the discussion of the Divine Warrior motif in Wis. 5.17-23 shows the following. First, it appears that the sage has conflated the

61. In addition to the reference to the δίκαιος as judge in 4.16, implied more generally by the exaltation of the δίκαιοι to royal status in 5.15, 16, note also the warfare of the ἀνὴρ ἄμεμπτος as πρόμαχος in 18.21. Mirroring the Divine Warrior, he fights off the Divine Warrior's ally or surrogate (λόγος and/or ὀργή) with his own λόγος (v. 22). He is clad, it should be noticed, in a long robe depicting the whole cosmos (cf. 5.20!) and wearing divine greatness upon the diadem of his head (v. 24; cf. 5.16 and Isa. 28.5, 6; cf. 62.3). That the ἀνὴρ ἄμεμπτος is allusive of Aaron in his capacity as priest does not lessen his paradigmatic role as warring δίκαιος. The connection of virtues to vestments of the priesthood can be observed in Exod. 28.23, 29; Lev. 8.8 LXX; Ps. 131.9, 16 LXX; 1 Esdr. 5.40; Sir. 45.10; *T. Levi* 8.2, and possibly 1 QSb 5.23-28 (which may or may not relate to a priestly figure). Furthermore, the relationship between the status of priest and exaltation is illustrated in Isa. 61.6 (cf. 1 Pet. 2.5, 9). Royal (messianic) and priestly language converge repeatedly in the New Testament as a way of ascribing status to Jesus and to his followers (e.g. Hebrews; cf. CD 20.1).

scenario of the abused δίκαιος as represented in the Fourth Servant Song with the scenario of Isaiah 59.

Secondly, by employing the image of the Divine Warrior as found in Isaiah 59, the author intends to convey some sense that the divine virtues, present in the exercise of human relationships either as victims or as hunters (see discussion of κρίσις and δίκη above), are an essential component of the Divine Warrior's intervention as judge and vindicator.

Thirdly, the author elaborates on what is a secondary and illustrative feature of the warrior as found in Isaiah 59 to show that the cosmos is not an immutable orderly creation, but an instrument or weapon in the hand of the Divine Warrior, profoundly related to the exercise of divine virtues. Thus the well-ordered universe is not a 'scientifically' predictable machine but a 'morally' predictable and thus malleable ὅπλον, constantly available to the Divine Warrior for vengeance and vindication. Creation is also not reliable in the sense that an apocalyptic calculus can predict when the ceiling will fall in on the ἀσεβεῖς. The shifts in tense and scene ensure only the certainty that the Divine Warrior intervenes on behalf of the just. The how and when are deliberately left to an awakened imagination. For example, a particulary shocking source of dismay for the ἀσεβεῖς is that those who are despicably weak and vulnerable to their violence turn out to be sons of God (or 'son' [corporate singular] as in 18.13), and thus implicitly participants in the exercise of divine kingship, judgment, and thus divine warfare. The last laugh is had by victims. This parallels the scenario of Isaiah 59.

Fourthly, by placing the virtues of Yahweh in the role of the abused and vindicated just one(s), Isaiah 59 is an adaptation of the wisdom tale of the vindicated, perhaps specifically of Second Isaiah's story of abuse and vindication of the servant of Yahweh. Isaiah 59 thus reinterprets the Isaiah 52–53 tradition, now not as an expression of generosity and reconciliation toward enemies but as a way to challenge and censure.[62] It is not the people who (corporately) inhabit that role of abused Servant, as in Isaiah 52–53, but Yahweh's own virtues. Thus it is the very people who have become used to seeing themselves as the recipients of Yahweh's help who in Isaiah 59 are painted as villains. The author of Wisdom of Solomon subsumes that reinterpretation of the

62. A vestige of generosity resides in the implicit call to repentance by picturing Yahweh as a redeemer for those who turn from evil (vv. 15a, 20). The 'turners' are gone from LXX. A further vestige of generosity resides in the redactional placement of ch. 59, located as it is between Isa. 58 and 60–62.

abused and vindicated Servant within the paradigmatic character and fate of the δίκαιος. The author reaches back to Isaiah 52–53[63] and reads it through the lens of Isaiah 59. This allows identification of the δίκαιος with the divine virtues, and, conversely, of the virtues with the true people of God. The line between divine and human realms is thereby smudged.

Fifth, in Isaiah 59 the motif of the Divine Warrior conjures Yahweh's warfare against his people and on behalf of his virtues and those who practice them. The mythological colours signify the magnitude and comprehensiveness of God's intervention against his human enemies—his own people. Nothing in the text suggests that the enemies of the Divine Warrior are superhuman, although mythological enemies do appear earlier in the Isaianic corpus.[64] Enmity against Yahweh is clearly pictured as having mythological stature, as it were, in that it is the messengers or surrogates of God in the 'persons' of the virtues who are abused and victimized. Nevertheless, the author of Isaiah 59 leaves no doubt that it is the practice of oppression within the context of human relations which constitutes this assault on Yahweh's friends and which elicits his intervention. The 'war', then, is between human enemies of God, on the one hand, and the mythological Divine Warrior, on the other.

Wisdom of Solomon represents much the same view. While Wisdom of Solomon is no stranger to hypostasization, or to *Kunstmythos*,[65] at no point are the enemies of God anything other than the ἀσεβεῖς. True, they are of the party of θάνατος (1.16, 2.24). But neither θάνατος nor διάβολος (2.24) take the offensive against God or the just, nor are they warred against.[66] At most they function behind the scenes. The ἀσεβεῖς have no alibi; that is to say, they cannot claim to be controlled in their enmity by some exterior force. Nor do they have supernatural allies: 'Hades has no kingdom on earth' (1.14). That is true even though the δίκαιος as true ἄνθρωπος takes on a paradigmatic, supra-specific, even docetic, and thus in some sense mythological quality. His reality and fate

63. See especially Nickelsburg's discussion in *Resurrection*, pp. 58-68.

64. Cf. e.g. Isa. 51.9-10; cf. 14.12; 27.1.

65. Georgi, 'Wesen der Weisheit', p. 75. Besides the mythological colouring of the δίκαιος (brought about by the expunging of all names, and by the docetic characterization of his 'passing') see not least the figure of σοφία, and of the characters of πνεῦμα, δίκη, κρίσις, λόγος and the various parts of the armour and weaponry of the Divine Warrior discussed above.

66. The only warring against a superhuman foe happens in the struggle of the ἀνὴρ ἄμεμπτος against the divine ὀργή in Wis. 18.20-25.

is constantly traversing the dividing line between this realm and the heavenly or transcendent one. It is not quite true to Wisdom of Solomon to refer to the enemies of God as 'human', since true humanity is reserved for the δίκαιος. Nevertheless, it is only within the mundane reality of the ἀσεβεῖς that God functions as Divine Warrior.[67]

To conclude, Wis. 5.17-23 represents a highly creative adaptation of, among other texts and traditions, Isaiah 59. In the preceding verses and chapters the author appropriates the essential building blocks of human sinfulness, reflected in the corruption and violence against the innocent, and the provocation of the Divine Warrior to intervene on behalf of victims who in one way or another function as God's representatives. Significant movement has taken place in the identification of the victim as the δίκαιος. The rising of the Divine Warrior has also been tied more tightly to the central concern of vindication and exaltation. Concomitantly, hostility to God's enemies is heightened. Not only are the ἀσεβεῖς punished; they are essentially excluded from the reality God and his δίκαιοι inhabit. The tradition of the Divine Warrior has thus been drawn into the dualism which comes to characterize gnostic writings.[68] However, the fact that the demise of the ἀσεβεῖς and the exaltation of the δίκαιοι is dependent on the *intervention* of the Divine Warrior means that his presence in Wisdom of Solomon also subverts this radical dualism. In traversing the boundary between the 'realities' of light and darkness, he represents the point of intersection between the realm in which the ἀσεβεῖς live and that of the δίκαιοι.

The way Wisdom of Solomon has employed Isaiah 59 recalls Hanson's reading of Third Isaiah as an abandonment of Second Isaiah's generosity of vision. In the end, however, one will need to recognize that underlying both Isaiah 59 and Wisdom of Solomon 5 are essentially sermonic interests. The diatribal character of the first section has been widely recognized.[69] Even Georgi's reading of Wisdom of Solomon as a gnostic

67. One should observe here as well that whatever vestige of lament was still present in the noting of the absence of an ἀνήρ as ἀντιλημψόμενος in Isa. 59.16 LXX, no such regret is present here. The vindication of the δίκαιοι is strictly κύριος's doing. The just participate in that warfare by virtue of their exaltation. Cf. discussion of the ἀνὴρ ἄμεμπτος in n. 61.

68. Cf. Georgi's understanding of Wisdom of Solomon as the earliest Gnostic document (*Weisheit*, p. 394; *idem*, 'Wesen der Weisheit', p. 80).

69. Georgi, *Weisheit*, p. 393, and the literature cited in n. 9; Reese, *Hellenistic Influence*, pp. 111-14. To identify Wisdom of Solomon as a *logos protreptikos* (Collins, *Between Athens and Jerusalem*, p. 182; Nickelsburg, *Jewish Literature*,

document suggests that the strategy informing the document is the acquisition of gnosis—*Bewußtsein.*[70] The intention of the authors of Isaiah 59 and Wisdom of Solomon 5, whatever the shock value of giving little if any play to those who repent, or to the salvific dimension of divine warfare, is not simply to reveal the fate of the ἀσεβεῖς and to confirm the audience's identification as either the damned or the saved, but rather to awaken, cajole to repentence, and prod to knowledge. The presence of the Divine Warrior tradition is an important instrument of such a strategy.

Athens and Jerusalem, p. 182; Nickelsburg, *Jewish Literature*, p. 175; Reese, *Hellenistic Influence*, pp. 117-21; and Winston, *Wisdom*, p. 18) may undervalue the confrontative nature of this document, seen especially in the use of the Divine Warrior motif.

70. Georgi, 'Wesen der Weisheit', p. 80.

Chapter 3

THE DIVINE WARRIOR IN 1 THESSALONIANS 5

1 Thessalonians 5 distinguishes itself from Isaiah 59 and Wisdom of Solomon 5 in that the circumstances surrounding the letter are clearly ascertainable. This study concurs with the critical scholarly consensus as to author (Paul [and Silvanus and Timothy]), date (50 CE),[1] provenance (Greece, specifically Corinth), audience (a new congregation of mostly Gentiles), and circumstance (Timothy's encouraging report, which evidently included issues specifically raised by the Thessalonians[2]). Paul and his colleagues desire to keep in touch, to encourage, and to buttress the confidence of a somewhat bewildered and anxious community of new believers.[3]

1. For a critical sifting of the scholarly discussion on date, including the proposal that the Thessalonian correspondence be dated around 40 CE (e.g., G. Lüdemann, *Paul, Apostle to the Gentiles: Studies in Chronology* [trans. F.S. Jones; Philadelphia: Fortress Press, 1984], pp. 205-38, especially 238), see P. Jewett, *The Thessalonian Correspondence: Pauline Rhetoric and Millenarian Piety* (Philadelphia: Fortress Press, 1986), pp. 49-60.

2. Note the use of 'περὶ δὲ...' in 4.13 and 5.1. Cf. Jewett, *Thessalonian Correspondence*, p. 92.

3. In addition to the work by Jewett cited above, see the extensive discussion of these issues in the introductions to the New Testament and the commentaries on 1 Thessalonians, notably E. Best, *A Commentary on the First and Second Epistles to the Thessalonians* (BNTC; London: A. & C. Black, 1972); F.F. Bruce, *1 & 2 Thessalonians* (WBC, 45; Waco, TX: Word, 1982); E. von Dobschütz, *Die Thessalonicher-Briefe* (ed. F. Hahn; Göttingen: Vandenhoeck & Ruprecht, 1974 [1909]); I.H. Marshall, *1 and 2 Thessalonians* (NCBC; Grand Rapids: Eerdmans 1983); A. Oepke, *Die Briefe an die Thessalonicher* (NTD, 8, *Die kleineren Briefe des Apostels Paulus;* Göttingen: Vandenhoeck & Ruprecht, 1970 [1933]), pp. 122-52; J.M. Reese, OSFS, *1 and 2 Thessalonians* (Wilmington, DE: Michael Glazier, 1979), and B. Rigaux, OFM, *Saint Paul: Les épîtres aux Thessaloniciens* [EBib; Paris: Gabalda, 1956]); studies by H. Koester, *Introduction to the New Testament.* II. *History and Literature of Early Christianity* (Philadelphia: Fortress Press, 1982),

1. *The Context of the Motif of the Divine Warrior's Armour*

The motif of the Divine Warrior's armour is taken up toward the end of the letter in 5.8, as part of the larger pericope of 5.1-11. Whether one identifies this pericope as part of the parenesis proper, as most scholars do,[4] or judges it with Koester to be part of the eschatological section following the parenesis or the body proper (4.12–5.11),[5] the use of the cohortative subjunctive in vv. 6 and 8 and the imperative in v. 11 indicate that this pericope has parenetic intent. This is the case even if, in Jewett's words, we find an 'interlacing of exhortation and topical material'.[6]

1 Thess. 5.1-11 is introduced by a phrase virtually identidical to 4.9: Περὶ δὲ τῶν χρόνων καὶ τῶν καιρῶν, ἀδελφοί, οὐ χρείαν ἔχετε ὑμῖν γράφεσθαι, suggesting the introduction of a new topic or concern. The distinctness of this pericope from the immediately preceding discussion of the parousia of Christ in 4.13-18 has led to the suggestion that 5.1-11 is an interpolation.[7] Whereas in 4.13-18 Paul intends to give

pp. 112-14; *idem*, 'Apostel und Gemeinde in den Briefen an die Thessalonicher', in D. Lührmann and G. Strecker (eds.), *Kirche: Festschrift für Günther Bornkamm* (Tübingen: Mohr [Siebeck], 1980), pp. 287-98; *idem*, '1 Thessalonians—Experiment in Christian Writing', in F.F. Church and T. George (eds.), *Continuity and Discontinuity in Church History: Essays Presented to George Huntston Williams* (SHCT, 19; Leiden: Brill, 1979), pp. 33-44; A.J. Malherbe's studies, most recently *Paul and the Thessalonians: The Philosophic Tradition of Pastoral Care* (Philadelphia: Fortress Press, 1987).

4. For an informative chart surveying the scholarly proposals on the epistolary structure of 1 Thessalonians, see Jewett, *Thessalonian Correspondence,* 220-21.

5. Koester, *Introduction*, II, p. 55.

6. Jewett, *Thessalonian Correspondence,* p. 78.

7. Gerhard Friedrich ('1 Thessalonicher 5.1-11, der apologetische Einschub eines Späteren', *ZTK* 10 [1973], pp. 288-315) has suggested that this is an interpolation, likely from a Lukan circle (pp. 307-309) intended to distance Paul from apocalyptic calculation. I have little difficulty with a view of Paul that distances him from apocalyptic calculation, but I see no reason why these verses cannot be from his hand. That Paul weaves traditions (e.g., like those found later in Lk. 12, 21 and Mt. 24, 26) into this pericope is recognized by everyone who argues for the authenticity of this section. Its force is indeed largely dependent on the familiarity of the language and the motifs, if not for his audience then certainly for Paul. The use of tradition in these verses has been studied with thoroughness, for example, by Rigaux (*Saint Paul*, pp. 552-74; 'Tradition et rédaction dans 1 Th. 5.1-10', *NTS* 21 [1974–75], pp. 318-40); J. Plevnik ('1 Thess. 5, 1-11: Its Authenticity, Intention and

worried Thessalonians a sense of security, in 5.1-11 he intends to take it away again. In contrast, I take the position that not only is Paul the author of this pericope but, what is more, the intentions underlying 5.1-11 are consonant with the strategies already employed in 4.13-18, which are to encourage and strengthen the believers. Paul is concerned, however, not only to meet the Thessalonians' need for reassurance as in 4.13-18, but to address on this occasion their sense of identity and mission. These verses are a next step, then, from reassurance to the shaping of consciousness, identity, and task. Therein lies the chief motive for the use of the divine armour in 5.8.

Paul responds in 5.1-11 to the issue of 'times and seasons' by first deflecting concern for it, initially by means of an ironic use of ἀκριβῶς. Whereas in 4.13-18 Paul has just provided a scenario of Christ's return that is intended to reassure the Thessalonians that they have not 'missed the train', in 5.1-11 he attempts to distance himself from a stance that would claim to know precisely (ἀκριβῶς) how and when events are to unfold. In 4.9 the Thessalonians have no need for information because God himself has taught them. On this issue they have no need for information because they know very well that the time of the coming of the day of the Lord is not knowable. With just a hint of sarcasm Paul reminds them in v. 2 that they know 'precisely' that the day of the Lord comes like a thief in the night, like the onset of labour, and thus that its coming cannot be known 'precisely'.[8]

Paul couples this reminder, secondly, with assurances about the identity of the Thessalonians as believers. They are neither *in* nor *of* darkness or night (vv. 4, 5); rather, they are 'sons of light' and 'sons of day' (υἱοὶ φωτός καὶ υἱοὶ ἡμέρας; v. 5). Furthermore, Christ has died for them and they are thus in a position to obtain salvation (vv. 9, 10). Their

Message', *Bib* 60 [1979], pp. 71-90); more recently L. Aejmelaeus (*Wachen vor dem Ende: Die traditionsgeschichtliche Wurzeln von 1. Thess 5.1-11 und Luk 21.34-36* [Suomen Eksegeettisen Seuran Julkaisuja, 44; Helsinki, 1985]). They argue compellingly against Friedrich for the authenticity of these verses.

8. Interestingly, the author of Wisdom of Solomon employs οἱ χρόνοι and οἱ καιροί as virtual synonyms in 8.8 and 7.18, but with no relation at all to divine intervention, except perhaps by implication resulting from the juxtaposition of divine intervention employing the forces of nature (κτίσις as weapon, 5.17) with Sophia's 'scientific' instruction regarding the (apparently) immutable structures of creation (ch. 7). See also Dan. 2.21; 7.12; Acts 1.7, where the overtones of χρόνοι and καιροί are clearly related to the set times of divine action; but only in Dan. 7.12 is it understood apocalyptically.

status and location renders their concern about times and seasons unnecessary. The Thessalonians are immune to the sudden invasion of the day of the Lord, because they are not even there, at least not as 'recipients' of the day. They are neither in nor of the darkness into which the day of the Lord comes. The appropriate stance for them is to be vigilant and sober, wearing the divine armour (v. 8). In light of the progression of Paul's argument, vigilance and sobriety (γρηγορῶμεν καὶ νήφωμεν; v. 6) should not be read, therefore, in relation to the threat of the day, but rather as the disposition of the invader, or, less dramatically, the stance of readiness for battle appropriate for those wearing the armour of the Divine Warrior.[9]

Two purposes converge: the divine armour serves to assure in the strongest possible terms the security with which the believers can look to a profoundly dramatic future (and present). Secondly, given its familiarity as the armour which the Divine Warrior wears, the summons to the Thessalonians to put on that armour serves as a startling signifier of status, and, by implication, task.

2. *The Appropriation of the Tradition*

While, as indicated above, the concerns of 4.13-18 and those of 5.1-11 are not in tension with each other, they should not simply be conflated.[10] 5.1-11 focusses not so much on the coming of Christ with all his saints to deliver 'us' from the coming wrath (ἐκ τῆς ὀργῆς τῆς ἐρχομένης; 1.10) as on the coming of ὀργή itself, alluded to in 5.2, 3 by the ἡμέρα κυρίου and the ὄλεθρος which come with unpredictable suddenness (αἰφνίδιος). It finds its echo in the ὀργή of v. 9. Expected is the ὀργή θεοῦ.[11] This does not mean that Paul intends clearly to distinguish the day of the Lord from the parousia of Christ, as 1.10 illustrates (cf. also Rom. 2.16). It is rather a matter of stress. In 5.1-11 the stress rests on the judgment of God. While it is often pointed out that 'Christ' and

9. It should be noted that in Lk. 21.34-36, a text which shares the tradition underlying Paul's argument here, watchfulness (ἀγρυπνεῖτε) is necessary in order to escape 'the day'; here the issue is not escape for those who live in the dark, since that is not where the readers of this letter find themselves, in Paul's view. For them 'escape' is irrelevant.

10. Most commentators do precisely that; e.g. Bruce, *1 & 2 Thessalonians*, p. 109; Marshall, *1 and 2 Thessalonians*, p. 132; Rigaux, *Saint Paul*, p. 556; Rigaux, 'Tradition', p. 326.

11. Cf. Rom. 1.18; 2.5, 8 (cf. Isa. 59.19); 5.9; 9.22.

'Lord' are synonyms in Paul, here he employs a traditional phrase. With few exceptions, when Paul refers to the day of the Lord without replacing 'Lord' with (or adding to it) 'Jesus' or 'Jesus Christ', the note of judgment is the predominant one.[12] The presence of ὄλεθρος as synonym for the ἡμέρα κυρίου is further proof that Paul is interested in addressing not so much the parousia of 4.13-18, but judgment more specifically.

Paul no doubt understands the judgment of God predominantly as an event of comprehensive finality. But the language with which this coming wrath is painted in 1 Thessalonians has its roots in the past events of God's judgment. The 'day of the Lord' already signified judgment for Amos.[13] Isaiah prefers ἐν τῇ ἡμέρᾳ ἐκείνῃ, but the connotations are the same. Notable is the explicit identification of the intervention of the Divine Warrior with the day of vengeance (יום נקם/ἡμέρα ἀνταποδόσεως) in Isa. 63.4, the poem that forms at least part of the background to ch. 59 (see earlier discussion). In the prophetic tradition the judgment of Yahweh is most often anticipated as a future event. That is, after all, where the prophet as harbinger of bad news is located vis-à-vis 'that day'. Nevertheless, prophets most often point to the certainty of future divine intervention on the basis of the past interventions of the Divine Warrior. Herein lies the attractiveness of painting the picture of the future by means of images of the imposing and familiar past, as is illustrated by, for example, Deuteronomy 32, Habakkuk 3, and not least Isaiah 59, where the intervention of the Divine Warrior is initially described in the past tense. By implication, then, in the prophetic tradition 'future' does not necessarily imply singularity or finality. It most certainly does not represent a loss of attention to a present reality marked by sin and rebellion. This attentiveness does not disappear from apocalyptic either, even if the means of expression are frequently drawn from the traditions of the cosmogonic warfare of the gods. This has the effect of ostensibly lifting the location of divine warfare beyond the immediate dynamics of historical existence. But as Daniel, Qumran's War Scroll, and John's Apocalypse show, mythological language does not represent

12. Cf. Rom. 2.5, 16; 1 Cor. 3.13; 5.5. 1 Cor. 1.8 and Phil. 1.10 are concerned with guiltlessness and purity on the day of Christ. This is not to suggest that in Paul's view Christ is absent from the exercise of judgment, as Rom. 2.16 shows. At issue is where the stress should be placed. The evidence suggests that when Paul refers to 'the day of the Lord' it represents judgment.

13. Amos 5.18; 8.9. Cf., e.g., Ezek. 30.2, 3; Joel 1.15; 2.1, 2; Zeph. 1.10-18.

a loss of interest in the here and now as the arena in which the Divine Warrior is active so much as a shift in perception of the nature and scope of that action.[14] To be sure, under impact of the eschatology informing apocalyptic writing, 'the day of the Lord' comes to signify the cataclysmic intervention of the divine warrior judge to bring about an end to the present evil. A frequent effect in apocalyptic thought is to render the faithful community largely passive while it waits for that intervention.

Paul draws on both prophetic and apocalyptic traditions, albeit critically. He shares with many of his contemporaries a sense of living in the καίρος of God's intervention. After all, Christ has been raised and is about to return (1.10; 4.13-18). Further, 1.10 explicitly anticipates the coming wrath (ἡ ὀργη΄ ἡ ἐρχομένη). But as this discussion of 5.1-11 will show, Paul's interest lies not in counselling passive readiness, but rather engagement in the arrival of 'the day', thus inviting the inference that 'the day' is not exclusively something to be awaited in the future, however imminent, but already a present reality.[15] The present tense of

14. Daniel is widely believed to reflect a radically critical stance toward Antiochus Epiphanes, Qumran (especially in the Hodayoth and the War Scroll) vis-à-vis both Jerusalem and the Romans, and John of Patmos over against Rome, no matter that the enemy is perceived in the shape and form that only a divine intervention of cosmic proportions can vanquish. The very use of pseudepigraphy, in particular the placing of revelation regarding the present on the lips of an ancient, intends to lay bare the truth about that present. The fact that a modern cosmology will find it difficult to recognize this as real interest in 'plain history' (see discussion of Paul Hanson's phrase earlier) only shows its distance from the apocalyptic understanding of evil and of power, not a lack of interest in apocalyptic writings as to what happens to real people and real power in real history.

15. 1 Thess. 2.14-17 suggests that wrath has come, or that the final coming of wrath has begun. However, the authenticity of 2.14-17 is embattled. For a clear position against authenticity see, e.g., H. Koester, *Introduction*, II, p. 113, and B. Pearson, '1 Thessalonians 2.13-16: A Deutero-Pauline Interpolation', *HTR* 64 (1971), pp. 79-94. Jewett has recently argued that the evidence does not allow for more than tentative conclusions either way, and decides in favor of Pauline authorship (*Thessalonian Correspondence*, pp. 36-41), a stance with which I concur. Even if 2.14-17 is not authentic, Paul will elsewhere speak of the ὀργή of God in ways which include its activity in the present. It is instructive to note that Paul is able to raise the issue of wrath in Rom. 12.19, drawing on a classic Divine Warrior text such as Deut. 32, and follow that immediately with a discussion of the ἐξουσία with its μάχαιρα as the διάκονος of God's ὀργή (13.4), concluding in 13.11-14 with language highly reminiscent of 1 Thess. 5.1-10. Of special importance for the tradition being pursued here is Rom. 1.18, where the ὀργὴ θεοῦ is revealed against all ἀσέβεια and ἀδικία of people who hold ἀλήθεια captive (cf. Isa. 59.14).

ἔρχομαι in v. 2, ubiquitous in the New Testament with a future meaning,[16] here directs attention to the present as the reality which the day of the Lord *qua* judgment invades with the suddenness (αἰφνίδιος) of a thief in the night or the onset of labour.[17] The 'day' invades the night while people sleep.[18]

Paul's intention is to heighten the sense of suddenness and unpredictability with which the Divine Warrior as judge invades the reality of sleep and darkness. But it becomes clear that his objective is not to strengthen the resolve of believers to endure until that day comes to surprise them, but to suggest that that day is already invading the night, moreover that the Thessalonians are centrally implicated in its arrival. They are to be a part of the surprise, however ironical the twist Paul will place on that notion.

Consonant with prophetic and sapiential traditions, and specifically the Isaianic corpus and Wisdom of Solomon, Paul views 'night' as the context of life apart from or in rebellion to God (vv. 2-5).[19] Amos characterizes the day itself as darkness (5.18; cf. Zeph. 1.15; Joel 2.2), playing on the irony of what had once been anticipated as the inbreaking of light. Amos thereby, however ironically, witnesses to the metaphorical freight of light and day as salvation. He turns it inside out, where day becomes the night of judgment. Third Isaiah describes the search for

16. Cf. BDF §323; J. Schneider, 'ἔρχομαι, κτλ.', *TDNT*, II (1964), pp. 670-75.

17. In this instance labour is not a metaphor for the birth of a new age. It is the ὀλέθρος which comes when least expected.

18. Paul appears to be drawing on a proto-Synoptic, perhaps even dominical, tradition. See especially Lk. 21.34-36: note drunkenness, day, suddenness (αἰφνίδιος); cf. also Mt. 24.43: see reference to watching and the coming of the thief and the reference to drunkenness during Noah's time in v. 38.

19. This does not need to contradict the note of suddenness, as Wis. 17.13, 14 (14, 15) illustrates. We find in Wis. 17 and 18 generally a similarity in context and vocabulary to 1 Thess. 5: night (and Hades; both characterized as ἀδύνατος; 17.14); sleep ('they slept the same sleep', τὸν αὐτον ὕπνον κοιμώμενοι, 17.14b); darkness (νύξ and σκότος, 17.21); the ἀσεβεῖς experience, the sudden (αἰφνίδιος) nightmares (17.15; this appears to be a psychologizing of the traditional *Gottesschrecken* of holy war). In 18.14-19 there is a sudden intrusion of the warrior λόγος, who arrives in(to) the middle of the night (19.14; cf. Rom. 13.12). The suddenness in 17.15 is thus related to the events of the plague and the destruction of the firstborn of the Egyptians. Whereas darkness and the light coexist in this passage (17.21-18.1) αἰφνίδιος relates more to the typical state of the ἀσεβεῖς being frightened by spectres in the night than it does to an impending future judgment, even if that is also present on the horizon.

light by the ἄνομοι as fruitless. Light has already fled the scene, leaving only the darkness of judgment (59.9). In Wisdom of Solomon darkness signifies not only the judgment of God, but the realm in which the ἀσεβεῖς 'live'.[20] Not surprisingly, the Gospel of John also uses darkness and light in this 'ontological' way.[21]

The language in 1 Thessalonians moves within these connotations.[22] In 5.4 believers are assured that they are not *in* darkness (ἐν σκότει), that is, they do not 'live' *in* the night. Their existence is not located there. Believers are neither *of* the night nor *of* darkness (οὐκ ἐσμὲν νυκτὸς οὐδὲ σκότους; v. 5). What defines their existence is that they are 'sons of light and sons of day' (υἱοὶ φωτός ἐστε καὶ υἱοὶ ἡμέρα; v. 5). Some of the 'parallelism of existence' characterizing the description of the ἀσεβεῖς and the δίκαιοι in Wisdom of Solomon[23] is thus present here as well.

Life in the dark is marked, first of all, by a false sense of security. 'Whenever[24] they say "Peace and Security!" (Εἰρήνη καὶ ἀσφάλεια) then destruction appears suddenly like labour pains for a pregnant woman (v. 3).' In view are not enthusiasts or gnostics who believe the end has come and passed, that is, that Christ has already returned.[25] To be sure, 2 Thessalonians does warn against that very teaching (2.2). That problem is not even on the horizon in this pericope, however, unless one sees 5.1-11 as an interpolation, in which case it would be arguing against

20. 'Live' needs to be placed in quotation marks, since as the discussion of Wisdom of Solomon showed, darkness and night are synonymous with death.

21. E.g. 1.4, 5; 3.19; 8.12; 9.4; 12.36.

22. This is true even if U. Schnelle ('Der erste Thessalonicherbrief und die Entstehung der paulinischen Anthropologie', *NTS* 32 [1986], pp. 217-18) is correct that one does as yet not find in 1 Thessalonians a fully developed anthropology, but rather a view of human life marked by presence of the Spirit, on the one hand, and the arrival of the Lord, on the other.

23. Cf. especially chs. 17 and 18.

24. Ὅταν with the present subjunctive normally means 'whenever.' There is, in my view, little justification exempting its usage here from that general convention, as does BAGD, p. 588.

25. See here especially Walter Schmithals, *Paul and the Gnostics* (trans. J.E. Steely; Nashville: Abingdon Press, 1972), pp. 164-67 and W. Harnisch, *Eschatologische Existenz: Ein exegetischer Beitrag zum Sachanliegen von I. Thessalonicher 4,13-5,11* (Göttingen: Vandenhoeck & Ruprecht, 1973), pp. 164-67. Cf. the extensive survey of the discussion in Jewett, *Thessalonian Correspondence*, pp. 96-100, and the critique by Rigaux, 'Tradition', pp. 336-37.

a 'realized eschatology' in quite a different mode than does 2 Thessalonians.

Most commentators go to Jer. 6.14, 8.11, Ezek. 13.10, 16, or to Mic. 3.5 for the source of this slogan,[26] where prophets accuse other prophets of fostering a false and fatal sense of peace and, by implication, security over against the judgment of God (security *per se* is notably not mentioned in those texts). No doubt such prophetic texts would come easily to mind for the scripturally literate hearer of this letter.

This slogan has resonance, further, with the way in which lawlessness and rebellion are characterized by the Wisdom of Solomon. The sage characterizes the ἀσεβεῖς as marked by a sense of power and security that is ignorant of the precariousness of injustice in light of the Divine Warrior's attentiveness (Wis. 2.11; 5.7-13). The ἀσεβεῖς believe they enjoy impunity and that their power over the weak, in particular the δίκαιοι, is real. It comes as a shock to them that their life was really not life to begin with, that the images of security, power and idols have been exposed as unreal. This is what the believers in Thessalonica have been liberated or called out from (cf. 1.9). But that 'reality' continues, marked by all of the symbols, rhetoric, and ideology of solidity and permanence.

This takes on special poignancy if one recognizes that far from being simply a well-worn cliché about the ignorant hubris of sinners before the divine judge, 'Peace and Security/*pax et securitas*' is an apt characterization and perhaps even a recognizable slogan signifying the best the pax Romana had to offer, 'einer ihrer wichtigsten Thesen'.[27] Paul's

26. E.g., Best, *Commentary*, pp. 208-18; Bruce, *1 & 2 Thessalonians*, p. 110; Marshall, *1 and 2 Thessalonians*, p. 134. Rigaux ('Tradition', p. 324) suggests rather that in the background lies an apocalyptic or even dominical saying which is then also taken up in Lk. 21.34, 36.

27. K. Wengst, *Pax Romana, Anspruch und Wirklichkeit: Erfahrungen und Wahrnehmungen des Friedens bei Jesus und im Urchristentum* (Munich: Chr. Kaiser Verlag, 1986), p. 98. Wengst has brought together a representative number of texts which illustrate the value of 'peace and security' to the empire. He points in particular to Aelius Aristides, Josephus, Seneca, Seutonius, and Tacitus (see pp. 32-4 and pp. 186-87 nn. 89-105 for specific literature). W.H.C. Frend refers to *pax et securitas* as 'the programme of the early Principate' (*Martyrdom and Persecution in the Early Church: A study of a Conflict from the Maccabees to Donatus* [Oxford: Basil Blackwell, 1965], p. 96). Friedrich ('1 Thessalonicher', p. 293) draws attention also to *Pss. Sol.* 8.16-18, where the entry of Pompey into Jerusalem is celebrated with this terminology. This reading of 1 Thess. 5.3 is seldom noted, as Wengst

taking up this slogan as an apt characterization of the present darkness becomes, in addition to an allusion to scriptural tradition, a brief but cutting critique of Rome. This would have been poignant in a Thessalonica enthusiastically beholden to Rome.[28] The horizon suggested by the slogan is thus both large and specific. Those mistaking a reality constructed on violence and oppression as peaceful and secure are in this case not faithless Jews (as in Amos, Jeremiah, or Third Isaiah), nor the ἀσεβεῖς as kings and judges of the earth (as in Wisdom of Solomon), but quite specifically those shaping and controlling the social, political, and religious milieu in which the Thessalonians are living out their faith. The pax Romana is thus not 'the day' which, in the view of Virgil's Fourth Eclogue, dawns with universal peace and prosperity. In Paul's view the pax Romana is night and darkness which, precisely because its claims to peace and security rest on a fateful misreading of reality, is marked by sleep (καθεύδειν) and drunkenness (μεθύειν).[29] With the slogan

rightly points out (216 n. 50), but it is determinative for Georgi's work on 1 Thess. 5.1-11 ('Gott auf den Kopf stellen: Überlegungen zu Tendenz und Kontext des Theokratiegedankens in paulinischer Praxis und Theologie', in J. Taubes (ed.), *Theokratie* [Religionstheorie und Politische Theologie, 3; Munich: Fink & Schöningh, 1987], pp. 163-66).

28. See H.L. Hendrix, 'Thessalonicans Honor Romans' (PhD dissertation, Harvard University, 1984).

29. Μεθύειν and καθεύδειν do not refer simply to licence and debauchery, and in that sense take up of the parenesis of 4.3-8. The horizon is much larger. At issue is the identity of the believers within the cosmic drama of the Divine Warrior's intervention. Μεθύειν is used metaphorically for those under judgment with great frequency in Isaiah: cf. 19.14 of Egypt; 24.20 of the whole earth under judgment; 28.1, 3, 7-8 of Ephraim against whom the Lord comes as a warrior; 51.17, 21-22, where getting drunk at the cup of the Lord's judgment is a characterization of exile (cf. here 63.3, 6, and 65.11). The image is used more widely than in Isaiah (cf. e.g., Joel 1.5). Amos 6.4 characterizes the recipients of woe as those who 'sleep (καθεύδοντες) on beds of ivory...and drink wine in bowls.' Sleeping and drinking marks the behaviour of those upon whom the day of the Lord comes (cf. ch. 5). Nevertheless, καθεύδειν is rarely used in a figurative sense in the New Testament. It is a *hapax legomenon* in the undisputed letters of Paul, but does appear, significantly, in the brief hymn fragment in Eph. 5.14. It would appear that Paul is employing language dependent on the prophetic tradition. In addition to Amos, he may also have in mind Isa. 29.9,10, where drunkenness and sleep characterize the state of those the Divine Warrior pursues, where sleep and drunkenness are the effect of his warfare, and 51.20-22, where καθεύδειν characterizes the sons of Jerusalem who are full of the wrath (θύμος) of the Lord. This in no way precludes resonance with gnostic characterizations of 'unconsciousness' (cf. Georgi, 'Gott auf den Kopf stellen', p. 19). But

Εἰρήνη καὶ ἀσφάλεια the entry of the day of the Lord is contextualized in a way immediately relevant to the Thessalonians. Moreover, this language evokes both the present hostile (and perhaps also attractive) world and the certainty of divine intervention. The scope of what is being named here is no smaller than that later found in the Apocalypse of John.

The statement 'you are not in the dark' in v. 4 thus cannot refer to ignorance of the coming of the day. While there is considerable fluidity in the way words shift their meaning or connotation within this text, it is quite clear that Paul intends to assure the Thessalonians that they are not in the dark where they would need to worry about the inbreaking day, because, says Paul in v. 5, they are sons of light and sons of day. As those who have been chosen (εἰδότες...τὴν ἐκλογὴν ὑμῶν; 1.4), who stand in the Lord (στήκετε ἐν κυρίῳ; 3.8; cf. Wis. 5.1), they need not fear judgment. Paul employs 'anthropological' or 'ontological' language in order to assure the believers that they are safe with respect to the events of judgment, to the 'day of the Lord'. The issue of identity is accentuated by the parallel statement that they are not *of* darkness nor *of* night. This is summarized finally in v. 9, where Paul asserts that God has not placed (ἔθετο; note the past tense) them εἰς ὀργή but εἰς περιποίησιν σωτηρίας. Whatever the eschatological dimension of this language, Paul can say of the Thessalonians that they are *presently* sons of light and sons of day, that they are not of darkness nor of night, that they are *presently* in a realm in which there is no need to be anxious about the invasion of the day of the Lord.[30]

This perspective does not in Paul lead to the abrogation of parenesis, however. In his view, identity or nature does not settle the issue of human decision making. The presence of this highly dualistic language fits the strategy of Paul, namely, to speak to matters of anxiety and life style not only by parenesis, but parenesis premised on identity.[31] In

the overall context here is one of judgment inclusive of socio-political dimensions.

30. Rigaux ('Tradition', p. 334) recognizes in the use of εις an eschatological orientation. The note of hope in salvation is sounded in the immediately preceding verse, and is no doubt retained here. But that in and of itself does not undo the dualistic nature of the language. Wis. 3.4 illustrates that 'hope of immortality' can sit alongside highly dualistic 'ontological' language. This leads Best to observe in relation to the Thessalonian text that 'Christians and non-Christians belong in different spheres of existence or possess different natures' (*Commentary*, p. 210).

31. There is also in Wisdom of Solomon a fusion of anthropology/ontology with the language of hope. It is in fact that peculiar combination which provides the

short, Paul is not so much interested in arresting the fears of the Thessalonians by telling them that Christ's work has provided them with escape from the day of judgment (vv. 9, 10) as he is in exhorting them to see themselves in a certain light and in relation to a certain task. That comes to expression most dramatically in the image of the divine armour and its surprising inhabitants in v. 8.

3. *The Transformation of the Divine Warrior*

Paul uses military imagery repeatedly in his correspondence with his churches, which no doubt reflects that he also would have done so in his teaching and preaching.[32] Malherbe's study of 2 Cor. 10.3-6 in particular illustrates the way the imagery would have been heard, given the Cynic tradition of the fortified philosopher.[33] Paul is clearly in conversation with that tradition. Paul is concerned also in 1 Thessalonians, especially in ch. 2, to define himself in relation to Cynics, as Malherbe's study on his pastoral language illustrates.[34] However, Paul does not there take up military imagery. In 5.1-11 the focus is not on Paul, or at least not on Paul in isolation or as distinct from the Thessalonian believers,[35] but squarely on the congregation as a whole. Moreover, the focus is not

meaningful context for the presence of divine intervention in Wis. While the juxtapostion of 'being' and 'hope' might be more aptly characterized as 'already' and 'not yet' in 1 Thess., the similarity should not be missed.

32. E.g. Rom. 6.13; 13.11-14; 2 Cor. 6.7; 10.3-6. The imagery appears also in the Deutero-Pauline writings, e.g. Eph. 6.10-18 and 2 Tim. 2.3,4; at times it is ambiguous as to whether the imagery is military or athletic, e.g. in 1 Tim. 6.12 and 2 Tim. 4.7. Cf. A. Oepke and K.G. Kuhn, 'ὅπλον, κτλ', *TDNT*, V, pp. 292-315; V.G. Pfitzner, *Paul and the Agon Motif: Traditional Athletic Imagery in the Pauline Literature* (NovTSup, 16; Leiden: Brill, 1967).

33. A. Malherbe, 'Antisthenes and Odysseus, and Paul at War', *HTR* 76 (1983), pp. 143-73. Cf. also H. Emonds, OSB, 'Geistlicher Kriegsdienst: Der Topos der militia spiritualis in der antiken Philosphie', in *Heilige Überlieferung: Ausschnitte aus der Geschichte des Mönchtums und des heiligen Kultes* (Münster: Aschendorff, 1938), pp. 21-50; reprinted as appendix to Adolf von Harnack, *Militia Christi: Die christliche Religion und der Soldatenstand in den ersten drei Jahrhunderten* (Tübingen: Mohr, 1905; Darmstadt: Wissenschaftliche Buchgesellschaft, 1963), pp. 133-62.

34. Malherbe, *Paul and the Thessalonians*, pp. 5-33; cf. his earlier, '"Gentle as a Nurse": The Cynic Background to I Thess. ii', *NovT* 12 (1970), pp. 203-17.

35. Notice the shift to 'we' in v. 5b and the subsequent first-person plural hortatory subjunctives in vv. 6 and 8.

on the individual Christian life and ministry as struggle, as in 2 Cor., so much as it is on the identity of the Thessalonians in relation to the day of the Lord, indeed on their identity in relation to God himself as Divine Warrior.[36]

The use of military imagery in 5.8 is more consonant with the way Paul will use it in Rom. 13.11-14, where the Roman believers are enjoined to 'put on the weapons of light' (ἐνδυσώμεθα τὰ ὅπλα τοῦ φωτός; v. 12), to walk in conformity (εὐσχημόνως) to being in the day (ἐν ἡμέρᾳ; v. 13), that is, not in carousing, drunkenness, sexual misbehaviour, and fighting.[37] Behaviour of this kind is obviously unbecoming soldiers who are to be ready for battle. Rather, believers are to put on Christ; that is, they are to don the Messiah and with him his identity and task. The theme of the readiness of the militia is parallel to identification with the messianic warrior.[38] All this is placed into the framework of imminent salvation, the replacing of night by day (vv. 11, 12).

In 1 Thess. 5.8 the connections with the tradition of the Divine Warrior are more explicit. The stress on readiness is present in the call to watchfulness and vigilance (γρηγορῶμεν καὶ νήφωμεν).[39] But that note of

36. I disagree with J.P. Brown's identification of 1 Thess. 5 as a transformation of a Semitic motif of an armed deity into the Stoic motif of the armed philosopher ('Peace Symbolism in Ancient Military Vocabulary', *VT* 21 [1971], p. 9).

37. The similarities between 1 Thess. 5.1-11 and Rom. 13.11-14 are commonly noticed. Friedrich ('1 Thessalonicher', pp. 305-306) identifies significant differences as well in the interests of showing 1 Thess. 5.1-11 to be later than Rom. 13. One need not agree with his conclusions to notice some important features, such as the fact that in Romans night and day do not coexist as *'Existenzweisen'* (Friedrich), but are understood sequentially; related is that in Romans believers are enjoined to put off the works of darkness, whereas in 1 Thessalonians the emphasis lies on believers not being in or of the dark.

38. Cf. the same combining of identity with Christ in baptism in Rom. 6.1-11 with the offering or presenting of the members as weapons (ὅπλα) of justice in 6.13.

39. In LXX γρηγορεῖν is the preparatory stance leading to the intervention of judgment (Jer. 38.28 LXX; Bar. 2. 9), 'watching' as in placing under siege (Jer 5.6), or explicitly as readiness for aggressive battle (1 Macc. 12.27). Cf. also 1 Cor. 16.13, where γρηγορεῖν stands in immediate relation to 'standing' (recall the discussion of 'standing' in Wis. 5.1). Νήφειν is not used in LXX, and appears in the New Testament only in metaphorical usage: in 2 Tim. 4.5 it marks the stance of teacher and prophet; in 1 Pet. 1.13, 4.7 and 5.8 it marks the stance of people caught up in the warfare of the last days. (1 Pet. 5.8 clearly utilizes the traditional scenario of the passive δίκαιος who is solely dependent on the Divine Warrior for vindication in the future.) Note also Oepke's comment ('ὅπλον', p. 310) that the putting on of the

readiness must be read in light of the more significant emphasis on the identification of the believers with God as Divine Warrior.[40] Christ plays a role here as well (vv. 9, 10), but largely one of having died for believers, thus preparing the way for them to identify themselves with God. The inhabiting of the divine armour must be at least in part what 'living with him (v. 10)' signifies.

A number of signals already implicate believers in the divine drama of intervention prior to v. 8. First of all, 'sons of light' would, at least in Paul's thinking, have implied militancy, as Rom. 13.12 attests. Familiarity with Qumran need not be assumed,[41] but the characterization of the militia as 'sons of light' signifies the overtones such language would have had in eschatological and specifically apocalyptic contexts. Secondly, for Paul to append to 'sons of light' the apparent synonym 'sons of day' indicates his desire to allow the meaning of 'sons of light' to be affected by the 'day of the Lord' in 5.2. That the use of 'day' quickly shifts its meaning from signifying punitive intervention to representing the opposite of 'darkness' and 'night' does not eliminate the lingering note of sudden divine intervention represented by 'day' in v. 2. To be 'sons of day' speaks to the issue of identity, but it also easily suggests implication of the Thessalonian believers in the divine invasion of darkness.

The explicit use of the motif of the divine armour dramatically identifies the community with the Divine warrior. Here, Paul is not simply employing a general tradition. He specifically reaches back to Isa. 59.17. There is no clear proof that Paul was familiar with Wisdom of Solomon[42] even if there is considerable resonance with language and concepts

armour implies an active engagement in battle, even if specific weapons are not mentioned in 1 Thessalonians.

40. Georgi observes this in radical terms: 'Der Vergöttlichung des Caesars steht die Vermenschlichung des paulinischen (biblischen) Gottes gegenüber'. ('Gott auf den Kopf stellen', p. 166). This is overstated if intended to reflect Paul's understanding of God. But it clearly does point to the surprise factor in placing the Thessalonians into the divine armour and thus into the role of the Divine Warrior. This step is decidedly not taken in 1QH and 1QM, where God remains the only true agent of divine warfare. Cf. e.g. 1QH 4, 6, 9, and especially the High Priestly prayer in 1QM 11.

41. 1QS 1.9; 2.16; 3.13, 24, 25; 1QM 1.1, 3; 9.11, 13.

42. See Larcher, *Études*, pp. 14-20, *Livre de la Sagesse*, p. 392. Cf., however, Oepke, 'ὅπλον', p. 309 n. 9, who sees Paul as dependent on Isa. 59.17, but knowing Wisdom of Solomon as well.

present there. With the author of Wisdom Paul retains Isaiah's breastplate (θώραξ), but in contrast to Wisdom of Solomon he also retains Isaiah's helmet of salvation (περικεφαλαία ἔλπις σωτηρίας[43]), suggesting that Isaiah and not Wisdom of Solomon functions as *Vorlage* for his appropriation.

Like the author of Wisdom of Solomon, Paul allows himself considerable freedom in the appropriation of this motif. He joins the triad of 'faith, love, and hope', already present in 1.3, to the armour of breastplate and helmet. This joining of the armour to the triad of cardinal virtues is often observed to be rather clumsy.[44] The clumsiness rests only, however, in the placing of a triad over a doublet. Surely Paul is aware of that. He must also be aware that that 'clumsiness' only draws attention both to the appropriation of a biblical tradition and its modification.[45] The familiar element in the appropriation rests in the relationship between the invading 'day of the Lord' and the image of God as Divine Warrior, who comes to judge and punish as well as to vindicate the innocent victims of oppression and violence.[46] The breaking in of the thief, the sudden onset of destruction, evokes the familiar motif of the fearsome Divine Warrior. That familiarity is the necessary premise for the modification Paul introduces.

The initially most noticeable modification is that the familiar Pauline triad of faith, hope, and love is combined with the two elements of armour taken from Isaiah 59. Thereby Paul intends the exercise of these virtues to be seen through the image of the Divine Warrior as encountered in Isaiah 59. The exercise of faith, hope, and love is drawn into the centre of the drama of divine warfare. These virtues are not simply the defensive arsenal of nurture, maintenance, and endurance. They

43. Isa. 59.17: περικεφαλαία σωτηρίου; Wis. 5.18: κόρυς κρίσις ἀνυπόκριτος.

44. Friedrich refers to this as *unorganisch* and *gewaltsam...eingepreßt* ('1 Thessalonicher', p. 295). So also E. Kamlah, *Die Form der katalogischen Paränese im Neuen Testament* (Tübingen: Mohr [Siebeck], 1964), p. 190.

45. Dobschütz (*Thessalonicher*, p. 211) recognizes the deliberateness, but nevertheless denies dependency on Isa. 59.

46. See earlier discussion of the degree to which this particular tradition of the Divine Warrior emphasizes the ultimately *sole* agency of God, an emphasis that is strengthened in the apocalyptic tradition (cf. literature cited earlier, especially Hanson and Cross). Note also that while Wisdom of Solomon implies in the exaltation of the δίκαιος a role as participant in the divine role of judge, the motif of God as ultimately sole warrior is retained in the taking up of Isa. 59.17-19 in Wis. 5.15-23.

represent, as do the virtues in Isaiah 59 and Wisdom of Solomon 5, the content and means of divine intervention. To say it another way, the divine armour and its implication of status and task is not 'emptied' of its militancy by the names given the pieces of armour in 1 Thessalonians. Rather, faith, love, and hope are pulled into the picture of the coming of the Divine Warrior as associated with the fearsome day of the Lord. Not only that, these virtues are exercised by a community which puts them on as the armour of *God*, which thus in the exercise of these virtues inhabits the role of Isaiah 59's Divine Warrior. The Thessalonians are called to take up a role even Wisdom of Solomon was not willing to offer the δίκαιοι directly—that of the Divine Warrior. Thus the exercise of faith, love, and hope is inextricably related to the invasion of the day of the Lord.

The nature of divine warfare is thus recast, both in terms of the nature of the armour and in who inhabits it. While Paul clearly intends 'the day of the Lord' to be understood as the invasion of the Divine Warrior into the realm of darkness, the movement from 'day of the Lord' to 'sons of day', from the terror of destruction to an armour of faith, love, and hope of salvation, suggests that some strain is being placed on the notion of vengeance as the sole meaning of judgment.

One would overstate the point, however, to say that the Divine Warrior's invasion is now to be understood exclusively in terms of the categories of faith, love, and hope as exercised by believers. God is not, finally, replaced. Nor does Paul give up on the notion of judgment, as his later letter to the Romans illustrates abundantly.[47] He has already alluded to this in 1 Thessalonians.[48] What sets Paul's thinking apart from Wisdom of Solomon, Qumran, and John's Apocalypse is that two things are being insisted upon at the same time: first, God is judge; second, the community participates in that judgment by virtue of its identity. The nature of that identity and calling is to participate in the most surprising aspect of God's judicial warfare, namely in the exercise of faith, love, and hope. Thessalonians are drawn into God, so to speak.

The intervention of the Divine Warrior by means of believers exercising the virtues of faith, hope, and love should be viewed, then, as part of the strategy of surprise. That is signalled by Paul's 'translating' (not replacing) of δικαιοσύνη as πίστις καὶ ἀγάπη.[49] Further, the absence

47. Cf. chaps. 1-3, 12, 13.

48. Cf. 1.10 and, if authentic, 2.14-17. Note also 4.6.

49. Paul will work with this irony again in Romans where the God before whose

of the cloak of vengeance must represent then a deliberate and important restriction of the image of the Divine Warrior's armour, contributing to the reinterpretation of divine warfare.[50] Even so, it could not have occurred to Paul to eliminate vengeance from the image of God as warrior.[51] But it does occur to him to identify those who imitate the Divine Warrior with that dimension of his militant δικαιοσύνη which they themselves have experienced, namely, grace.[52] So, while in 1 Thessalonians God remains in the picture as warring judge who brings wrath, the sons of light and day are enjoined to participate in a specific dimension of this invasion of the day of the Lord. Their exercise of divine warfare consists of the radical exercise of faith, love, and the hope of salvation.

It is in light of this irony that the fluidity of not clearly marking off the meanings of day, night, sleep, and wakefulness, must be appreciated. The phrase εἴτε γρηγορῶμεν εἴτε καθεύδωμεν in 5.10 does not simply reiterate the assurances of 4.13-18 that both the dead and the still living will meet and live with Christ.[53] Paul could have taken up the unambiguous vocabulary of 4.13-17 (ζῶντες and κοιμώμενοι).[54] Here, however, he repeats the vocabulary of vv. 6 and 7 (γρηγορεῖν and καθεύδειν), where it clearly defines classes of people, or at least modes of

δικαιοσύνη both Jew and Gentile are fatally culpable manifests that δικαιοσύνη 'χωρὶς νόμου...διὰ πίστεῶ Ἰησοῦ Χριστοῦ' precisely for the sake of those who are subject to judgment (3.5, 21, 22; cf. ch. 5).

50. It should be noted that Wisdom of Solomon also dispenses with the cloak and mantle of vengeance, but it expands the armour to include the sword of ἀπότομος ὀργή (5.20), aided by creation transformed into weaponry (vv. 17, 20-23).

51. Cf. 1.10 and the texts from Romans cited above.

52. Note that in Rom. 5 it is God who because of his love saves his enemies from his wrath (vv. 6-11). Those same recipients of grace are to exercise their own dominion in accordance with that grace, albeit 'through the one man Jesus Christ' (v. 17); that is, they are to present their members to God as weapons of righteousness (ὅπλα δικαιοσύνης; 6.13).

53. There is virtual consensus among commentators that v. 10 reiterates the assurance of salvation in 4.13-17, whether believers are alive or dead at the parousia. Jewett (*Thessalonian Correspondence*, pp. 190-91) suggests instead that one read v. 10 as a reference to watchfulness, but that Paul is concerned to clarify for readers that he is not suggesting an eschatologically motivated insomnia. T.R. Edgar ('The Meaning of Sleep in 1 Thessalonians 5.10', *JETS* 22 [1979], pp. 344-49) suggests that sleep in this case really does refer to lack of vigilance, but that there is a strong note of grace which relativizes its importance with regard to salvation. He comes closest to seeing the direction of the language in this passage.

54. Paul uses similar language in Rom. 14.8-9: ζῆν and ἀποθνήσκειν.

existence. It is not insignificant that καθεύδειν is a *hapax legomenon* in the Pauline corpus, with the exception of Eph. 5.14, where it appears in a baptismal song fragment. Here, then, is an unavoidable hint of the generosity of a Divine Warrior who loves enemies.[55] It is in keeping with this irony that Paul attributes this status and participation in divine warfare to those who come from the class marked for wrath in Wisdom of Solomon. Those who once worshiped idols[56] have become participants in the intervention of the Divine Warrior.

This profound recasting of divine warfare does nevertheless not allow for an unqualified universalism. That would only remove the surprise element endemic to grace,[57] and thus also the surprise element at the heart of Paul's reinterpretation of divine warfare. The generosity implicit in the placing of erstwhile sons of night and darkness into the armour of the Divine Warrior, whose task it now becomes to wage war with the means of their own salvation, should be seen rather as the resourcefulness of 'warfare'. It is fitting here to recall Rom. 11.33-36, which follows a sketch of the resourcefulness of God in bending even wrath and judgment to the purposes of salvation (chs. 9–11). Grace, in Paul's view, cannot be systematized. Indeed, its reality requires the intactness of a notion of δικαιοσύνη which sees punitive warfare and destruction as the predictable and justifiable outcome of apostasy and hubris.

The restating of the names of the armour and the restriction of the image of the warrior to that of breastplate and helmet can therefore not be read simply as evidence of casual, let alone thoughtless, use of a well-worn aphorism. That it would have been repeatedly used in sermon and teaching, or more specifically in baptismal homily or charge is not thereby denied. That sense is strengthened if the aorist participle ἐνδυσάμενοι in v. 8 is read as referring to the past event of baptism, recalled here as motivation for a stance of readiness.[58] True, the image of the Divine Warrior as derived from Isaiah 59 lends itself to a certain play-

55. Cf. the similar sentiment in similar language in Phil. 1.18: πλὴν ὅτι παντὶ τρόπῳ, εἴτε προφάσει εἴτε ἀληθείᾳ, Χριστὸς καταγγέλλεται, καὶ ἐν τούτῳ χαίρω.

56. 1 Thess. 1.9; cf. Wis. 13–15.

57. Cf. Rom. 2.5, and especially also 3.5 in relation to 3.21.

58. Many (e.g. Best, *Commentary*, p. 213; Rigaux, *Saint Paul*, p. 567; Dobschütz, *Thessalonicher*, p. 210) suggest that the aorist be read as a 'coincident aorist participle' (Smyth §1872.c.2), further elaborating on what is meant by sobriety or vigilance. I take the use of the aorist to indicate an element of recall, alluding to the experience of baptism as the entry into the armour (cf. in particular Rom. 6.1-14).

fulness or looseness. Wisdom's appropriation of Isa. 59.17 illustrates the ease with which the representational character of the armour can be exploited. But it is unlikely that Paul could have used casually an image rooted in the biblical tradition which accentuates the power and intervention of the Divine Warrior against oppression and violence. 1 Thess. 5.8 represents an intentional and significant reinterpretation and recasting of the tradition of the Divine Warrior in armour, indeed of the tradition of divine warfare generally.

The image of the divine armour as presented here must therefore not be read as a recasting of an image of power and warfare into familiar, domestic, 'normal' virtues, or more generally from offence to defence.[59] That would be seriously to misread the inherent force of the image, namely, that it is and remains ultimately the armour of the Divine Warrior. Certainly, given Paul's pastoral concerns throughout the letter, the matter of developing a sense of security in light of the time and the situation of darkness is present (cf. esp. 4.13-18). Armour is clearly a defensive phenomenon. But that is not its chief meaning, especially in light of its origin in Isaiah 59. Rather than to assure the believers of protection, Paul's concern as pastor is to prod the Thessalonians into action. The taking up of this image, especially since its usage presupposes scriptural familiarity, cannot have been heard in any other way than as an invitation for the Thessalonians to see themselves as enjoying the status of the exalted already now, *prior to*, or better, as *part of* the fulfillment of the eschatological scenario. Watchfulness and sobriety are here not a stance of readiness of passive and worried bystanders awaiting the arrival of the Lord, but the stance of the divine combatant, ready to seize every opportunity to exercise the warfare of love.

4. *Observations*

The way Paul employs the image of the Divine Warrior in this passage suggests some important points of contact with the ways the motif has been taken up previously. Those who live in the light are juxtaposed with those who dwell in darkness. Further, the armour of the divine warrior is identified with specific virtues or covenant dynamics which identify in a more or less cryptic fashion the nature of divine warfare.

59. *Contra*, among others, Plevnik, '1 Thess. 5,1-11', pp. 86 n. 59, 89, and Rigaux, *Saint Paul*, p. 567, who tend to view the believers as under siege, rather than, as Paul does here, to see the believers putting darkness under siege.

1 Thessalonians shows that Paul builds on the precedent set by Isaiah 59 LXX and Wisdom of Solomon 5 of adapting the shape and content of the armour of the Divine Warrior to his vision and needs.

It is here, however, that the points of departure become most evident. First, the sons of light and of day are conscripted (elected) among those who were once in darkness and night. Their election in and of itself anticipates the surprising interpretation of the Divine Warrior motif, and in that way, the day of the Lord. They are assured that they do not (or no longer) belong to the dark and to the night. The means of this assurance are the old and familiar categories of darkness and light, in other words, the kind of dualism familiar to us from Wisdom of Solomon, but which normally serves to disfranchize the category of people the Thessalonians represent.

Familiar from Wisdom of Solomon, and to a highly modified degree from Isaiah 59, is also the notion of the vindication and exaltation of the just to the status of kingship, of divine sonship. But in 1 Thessalonians it is erstwhile ἀσεβεῖς who are not only exalted to the status of monarchs and sons of God, but invited to put on God's armour and thus to take on the role of the Divine Warrior. The sons of God participate in the warfare of God.

1 Thessalonians is pervaded by a profound sense of expectancy, more so than can be observed in either Isaiah 59 or Wisdom of Solomon. The community and imagination out of which this text emerges is, after all, thoroughly shaped by a conviction that the messianic scenario has begun to unfold with the death and resurrection of Jesus. His return is expected at any time (4.13-18), and so is the judgment of God (1.10; 5.1-3). The appropriation of the motif of the Divine Warrior in armour reflects that mindset. No doubt it is this that has led scholars to read 5.8-10 as chiefly defensive. But as this study has shown, this text is concerned with assuring the believers in Thessalonica that they are not passive victims or beneficiaries of that day, but victors inhabiting the armour of the divine invader.

The warfare of this Divine Warrior is highly ironical. But warfare it is, requiring the divine armour, with its full connotation of divine power, and full vigilance and sobriety. Related to this is the specification of the enemy and the context of battle as the pax Romana. Paul lays the groundwork for a critical and confrontative ethic vis-à-vis the security state and its ideology, even if the means of that confrontation are faith, love, and hope. The fact that the author of Ephesians, given a quite different eschatological outlook, will find it suitable to accentuate precisely this element in 1 Thessalonians speaks volumes about the interpretive possibilities Paul's choice of imagery and language allow.

Finally, it is clear that in 1 Thessalonians 5 Paul moves in the direction of minimizing the distance between the Lord and his sons of light and day. As such Paul participates in what Georgi has called an 'experiment in transcendence'.[60] In this instance Paul quite literally (*buchstäblich*) democratizes the Divine Warrior.[61]

60. Georgi, *The Opponents of Paul in Second Corinthians* (ET; *Die Gegner des Paulus im 2. Korintherbrief: Studien zur Religiösen Propaganda in der Spätantike*, with 1984 'Epilogue'; Philadelphia: Fortress Press, 1984 [1964]), p. 390.

61. *Idem*, 'Gott auf den Kopf stellen', p. 164.

Chapter 4

THE DIVINE WARRIOR IN EPHESIANS 6

The assumption underlying this study of Eph. 6.10-20 is that the letter as a whole is pseudepigraphic.[1] The letter dates from the end of the first century, its provenance likely Asia Minor. Ephesus may in fact be its

1. The arguments centre on vocabulary and style, theological and doctrinal orientation, and dependency on undisputed Pauline letters, and most especially on Colossians. The arguments are well rehearsed in introductions such as H. Koester, *Introduction*, pp. 267-72; W.G. Kümmel, *Introduction to the New Testament* (trans. H.C. Kee; Nashville: Abingdon Press, 17th rev. edn, 1975), pp. 350-66; see commentaries, notably J. Gnilka, *Der Epheserbrief* (Freiburg: Herder, 1971), pp. 1-21; J.L. Houlden, *Paul's Letters From Prison: Philippians, Colossians, Philemon, and Ephesians* (Westminster Pelican Commentaries; Philadelphia: Westminster Press, 1977), pp. 235-55, and R. Schnackenburg, *Der Brief an die Epheser* (EKKNT, 10; Zürich: Benziger; Neukirchen-Vluyn: Neukirchener Verlag, 1982), pp. 17-34; special studies such as E.J. Goodspeed, *The Meaning of Ephesians* (Chicago: University of Chicago Press, 1956); C.L. Mitton, *The Epistle to the Ephesians: Its Authorship, Origin and Purpose* (Oxford: Clarendon Press, 1951); and more recently D.G. Meade, *Pseudonymity and Canon: An Investigation into the Relationship of Authorship and Authority in Jewish and Earliest Christian Tradition* (WUNT, 39; Tübingen: Mohr, 1986), pp. 139-42. The arguments in favor of Pauline authorship in H. Schlier's *Der Brief an die Epheser: Ein Kommentar* (Düsseldorf: Patmos, 7th edn, 1971) appear to be motivated by doctrinal or ecclesiastical concerns (cf. in contrast his earlier studies on Ephesians; cf. also E. Käsemann's critique in 'Das Interpretationsproblem des Epheserbriefes', *TLZ* 86 [1961], pp. 1-8); for other defences of Pauline authorship cf. also the earlier study by Ernst Percy, *Die Probleme der Kolosser- und Epheserbriefe* (Lund: Gleerup, 1946); A. van Roon, *The Authenticity of Ephesians* (Leiden: Brill, 1974). Markus Barth's two-volume commentary (*Ephesians: Introduction, Translation, and Commentary* [AB, 34, 34A; 2 vols.; Garden City NY: Doubleday, 1974], pp. 4-52 and *passim*) makes the issue of Pauline authorship central to interpreting Ephesians, with the effect that distinctives and peculiarities are consistently played down or harmonized with Pauline thinking and expressions in the undisputed letters.

place of origin, rather than its intended destination.[2] The 'letter' somewhat superficially imitates the Pauline letter form, enough to render it 'typical' authoritative communication within Pauline church circles, and in that way commending it for serious consideration by its first readers. It consciously participates in the reflection upon and rearticulation of the Pauline inheritance, both by taking up many of the notes sounded in the undisputed letters of Paul and by critically taking issue with the pseudepigraphical articulation of Pauline theology in Colossians. It is most attractive to see Ephesians, much as has been proposed for both Third Isaiah and Wisdom of Solomon, as a product of a communal process of reflection on a prophetic/apostolic inheritance.[3] It participates in that prophetic and apostolic task, but in the derivative sense of interpretation and rearticulation, in effect up-dating and critically restating that inheritance. As the following study will show, this does not curtail its creativity or its critical engagement with the prophetic task. By letting 'Paul' speak it is doing what the contemporaneous Gospel writers are doing with the traditions of and about Jesus. In a sense, it is the 'risen Paul' who continues to address the churches of his mission. Paul's mouth remains open (cf. 6.19). But it is the Pauline 'school', in particular one or several of its 'members', that now speaks for or through him.[4] In some respects Ephesians marks the sapientialization of Pauline prophecy, inviting by its obvious citations of and allusions to previous Pauline writings, even if in very fragmentary fashion, an ongoing

2. This is suggested by, among others, Gnilka, *Epheserbrief*, p. 6, and H.-M. Schenke; K.M. Fischer, *Einleitung in die Schriften des Neuen Testaments I: Die Briefe des Paulus und Schriften des Paulinismus* (Gütersloh: Gütersloher Verlagshaus/Gerd Mohn, 1978), p. 236. The identification of addressees in Eph. 1.1 enjoys very poor manuscript support (P^{46}, a, and B mention no addressee at all).

3. M. Barth, who defends Pauline authorship of Ephesians, nevertheless provides a rich inventory of the traditions appropriated in Ephesians, only to ask who else but Paul himself could have done that as creatively ('Traditions in Ephesians', *NTS* 30 [1984], pp. 3-25).

4. Whether one should speak homogenously of such a 'school' is questionable, since it appears that Colossians would also have emerged from such a context. Either Ephesians represents later 'second thoughts' or it represents a taking issue with others within the circle of Paulinists. Cf. Schenke, *Einleitung*, p. 243, who characterizes the 'school' as *'eine sehr komplexe und verzweigte, in der Entwicklung befindliche Größe'*. As in previous chapters, the use of the singular 'author' is strictly for the sake of convenience; it is not meant to mask the likelihood that this letter, like the previous texts studied, is at heart collaborative.

engagement with Paul's prophetic legacy. Such engagement is considerably more participatory than is the collecting of Paul's own writings.[5] Ephesians is evidence both of the author (or authors) being thoroughly steeped in Paul's writings and, at the same time, of taking seriously the Pauline conviction regarding life 'in Christ', expressed in the freedom to speak again, not only as the corporate Christ, but in a sense as the corporate Paul.[6]

It is in this light that the taking up of the motif of the divine armour must be understood. As the study of 1 Thessalonians shows, Paul already laid the groundwork for the reappropriation of the motif found in Isaiah 59. This motif and especially the Pauline way of reading it did not, however, find automatic or widespread echo in the immediate subsequent tradition.[7] It is absent from 2 Thessalonians, where the idea of participation in the eschatological struggle gives way to heeding the signs of the times, while not letting the certainty of the final divine intervention of God drive a wedge into the performance of everyday obligations.[8] 2 Thessalonians does know about eschatological warfare, but the warrior

5. Cf. Schenke's thesis of two comensurate processes: first, the collecting of Paul's own writings centered in Corinth; secondly, the rearticulation of Paul's thought in the deutero-Pauline writings centered in Ephesus (*Einleitung*, p. 244). Cf. also Meade, *Pseudonymity*, pp. 148-61.

6. A. Lindemann (*Paulus im ältesten Christentum: Das Bild des Apostels in der frühchristlichen Literatur bis Marcion* [BHT, 58; Tübingen: Mohr, 1979], pp. 122-30) suggests that there is no polemical or even apologetic motive underlying this pseudepigraphical letter, only a theological interest in explicating an ecclesiology in dependence if not always on Paul's thought, then at least on his authority. So also E. Dassmann, *Der Stachel im Fleisch: Paulus in der frühchristlichen Literatur bis Irenäus* (Münster: Aschendorff, 1979), pp. 52-3. The following discussion will show that while there may be no *specific* occasion which prompts the writing, and no specific heresy plaguing a particular congregation, the author of Ephesians positions himself over against Colossians in such a way, most particularly with the image of the Divine Warrior, as to suggest that intra-Pauline school or mission trends and debates may provide the occasion for the writing of Ephesians. In such a case it would be fitting to speak of a polemic, albeit one couched in the careful restating of both Pauline and Colossian themes, as would be appropriate where the battle is over the shape of the Pauline legacy.

7. The Pastorals do take up the image of Paul as struggler and mention the soldier as model for the Christian leader (1 Tim. 6.12; 2 Tim. 2.3, 4; 4.7), but the ideal of the church community wearing *God's* armour is absent.

8. See the discussion of the transformation of Pauline apocalyptic thought in 2 Thessalonians in Koester, *Introduction*, II, pp. 241-46.

is clearly and only ὁ κύριος Ἰησοῦς (1.7; 2.8). Furthermore, Colossians argues that there is no cosmic threat. The heavens are empty of hostile powers; the cosmos is safe.[9] There is a call to vigilance (4.2), but there is no indication that it relates to a context of struggle, let alone battle. Furthermore, while eschatology is not completely absent from Colossians, the focus has shifted from a temporal to a spatial paradigm. Believers are to seek τὰ ἄνω (3.1, 2), counsel that could be seen to offer support for a gnostic understanding of salvation divorced either from the future or from a radical struggle with τὰ ἐπὶ τῆς γῆς (3.2). There is thus little motivation for the reappropriation of the democratized Divine Warrior of 1 Thessalonians 5.

Ephesians 6 represents therefore not only a reappropriation of an important Pauline motif, but also a critique of fellow tradents of the Pauline inheritance. One might well characterize Ephesians as a 'third way', one which rejects dissolution of eschatological tension, whether as a result of rendering divine intervention as a 'permanently' future event *à la* 2 Thessalonians,[10] or as a result of conceiving salvation largely as a past and completed event *à la* Colossians. To be sure, Colossians retains an emphasis on hope (1.5, 11[?]) and on awaiting the revealing of the Christ (3.4), but its underlying argument is largely that all issues are settled (1.13) and that all enemies have been vanquished (2.15). The pastoral intention is to remove any sense of anxiety. In contrast, the author of Ephesians appropriates apocalyptic language of urgency and contrast and conflates it with that of certainty and completion. The intended effect is to confront the believers within the Pauline circle of churches with both their status as co-regents with Christ and with the urgency of the still unfinished task of cosmic struggle and victory. The motif of the Divine Warrior plays a central role in that strategy.

1. *The Context of the Divine Warrior in Ephesians*

Before undertaking a discussion of the motif of the Divine Warrior, it is useful to locate that image within the strategy of Ephesians as a whole. It

9. Both Col. 2.20 and 2.15, and the insistence that Christ created the powers in 1.16, share the intention to render the cosmos safe in the mind of the hearers or readers.

10. There is no evidence that the author of Ephesians knows of 2 Thessalonians. The claim made here is solely that the author is in critical dialogue with the apocalyptic inheritance, one expression of which is found in 2 Thessalonians.

represents the convergence of two important strands in the Ephesian presentation, namely, ecclesiology[11] and power.

Ephesians begins with a eulogy to God for having blessed 'us' with every blessing already before the foundation of the world (1.3-4), appointed us for sonship and bestowed on us insight into the mystery, namely, the subsummation or recapitulation of all things in Christ (ἀνακεφαλαιώσασθαι τὰ πάντα ἐν τῷ Χριστῷ; v. 10). The chief focus appears to be on knowledge and insight (σοφία καὶ φρόνησις; v. 8) into this mystery. However, this knowledge (πνεῦμα σοφίας καὶ ἀποκαλύψεως ἐν ἐπιγνώσει αὐτοῦ; v. 17) is immediately related to the awareness of the possession of power (τὸ ὑπερβάλλον μέγεθος τῆς δυνάμεως αὐτοῦ εἰς ἡμᾶς τοὺς πιστεύοντας κατὰ τὴν ἐνέργειαν τοῦ κράτους τῆς ἰσχύος αὐτοῦ; v. 19). This power is measured by the raising of Christ from the dead and his victorious enthronement over all his enemies (vv. 20-22). In focus is not Christ as distinct from the church, in contrast to Col. 1.15-20, but the church itself as the σῶμα Χριστοῦ. Verse 23 is perhaps intentionally enigmatic, but the impression is created that the σῶμα is also the πλήρωμα of the one who fills all things with everything. The puzzling dative 'τῇ ἐκκλησίᾳ' in v. 22 might then suggest on second and third hearing or reading (something surely intended with a document of this kind) an instrumental dative. This impression is strengthened by the use of διά in 3.10, where it is explicitly the church through which the powers are informed of God's wisdom.

The author now elaborates on the theme of the exaltation and enthronement of those who once belonged to what Wisdom of Solomon called the 'party of death.' In ch. 2 the once dead (v. 5), the τέκνα φύσει ὀργῆς (v. 3), have been brought to life with Christ due to the grace and mercy of God (vv. 5-9). Moreover, they have been raised and seated ἐν τοῖς ἐπουρανίοις ἐν Χριστῷ Ἰησοῦ (v. 6). This bestowal of status is then recalled and celebrated with the hymn to Christ as peace,

11. Cf. here the treatment of this issue in, for example, F. Mußner, *Christus, das All und die Kirche* (Trier: Paulus, 1955); H. Schlier, *Christus und die Kirche im Epheserbrief* (BHT, 6, 1930; repr. 1966); E. Schweizer, 'Die Kirche als Leib Christi in den paulinischen Antilegomena', *TLZ* 86 (1961), pp. 241-56. Ecclesiology is often characterized as the central concern of the author and taken to reflect growing institutionalization of Pauline communities at the turn of the century. Much could be said about this, but I am here restricting myself to the way ecclesiology motivates the usage of the Divine Warrior and divine armour traditions at the climactic end of the letter.

who through death on the cross has overcome all divisions (τὰ ἀμφότερα; v. 14). Specified is the inclusion of the once excluded—the Gentiles, strangers, atheists (v. 12; cf. οἱ ἀμφότεροι, v. 18). The erstwhile rejects are now, together with the old insiders, fashioned into a new ἄνθρωπος (v. 15), into one σῶμα, into the holy dwelling place of God (v. 21). God has moved into the court of the Gentiles and rendered it the holy of holies, as it were.

It becomes clear that the emphasis on power in Ephesians 1 results from the author's drawing out the implications of believers being the body of the cosmic Christ. This emphasis on the status of the church also explains the presentation of Paul in ch. 3. He is introduced as ὁ δέσμιος τοῦ Χριστοῦ (v. 1),[12] the one to whom the μυστήριον has been revealed. But in v. 8 the self-deprecation of Paul in 1 Cor. 15.9—as ὁ ἐλάχιστος τῶν ἀποστόλων—is intensified; he is placed not only behind the rest of the apostolic elite, but behind the recipients of the letter—ἐλαχιστοτέρῳ πάντων ἁγίων.[13] Not surprisingly, it is not Paul the custodian of the μυστήριον who informs αἱ ἄρχαι καὶ αἱ ἐξουσίαι ἐν τοῖς ἐπουρανίοις of God's πολυποίκιλος σοφία but the church (3.10). For that task the church needs παρρησία καὶ προσαγωγή (3.12[14]), but it also needs power.

Eph. 3.14-19 represents the capstone of the sustained attempt in the first three chapters to speak to the issue of status and identity. The fact that this status and identity is informed by that of the Messiah means that knowledge and power are needed in abundance. Concluding this section is appropriately a prayer that the readers might be filled with power and might, so as to be able to grasp (καταλαβέσθαι, v. 18) what is the breadth and width, height and depth, and the incomparable knowledge of the love of Christ, and climactically to be filled with the very πλήρωμα τοῦ θεοῦ (v. 19).[15]

12. This plays on the hagiographic image of Paul the suffering apostle for the sake of the Gentiles.

13. Schenke has pointed out that Ephesians distinguishes itself from the other deutero-Pauline writings by allowing that there are other apostles than Paul in 2.20 (*Einleitung*, p. 244). Schenke suggests that this is faithful to Paul's own way of thinking. As such it conforms to the strategy of the author of Ephesians: namely, to force those who are by now used to viewing Paul as a singular hero to see themselves pushed into a position ahead of him.

14. Cf. here again Paul as exemplar in 6.19; cf. also 2 Cor. 3.12.

15. The strategy of the author of Ephesians to place the church front and centre emerges in comparing this phrase with how it is used in Col. 1.19, where the whole

In ch. 4 the view shifts from identity and status to task, signalled formally with the typical parenetic introduction παρακαλῶ οὖν in 4.1. The reconciling work of Christ in ch. 2 is now mirrored in what his σῶμα is called to do, namely, to preserve the bonds of unity and peace (vv. 1-6). This turns out to be nothing short of continuing the work of Christ in building up the σῶμα until it reaches the full and mature stature of Christ, that is, the cosmos reconciled (v. 13).[16] The building up of the body of Christ (v. 12) becomes a way of implicating the church in the ἀνακεφαλαίωσις of the cosmos (1.10).

The strategy of pushing to the limits the issue of status and task is illustrated by the image of Christ giving gifts. Ps. 68.18 (68.19 MT; 67.19 LXX) is turned on its head in 4.7-11. Whereas in Ps. 68 the Divine Warrior *ascends* the mountain in victory, receiving gifts and booty from either enthusiastic supporters or the vanquished, in Eph. 4.9-10 the psalm is reinterpreted in two ways: first, it is Christ who ascends the mountain. That represents an important restatement, given that Christ has already been 'democratized' in Ephesians (see especially ch. 2). Second, the image is exploited ironically: that which goes up must have come down (v. 9). The author introduces this notion to indicate that Christ came down not to *receive* gifts but to *give* them (vv. 10, 11).[17] The attention

fulness dwells in Christ—ἐν αὐτῷ εὐδόκησεν πᾶν τὸ πλήρωμα κατοικῆσα.

16. I disagree with Schnackenburg (*Brief an die Epheser*, p. 191) and Gnilka (*Epheserbrief*, p. 218) who read the image as intensive and internal. True, 'οἱ πάντες' following the first person plural in v. 13 makes sure that 'we' is understood as inclusive of everyone within the group (cf. 2 Cor. 3.19). But the building up of the body as continuation of the creation of that body in ch. 2, and the persistent depiction of Christ as cosmic reality (not least in 1.10) ensures that it be read as an image of extensive growth. Closer to my reading are Schlier (*Brief*, p. 206) and F.-J. Steinmetz (*Protologische Heilszuversicht: Die Strukturen des soteriologischen und christologischen Denkens im Kolosser- und Epheserbrief* [Frankfurter Theologische Studien, 2; Frankfurt am Main: Josef Knecht, 1969], p. 120).

17. It matters little that there already was a precedent for such a version or alteration of the text. R. Rubinkiewicz ('Ps LXVIII 19 [=Eph IV 8]. Another Textual Tradition or Targum?' *NovT* 17 [1975], pp. 219-24) posits a Jewish rabbinic tradition that had already changed 'receiving' into 'giving' and also related the verse to Moses receiving the Law and then offering it to Israel. The author of Ephesians thus draws on this tradition, now replacing Moses with Christ. Assuming this were so (Schnackenburg [*Brief*, pp. 179-80] is persuaded), the use made of this interpretation in Eph. 4.8 would still serve the purpose I am identifying. It would only mean that the author found an interpretation compelling for his own purposes.

is thus drawn away from the ascending victor to those below who receive his gifts.

This attention to the people 'below' is at work also in the way the author treats the gifts. The list of 'gifts' in 4.11 consists of various ecclesiastical functionaries, often taken as evidence for the institutionalization and hierarchicalization of the church.[18] No doubt the text reflects such a reality. However, in my opinion this text stands in a critical relationship with that development. Much as Paul is placed at the back of the saintly line in 3.8, so now too the ostensibly important members of the church are to equip the saints for ministry. They are, so to speak, coaches and trainers. The 'players' in the διακονία of building the σῶμα are the ἅγιοι generally.[19] Once again the tendency to shift focus onto the church and the status of its (ordinary) members is apparent. The point of the image of the ἅγιοι building the body of Christ is precisely not hierarchy but the empowerment of the saints.

Chapter 5 follows, appropriately, with a call to imitation: not of Paul, and through him of Christ, but directly of God. Thus the 'demotion' of Paul to fellow saint and the shifting of the focus from Christ as head to Christ as body is now complemented by raising the stakes as to who is to be imitated.[20] Highly dualistic language, now familiar from the previous study of Wisdom of Solomon 5, and of 1 Thessalonians 5, is now introduced. As τέκνα ἀγαπητά (v. 1), as τέκνα φωτός (v. 8), indeed as φῶς itself (v. 7), the ἅγιοι are to keep themselves from alliances with the υἱοὶ τῆς ἀπειθείας (μὴ οὖν γίνεσθε συμμέτοχοι αὐτῶν; vv. 6, 7) and

18. Schnackenburg (*Brief*, pp. 185-86 and literature cited there, pp. 194-95) argues that the building up of the body describes the activity of the offices, which are thereby given the permanent legitimacy in the post-apostolic age once enjoyed by the prophets and apostles. Cf. Houlden, *Paul's Letters*, pp. 312-14.

19. I take both instances of εἰς to relate to the ἅγιοι. So also Meade, *Pseudonymity*, p. 156 and n. 159.

20. The imitation of God is rooted in the notion of holiness (Lev. 19.1; cf. Matt. 5.48). It is a concept familiar also to Jewish, in particular Philonic, thinking, as H.D. Betz (*Nachfolge und Nachahmung Jesu Christi im Neuen Testament* [BHT, 37; Tübingen: Mohr (Siebeck), 1967], p. 132) and R.A. Wild, SJ ('"Be Imitators of God": Discipleship in the Letter to the Ephesians', in F.F. Segovia [ed.], *Discipleship in the New Testament* [Philadelphia: Fortress Press, 1985], pp. 128-32) have shown. However, given the critical dialogue Ephesians carries on with the Pauline writings, the shift from the imitation of Christ via imitation of Paul (1 Thess. 1.6; 1 Cor. 4.16, 17; 11.1; Phil. 3.17) to the imitation of *God* must be seen to conform to the Ephesian strategy of inflating the church's sense of status and task.

all the works of darkness (μὴ συγκοινωνεῖτε τοῖς ἔργοις τοῖς ἀκάρποις τοῦ σκότου; v. 11; cf. vv. 3-7).[21] In essence they are to live like σοφοί (v. 15) and δίκαιοι.

The specific term δίκαιοι does not appear in Ephesians, but the vocabulary and the especially the tone of confrontation has clear resonance with the image of the δίκαιος in Wisdom of Solomon. There are, however, some significant differences. First, the separation from darkness and the sons of disobedience does not result in the isolation of the community from encounter with darkness, this despite the use of the past tense in 2.5, 6. As the following verses indicate, and as the image of the church in the divine armour in ch. 6 will show most dramatically, the community remains in direct contact with darkness and the sons of disobedience. The darkness is, after all, the realm from which the τέκνα φωτός have themselves been recruited, and from where they continue to draw recruits. It is perhaps for that reason that the antipathy between the party of death and the ἅγιοι *qua* δίκαιοι is not played up in Ephesians as it is in Wisdom of Solomon.[22] Secondly, the ἅγιοι are not described as innocent victims whose suffering stokes the fires of retribution against the ἄθεοι. Instead, much as in Wisdom of Solomon their role with respect to sin and darkness is one of radical confrontation (ἐλέγχειν, v. 11[23]), the purpose of which is the transformation of darkness into light (v. 13).

The build-up to divine warfare and in particular to the introduction of the Divine Warrior is suggested further by the baptismal hymn fragment in 5.14.[24] While the hymn suggests gnostic, mystery, and Qumranic similarities, the context here draws attention to its relationship to battle and warfare. The use of ἔγειρε recalls the summons (*Aufgebot*; von

21. Cf. also Rom. 13.12. The close relationship of Rom. 13.11-14 to 1 Thess. 5.1-11 was discussed above. It enjoys many points of contact with Ephesians as well, most particularly with ch. 5.

22. Ch. 2 has already made the leap of identifying οἱ μακράν not with the exiled people of God but rather with the ἄθεοι, those who, like 'we', were once under the authority of the prince of the air. In making this leap the author of Ephesians shares in the attitude of Paul as reflected in the previous study of 1 Thessalonians; cf. especially also Romans.

23. Cf. Wis. 2.12; Amos 5.19 LXX.

24. Schnackenburg (*Brief*, pp. 232-34), Gnilka (*Epheserbrief*, pp. 259-63) and Houlden (*Paul's Letters*, p. 327) argue with the majority of commentators for a baptismal matrix of the song.

Rad) of the Divine Warrior to do battle,[25] as does the virtual synonym ἀνάστα.[26] Furthermore, the reference to believers as awakened καθεύδοντες suggests familiarity with 1 Thessalonians 5. In the Pauline corpus καθεύδων is only used here and in 1 Thess. 5.6, 7, 10.[27] Given that the author is citing a hymn fragment, and that its language is unlikely to have been shaped specifically by 1 Thessalonians 5, one should hesitate to claim direct dependency here on 1 Thessalonians 5. More likely is that in 1 Thessalonians 5 Paul drew language with which to characterize the realm from which the members of the Divine Warrior are recruited from the same well as does the hymn in Eph. 5.14. It is also likely that the author of Ephesians recognizes the allusive possibilities of citing that hymn within a context in which darkness and light are pitted against each other, thereby evoking 1 Thessalonians 5. He is building up to the motif of the community in the divine armour, as does Paul in 1 Thessalonians 5.[28]

25. The more frequent form in the LXX is ἐξεγείρειν (e.g. Num. 10.35; Judg. 5.12; Pss. 7.6; 34.23; 43.24; 77.65 LXX (notice the Divine Warrior arising as a sleeper; ἐξηγέρθη ὡς ὑπνῶν κύριος); Isa. 51.9 is interesting in that the MT implies that Yahweh is being roused to battle, whereas LXX parallels here the call in v. 17 for Jerusalem to rise. Ziegler's apparatus shows later attempts to harmonize the text to the MT by deleting reference to Jerusalem (*Isaias–Septuaginta* [Vetus Testamentum Graecum Auctoritate Academiae Litterarum Gottingensis editum, 14; Göttingen: Vandenhoeck & Ruprecht, 1967]).

26. It is clear that this hymn fragment refers to participation in the resurrection of the dead, where the experience of baptism is either anticipation of the resurrection at the time of the eschaton (cf. Rom. 6.3-11), or itself already participation in resurrection. The strategy of the author of Ephesians is to accentuate as much as possible the present status of the baptized. So the hymn fragment plays well into the note already sounded in 2.5, 6, which places the believers onto the heavenly throne. But 'militant' overtones of such royal status are suggested by the frequency with which ἀνίστημι describes the rising of the warrior for battle in LXX, often together with ἐξεγείρειν (e.g., Num. 10.35; Judg. 5.7, 12; Pss. 3.7; 9.19; 34.2; 43.24, 27; 67.2; 73.22; 81.8 LXX; Isa. 33.10; and the references to 'rising' in Isa. 51). Rom. 6.13 shows clearly the connection between baptism, resurrection, and participation in divine warfare (παραστήσατε...τὰ μέλη ὑμῶν ὅπλα δικαιοσύνης τῷ θεῷ).

27. See discussion on this in the chapter on 1 Thess. 5 above. Rom. 13.11 shows familiarity with this theme, only in Ephesians it is reminiscent not only of sleep as living in darkness but also of usage as in Ps. 77.65 LXX, where the Lord is awakened from sleep to do battle (cf. note above on ἐξεγείρειν).

28. The exact nature of the dependency of the author of Ephesians on 1 Thessalonians is difficult to determine, since here, as in the case of its relationship to Colossians, there is no 'copying' of the sort that would make the dependency obvious. Instead one finds similarities in vocabulary, ideas, progression of ideas and themes

Only in 1 Thess. 5.2 and here in Eph. 5.15 does ἀκριβῶς appear in the Pauline corpus. Whereas there it refers to knowing precisely that one cannot know when the day of the Lord will invade, here it refers to walking (περιπατεῖν) 'carefully' (ἀκριβῶς) as σοφοί (not as ἄφρονες; vv. 15, 17), 'buying out the time' (ἐξαγοραζόμενοι) since the days are evil (αἱ ἡμέραι πονηραί εἰσιν). This is clearly not an aping of 1 Thessalonians 5, but the resonance is palpable. Whereas the 'day of the Lord' has given way to 'evil days', allowing a much wider latitude of interpretation, the sense of 'day' as threat and as time of battle is present. Whereas in 1 Thess. 5.6-8 the sons of light are to be alert and sober soldiers prepared for battle, not drunk and asleep like those who live in the night, here the readers are not only to walk carefully, but not to be drunk with wine (Eph. 5.18). This call to sobriety gives way to the command to be filled with spirit, which is then elaborated upon with a catena of participles, the last of which is mutual subordination (ὑποτασσόμενοι ἀλλήλοις), taking the place of mutual (ἀλλήλους) exhortation and edification in 1 Thess. 5.11.

Ephesians is in critical interaction with other texts as well. Colossians, first of all, contains many phrases and words found here. Eph. 5.3-5 draws part of its catalogue of vices from Col. 3.5 (πορνεία, ἀκαθαρσία, πλεονεξία, εἰδωλολατρία). In Colossians this is followed by a call to put on (ἐνδύσασθε; 3.12) a set of virtues exercised in the community of the elect (cf. Eph. 4.32). It is within this context of letting the λόγος τοῦ Χριστοῦ dwell within the community that the singing of psalms and spiritual songs is mentioned (3.17). There is no hint of struggle or battle. The call to 'buy out the time' in 4.5 comes within the context of apology and evangelism, not within the context of evil days as in Ephesians.

Given the significant degree to which Colossians finds an echo in Ephesians, the author must intend a critical recasting of the Colossian agenda. The exercise of virtue is drawn into the confrontation with darkness, and leads to and constitutes divine warfare itself. Hence ἐνδύσασθε is taken out of the Colossian sequence and held in reserve until after the *Haustafel* and appears in 6.11. However, it has been intensified by describing not the putting on of Christ *per se* (Col. 3.9, 10)[29] but the

that give the clear impression that Ephesians represents a critical recapitulation of the Pauline legacy.

29. Ephesians can make that same point strongly; cf. 4.24 and the putting on of the new ἄνθρωπος.

putting on of the divine armour and thus the imitation of God as Divine Warrior. This 'militarizing' of the Colossian *Vorlage* is accomplished in some measure by overlaying it with vocabulary and themes from 1 Thess. 5.1-11, most particularly its central motif of the Divine Warrior's armour. For example, 'walking' not as ἄσοφοι and ἄφρονες but as σοφοί (v. 15) implies watchfulness and sobriety in the light of dangerous days, serving thus largely as synonym for the γρηγορεῖν (and νήφειν), not as used in Col. 4.2, where it follows immediately the *Haustafel* and has no relation at all to struggle and warfare, but as it functions in 1 Thess. 5.6.[30]

Parenthetically, whereas the injunction not to be drunk with wine but rather to be filled with the spirit (5.18) might be seen at first glance as little more than parenesis regarding sobriety,[31] that would be to ignore its context. First, the author adds this item to those drawn from Col. 3.16. 'Being filled with spirit' replaces the indwelling λόγος τοῦ Χριστου of Col. 3.16. Prov. 23.31 supplies some of the vocabulary as well. Strikingly resonant with Ephesians 5 is what replaces the drinking of wine in Proverbs, namely, conversation (ὁμιλῶ) with just persons (ἄνθρωποι δίκαιοι) and with (ἐν) 'walkers' (περιπάτοι). Compare the Ephesian stress on 'walking as the wise' (5.15) and on the singing to each other of hymns and spiritual songs (5.19, 20). But the injunction to sobriety, specifically to be filled with the spirit, opens up into images of readiness for participation in battle.[32] If that context is kept in view, then

30. Cf. the very similar note in Rom. 13.13, where the value of sobriety is implied in the list of vices, including drunkenness. Those who have taken off τὰ ἔργα τοῦ σκότους and have put on τὰ ὅπλα τοῦ φωτός (v. 12) are to 'walk conformed to being in (of) day' (ὡς ἐν ἡμέρᾳ εὐσχημόνως).

31. Barth, *Ephesians 4–6*, pp. 580-82.

32. Not surprisingly this image resonates with the gnostic characterization of life without consciousness or knowledge as a state of drunkenness or intoxication: e.g. *Ap. Jas.* 3.8-14; *Gos. Thom.* Logion 29; *Auth. Teach.* 24.14-20; *Corp. Herm.* 1.27; 7.1-3. Cf. *Teach. Silv.* 94.19-22; note the alternative of drinking from the vine of Christ, which gives joy through the spirit of God; 107.26–108.3. (Peel and Zandee suggest *Teach. Silv.* is non-Gnostic ['The Teachings of Silvanus', *The Nag Hammadi Library in English* (intr. and trans. M.L. Peel and J. Zandee; ed. F. Wisse; New York: Harper & Row, 1977), p. 346].) Whatever the attractiveness of the language of Ephesians for subsequent gnostic writing, and whatever points of contact Ephesians has to gnostic thinking, the point here is to explore the relationship of this language to the tradition of divine warfare. That this tradition can feed into the gnostic notions of drunkenness, sleep, awakening, and finally conflict with hypostases, is by no means denied.

there is also some resonance with Isaianic texts such as 29.9 and 51.21, where drunkenness ('be drunk but not with wine') is an image of reeling under the impact of judgment, virtually synonymous with living in darkness.[33] The author of Ephesians intends, then, to take up the image of drunkenness as a metaphor for a life subject to judgment and to place against it a life of being filled, being 'drunk', with spirit. This becomes then a description of a community filled with spirited singing,[34] thankful praying, and mutual subjection, ready to do battle against the forces of darkness and drunkenness.[35]

The last participle in the catena introduces subordination, subsequently elaborated in the *Haustafel*. It is attractive to think of the *Haustafel* as interrupting a flow of thought that moves from identification with Christ, to imitation of God, to confrontation with darkness, and finally to the taking up of the armour of God itself. The suggestion that the *Haustafel* represents an interpolation both here and in Colossians has been argued by, among others, Winsome Munro on the grounds that it reflects the hierarchical thinking of the second-century Pastoral letters.[36]

33. The image of drunkenness is closely related to divine judgment in Isaiah; it can describe a life of injustice and oppression: 5.11; 22.13; 28.1, 3, 7, 8 (see how the 'crown of the drunkards of Ephraim' is juxtaposed with the Lord as crown and diadem, paralleled by the 'spirit of justice'), and 56.12. At other times it becomes a metaphor for the experience of judgment: e.g., 24.20; 34.5; 51.17, 22, and also 63.3, 6 (the image of judgment as the wine press).

34. The singing of hymns is a frequent part of the tradition of divine warfare. Most obvious are classic divine warfare hymns such as Exod. 15, Deut. 32, Judg. 5, Pss. 18 and 68, and Hab. 3. Many of these songs celebrate the past victory of the Divine Warrior and his people, but their repetition functions as a renewed call for divine intervention. One can also cite late texts which illustrate this: e.g., 2 Chron. 20.21-28; 1 Macc. 4.24; 13.51; 1QM 4.4, 5, 4; Rev. 15.3, 4; 18.2–19.3. Cf. F. Schwally, *Semitische Kriegsaltertümer*. I. *Der heilige Krieg im alten Israel* (Leipzig: Dieterich'sche Verlagsbuchhaltung, Theodor Weicher, 1901), p. 25, and G. von Rad, *Heilige Krieg*, p. 11.

35. Cf. Schwally's discussion of the military meaning of sobriety in holy war texts (*Semitische Kriegsaltertümer*, p. 109). It is also interesting to note Livy's description of the Bacchanalia as a night culture marked by debauchery and drunkenness. He asks: 'Do you think, citizens, that youths initiated by this oath should be made soldiers? That arms should be entrusted to men mustered from this foul shrine? Will men covered with the signs of their own debauchery and that of others fight to the death on behalf of the chastity of your wives and children?' (Livy 39.15; trans. E.T. Sage [LCL; Cambridge, MA: Harvard University Press, 1936], p. 261).

36. W. Munro, *Authority in Paul and Peter: The Identification of a Pastoral*

There is no compelling reason, however, to hold that the *Haustafel* tradition post-dates Ephesians or that the author does not intend to place the tradition in precisely this spot in the letter. On the contrary, in keeping with the strategy already observed, the author also attempts to subject this tradition to critique and to employ it in relation to the call to arms, as it were.

First, the call to be mutually subject to each other can be taken to suggest a call for good military order. The author of 1 Clement recognizes as much when he speaks of ὑποταγὴ μία (37.5), combining the motifs of a well-ordered (εὐτάκτως; 37.2) army and an integrated body to support a hierarchy of authority (37.1-38.1). However, the intentions of the author of Ephesians are closer to those of Paul in 1 Cor. 12.12-31 and Rom. 12.3-8. I have already noted the upending of hierarchical notions with respect to the 'gifts' in 4.7-12. In 5.21 ἀλλήλοις is meant to signal that the *Haustafel*, familiar to readers (or at least to fellow members of the Pauline 'school') from Colossians, is to be read in the light of *mutual* subjection.[37] It is debatable whether the author is successful in giving the *Haustafel* such a twist.[38] But the attempt illustrates the intention of the author once again to push the church to view its task and its mutual relations in the light of the overall task of being centrally implicated in the process of 'recapitulating' all things in Christ (1.10). The fact that in subsequent history this text effected the opposite does not preclude that the author intended to draw the conservative tradition into the overall dynamic of equipping the saints for the role of the Divine Warrior.[39]

Stratum in the Pauline Corpus and 1 Peter (Cambridge: Cambridge University Press, 1983).

37. It is important that whereas ἀλλήλων is ubiquitous in the undisputed writings of Paul it appears only seldom in the rest of the Pauline corpus: 2 Thess. 1.3; Col. 3.9, 13; Tit. 3.3. In Ephesians it plays a larger role: 4.2, 25, 32; 5.21; cf. also 1 Thess. 5.11.

38. For an evaluation of the *Haustafel* as essentially conservative or reactionary, see, e.g., D.J. Balch (*Let Wives be Submissive: The Domestic Code in 1 Peter* [SBLMS, 26; Chico, CA: Scholars Press, 1981]); J.E. Crouch (*The Origin and Intention of the Colossian Haustafel* [FRLANT, 109; Göttingen: Vandenhoeck & Ruprecht, 1971]), and Munro (*Authority*).

39. If, as is often asserted, at the time of the writing of Ephesians the implied radicalism of Gal. 3.28 is no longer appreciated or practised in Pauline communities, then it is significant that Ephesians loads the *Haustafel* with christological freight. If my reading of Ephesian Christology is correct, and this is pivotal, then the insertion

Second, the raising of domestic relationships within a context of impending battle is not without precedent within the scriptural warfare traditions. Deuteronomy 20 gives instructions for preparations for battle. First there is to be an exhortatory speech by a priest,[40] who is then to cull appropriate warriors from those assembled. The criteria are household circumstances and relationships. The sequence of assurance of victory and the subsequent culling of worthy warriors in Deuteronomy is paralleled by the sequence of blessing, assurance, and parenesis in Ephesians. However, in Ephesians it is exactly *not* the case that the warriors are to be *without* familial and domestic ties. So no more can be claimed here than that the placing of domestic relationships into a context of a call to readiness for battle has biblical precedent. In Ephesians familial ties are to be marked by mutual subordination, by obedience, and by self-sacrificial love. In short, in the view of the author of Ephesians, 'normal' social relationships are the context in which the battle order is to be set up, in which the troops are mustered, and where or from where the battle is fought.

In the end, an evaluation of the *Haustafel* is not critical for this reading of Ephesians. But it needs at least to be stated that its presence following the dualistic confrontational language of ch. 5 and immediately preceding the call to put on the divine armour does not mitigate the interpretation given here to the whole of Ephesians. To see the critical note in the Ephesian *Haustafel* residing chiefly in the redactional exploitation of its paradigmatic function means that one can recognize the conservatism in the tradition and, at the same time, appreciate the critical element in how the *topos* is employed and nuanced.[41] So, while the

of the *hieros gamos* into the traditional household carries a certain challenge to patriarchal assumptions of power and privilege. How deep that challenge goes is a matter of debate. Note that only Ephesians locates the *Haustafel* as an elaboration of mutual (ἀλλήλων) subordination, which is in turn a specification of what it means to be filled with the spirit. While in the undisputed letters Paul does not refer to Christ as 'head' of the body (he does remain unequivocally its Lord), in Ephesians 5, quite in keeping with Pauline Christology, Christ as head performs what are seen as the marks of oppression: he loves, he washes, and he gives his life for his spouse. E. Schüssler Fiorenza recognizes this (*In Memory of Her: A Feminist Theological Reconstruction of Christian Origins* [New York: Crossroad, 1983], pp. 269-70), even if she also correctly perceives that the 'wedding' of the relationship of husband and wife to Christology spelled trouble, given the directions Christology was to take.

40. Cf. 1QM 7.3, 11.

41. Cf. here J.H. Elliott, *A Home for the Homeless: A Sociological Exegesis of*

Haustafel appears initially to be a diversion from the steady intensification of militancy in the tone of this letter, it is the author's intention, visible especially when compared to the treatment of the *Haustafel* in Colossians, to draw the everyday, which was by all indications becoming more conservative within Pauline circles, into his vision of a church centrally engaged in the conflictual divine programme to set things right—divine warfare. Thus, immediately following the instructions to the κύριοι in 6.9, the author of Ephesians calls the whole community to put on the armour of God and enter the fray of battle.

2. *The Call to Divine Warfare*

Ephesians 6.10 sets the tone for the whole of 6.10-20 by summoning the church to imitate God (cf. 5.1) by taking up God's power. The verse begins with Τοῦ λοιποῦ, which is either translated as 'Finally...' or as 'Henceforth...' Most scholars read τοῦ λοιποῦ as synonymous with the more frequent accusative τὸ λοιπόν and translate it then as 'Finally...' (lit., 'with respect to the rest...').[42] Eph. 6.10-20 would then be the last in a chain of exhortations, the horizon having shifted from the οἶκος in 5.21–6.9 to the κόσμος. Such a shift requires some sort of a rhetorical signal to mark the shift (*Übergangsfloskel* [43]). According to this view a sufficient tone of urgency is not present in Ephesians to have τοῦ λοιποῦ signal a warning for the future.[44]

There are, however, some compelling reasons for preferring the temporal 'Henceforth,...' as in Gal 6.17, where χρονοῦ is understood (lit.,

1 Peter, its Situation and Strategy (Philadelphia: Fortress Press, 1981), pp. 165-266; D. Lührmann, 'Neutestamentliche Haustafeln und antike Ökonomie', *NTS* 27 (1980), pp. 83-97; S.F. Miletic, *'One Flesh': Eph. 5.22-24, 5.31: Marriage and the New Creation* (AnBib, 115; Rome: Editrice Pontificio Istituto Biblico, 1988); W. Schrage, 'Zur Ethik der neutestamentlichen Haustafeln', *NTS* 21 (1974/75), pp. 1-22, and the early study by D. Schroeder, 'Die Haustafeln des Neuen Testaments: Ihre Herkunft und ihr theologischer Sinn' (DTheol dissertation, Hamburg University, 1959).

42. E.g., M. Dibelius and H. Greeven, *An die Kolosser, Epheser, an Philemon* (HNT, 12; Tübingen: Mohr [Siebeck], 3rd edn, 1953), p. 74; Gnilka, *Epheserbrief*, p. 304; F. Mußner, *Der Brief an die Epheser* (Ökumenischer Taschenbuchkommentar zum Neuen Testament, 10; Gütersloh: Gerd Mohn, Echter Verlag, 1982), p. 165; Schnackenburg, *Brief*, p. 272; note the variant reading τὸ λοιπόν in a^2 D F G Y *Byz*.

43. Schnackenburg, *Brief*, p. 277.

44. Gnilka, *Epheserbrief*, p. 304 n.1.

'for the remaining time').[45] As I have attempted to show, within the rhetorical framework of Ephesians the battle is about to ensue.[46] To the extent that this *topos* reflects baptismal parenesis,[47] the eschatological context of readying for battle would have suggested itself to Pauline readers (cf. Rom. 6.3-5; cf. Rom. 13.11-14). The genitive of time is thus to be preferred.[48]

Eph. 6.10-20 is the final in a series of exhortations beginning in 4.1. It constitutes the climax of the parenesis of the letter, indeed, of the letter as a whole. With respect to rhetorical analysis, Taylor contends that Ephesians as a whole is epideictic, and that 6.10-24 represents the *peroratio* of the letter.[49] As Kennedy notes, the genres of rhetoric can become quite mixed, but generally one of the three types of rhetoric—deliberative, forensic, and epideictic—will be the determining one.[50] The epideictic sections of Ephesians, such as the eulogy at the outset of the document, thus serve what is chiefly a deliberative purpose, as is indicated by the strong imperative tone of the *peroratio*. Verses 10-20

45. E.g. Schlier, *Brief*, p. 289; Barth, *Ephesians 4–6*, p. 760.

46. Cf. the previously cited examples of Deut. 20 and 1QM 10 and 11 as speeches prior to battle calling for courage and fortitude.

47. Cf. P. Carrington, *The Primitive Christian Catechism* (Cambridge: Cambridge University Press, 1940); inexplicably, to my thinking, W. Meeks (*The First Urban Christians: The Social World of the Apostle Paul* [New Haven: Yale University Press, 1983], pp. 154, 155, 238 n. 68) rejects the connection between the putting on of armour and baptism.

48. BDF §186(2), Smyth §1444. Barth (*Ephesians 4–6*, p. 760) suggests that the silent χρονοῦ implies a limitation on the future as in 'for the time that remains'. His reading is correct, even if I do not share his assumption of Pauline authorship and the concomitant reading of Ephesians through the eyes of Paul's apocalyptic eschatology. A limit to the future is called for by the strong 'already' that in Ephesians functions as the fundamental premise to the call to battle. If the sense of urgency is here not unambiguously shaped by a sense of impending apocalyptic crisis, there is nonetheless a sense of urgency, a sense of a future in need of resolution. This sense is rooted in the necessary tension between the assurance of victory and the subsequent call to battle. That tension, illustrated in Ephesians by the preceding assurance of victory implied by the identification of the community with a victorious Christ, is endemic to Divine War. One should note the past tense in the ubiquitous formula, 'I have given them into your hand!', which necessarily precedes holy battle.

49. W. Taylor, 'Ephesians 6:10-24 and the Genre of Ephesians' (Pauline Epistles Section, SBL, 1985).

50. G.A. Kennedy, *New Testament Interpretation Through Rhetorical Criticism* (Chapel Hill: University of North Carolina Press, 1984), p. 19.

are thus a forceful concluding summation of the burden of the oration as a whole, as well as a final call to action in light of the impending future.[51]

The whole community[52] is called to be empowered: ἐνδυναμοῦσθε![53] The imperative is noteworthy. On most other occasions where ἐνδυναμοῦσθαι (and δυναμοῦσθαι) appears the imperative is not used, perhaps because divine empowerment is generally understood to be a passive experience.[54] It is of interest that ἐνδυναμῶ appears in the LXX only as

51. The very fact that documents such as Ephesians were meant not only to be studied but to be heard, and to have impact on first hearing, suggests the relevance of rhetorical observations. Cf. Kennedy, *New Testament Interpretation*, p. 30.

52. Τοῦ λοιποῦ signals the conclusion of the *Haustafel* and resumption of the parenesis to the whole community. This should not be understood, as it usually is, in individualistic terms. The whole letter is preoccupied with the movement toward unity and oneness. That is the central concept underlying ch. 2, both with respect to being seated with Christ and to the creation of the καινὸς ἄνθρωπος, the σῶμα τοῦ Χριστοῦ. It is thus in keeping with Ephesians to see the community addressed corporately. So also W. Wink, *Naming the Powers: The Language of Power in the New Testament* (Philadelphia: Fortress Press, 1984), p. 88.

53. There is relatively good manuscript support for δυναμοῦσθε (P^{46} B 33). This variant likely came about under the influence of Col. 1.11. Ἐνδυναμοῦσθε is more suited to Ephesians with its unusually persistent use of ἐν, both in absolute and in construct form.

54. Rom. 4.20: Abraham was empowered in or by faith; Phil. 4.13: Paul can do all things through the one who empowers him; 1 Tim. 1.12: 'Paul' gives thanks that he is empowered through Christ Jesus. 2 Tim. 2.1 constitutes an exception to the rule: 'Timothy' is called upon to be empowered in or by the grace which is in Christ Jesus. Acts 9.22 has little if any relevance since little more is meant than that Saul is convalescing.

Δυναμοῦσθαι: Col. 1.11: believers are to be 'powered' with all δύναμις according to the κράτος of God's glory for all ὑπομονή and μακροθυμία. Ephesians may be dependent on Colossians here; but the participle δυναμούμενοι elaborates the prayer in 1.9 that the Colossians might be filled, implying that the empowerment comes from the one who can answer the prayer. Cf. finally Heb. 11.34, where heroes and prophets are said to have been 'powered' ἀπὸ ἀσθενείας. This is given further support by the occurrences in the Apostolic Fathers, the bulk of which appear in the Shepherd of Hermas. While *Herm. Sim.* 9.1.2 speaks of the visionary Hermas being empowered by the Spirit so as to be able to receive a vision, most frequently the sense is one of being empowered to be able to keep the ἐντολαί. The keeping of the ἐντολαί is in turn part of the arsenal with which to resist (ἀντιστῆναι) the διάβολος (*Herm. Man.* 12.5.1, 2; 12.6.1-4; 5.2.8). Hermas might represent a moralizing of the tradition which has its origins in Ephesians; cf. here also CD 16.5, where to keep the laws of Moses results in the angel of enmity taking his leave. Ignatius speaks of being empowered by the τελείος ἄνθρωπος (Ign. *Smyrn.* 4.2).

a variant for ἐνδύω (cf. Judg. 6.34 and 1 Chron. 12.19). Individuals are empowered or clothed by the spirit within contexts of warfare.[55]

'Ενδυναμοῦσθε is a middle imperative, in keeping with the strategy of Ephesians. For theological reasons Barth suggests one read this as a passive, since a middle would be inappropriate given that God is the source of power.[56] In most instances it is in fact God or Christ who is described as the one who empowers. However, the author of Ephesians has already pushed the Pauline and deutero-Pauline language of identification of believers with the Christ to the limit; tellingly, in 5.1 the author calls for the imitation of God. So 6.10 can and should be read as a call to the community to take up divine power. Such a call is made most forcefully with a middle imperative, which then also parallels the middle ἐνδύσασθε in 6.11.[57]

This is illustrated further by the fact that, with the exception of Col. 1.11, in the Scriptures those who are 'empowered' are all exceptional individuals such as Abraham, Paul, Timothy, or the warriors and prophets in Heb. 11.32.[58] This is consistent with the notion of the special empowerment of charismatic individuals by God for a particular task such as holy war. In Ephesians the exceptional persons, whether Paul or the 'gifts' of 4.11, are placed in a position *behind* that accorded the community as a whole—saints, women and men, children and parents, slaves and masters.

This call to take up power, specified in 6.11 as a call to put on the

1 Clem. 55.3 utilizes the term in an interesting fashion by referring to heroic women (Judith and Esther, 55.4,6) who were empowered to perform masculine feats or virtues (ἀνδρεῖα; cf. Prov. 31.10,25).

55. It will be important to keep this in mind for the relationship of ἐνδύσασθε in 6.11 to ἐνδυναμοῦσθε in 6.10, in particular as to whether there might be some sort of wordplay here. (Cf. *Herm. Sim.* 6.1.2 for a similar case.)

56. Barth, *Ephesians 4–6*, p. 760 n. 7; so also T.K. Abbott, *Epistles to the Ephesians and to the Colossians* (ICC; Edinburgh: T. & T. Clark, 1897), pp. 180-81; E. Gaugler, *Der Epheserbrief* (Auslegung Neutestamentlicher Schriften, 6; Zürich: EVZ, 1966), p. 217.

57. Cf. the similar dynamic in the NHC, notably *Teach. Silv.* ('Open for yourselves…') and *Ep. Pet. Phil.* 137.27, 'gird yourselves with power from the Father'. ET: *The Nag Hammadi Library in English* (San Francisco: Harper & Row, 1977).

58. One will want to keep in mind the relationship of the extraordinary individual to the whole of the community in which he or she functions as exemplar of virtue, obedience, or courage. See here, for example, the explicit generalization in *Herm. Man.* 5.2.8. Nevertheless, exemplars remain exemplars inasmuch as they continue in some sense to be extraordinary.

armour of God, recalls the ubiquitous demand in the Scriptures for God as the איש מלחמות/συντρίβων πόλεμος to arise for battle (Exod. 15.3; Isa. 42.13; cf. Pss. 9.20; 43.24 LXX). As indicated earlier, the call to wake up and arise also on occasion summons the people, first individual charismatic warriors, but then also the people as a whole (cf. Judg. 5.12). However, in such cases the people arise at most to participate in what remains the prime warring of יהוה/κύριος (Deut. 20.1-4; cf. 1QM 11 and 12).

This is, parenthetically, the context of the μὴ φοβοῦ/μὴ φοβεῖσθε formula in traditional Divine Warrior texts. The command not to fear is present both in situations in which God alone is the warrior, that is, in contexts of strict human passivity,[59] and in contexts in which human warriors fight but are outnumbered and ostensibly outpowered by their enemies. Relevant here are those instances in which the call not to be afraid is combined with the order to be strong.[60] But it should be noted that in none of the texts cited is ἐνδυναμοῦ/ἐνδυναμοῦσθε used. Rather we find ἴσχυε/ἰσχύετε (ἀνδρίζου/ἀνδρίζεσθε), suggesting not so much active exercise of power as the strength, fortitude and courage to 'stand still', to hold one's ground.[61] Thus, typically, the call to be strong is accompanied by the assurance that God will fight for the people.

Significantly, the formula μὴ φοβοῦ does not appear in Ephesians, nor would it be relevant, given where the author of Ephesians locates the church. Instead, it is the pervasive emphasis on power in the first three chapters, in particular 1.19 and 3.16-20, which provides the motive for the call to be empowered in 6.10. Indeed, the pleonastic heaping up of power terms in 6.10 echoes the wording in 1.19: τὸ ὑπερβάλλον μέγεθος τῆς δυνάμεως αὐτοῦ εἰς ἡμᾶς τοὺς πιστεύοντας κατὰ τὴν ἐνέργειαν τοῦ κράτους τῆς ἰσχύος αὐτοῦ. In 1.19 power exists *for* the community (εἰς ἡμᾶς).[62] 6.10 represents then the complement to 1.19. In 1.16 and 3.14-19 'Paul' prays that the community might have

59. E.g. Exod. 14.13, Deut. 3.22.

60. E.g. Deut. 31.6; Josh. 8.1; 10.25; 2 Sam. 13.28; 2 Chron. 20.15-17, 26; Isa. 35.3, 4; 41.10.

61. See here BAGD, p. 383, and W. Grundmann, 'ἰσχύω, κτλ.', *TDNT*, III, pp. 397-402; note Sir. 17.2 where clothing with ἰσχύς gives fortitude for life, as in creation.

62. It is ambiguous as to whether the εἰς ἡμᾶς implies something as yet outstanding, or whether it is the equivalent to ἐν ἡμῖν in 3.20.

knowledge of such power.[63] In 6.10 the author now clarifies that the seizing of power and with it the full realization of divine power demands the initiative of the community. The community is precisely not asked to wait and watch. It is rather to seize the initiative. The community is to take up and exercise that power which raised Christ.

The community is to 'empower itself' ἐν κυρίῳ καὶ ἐν τῷ κράτει τῆς ἰσχύος αὐτοῦ. More than a habitual turn of phrase or typical formula in Pauline letters and especially in Ephesians, ἐν κυρίῳ is here fraught with meaning.[64] Whereas ἐν 'utterly defies definite interpretation,'[65] it should be translated here as causal or instrumental rather than local. More frequent for Pauline usage is the local sense, which would render ἐν κυρίῳ synonymous with ἐν Χριστῷ, signifying participation in and identification with Christ, imagery no doubt shaped by baptismal experience and teaching.[66] It has been suggested that the largely instrumental use of ἐν in Ephesians indicates to what an extent a once significant expression of Pauline 'mystical' participation 'in Christ' has come to be formulized, its meaning largely exhausted by an instrumental sense.[67] There is, however, no reason to see in this a weakening of connotative power. When the pervasive spatial sphere-like language is combined in Ephesians with an instrumental use of ἐν, space takes on life, space becomes eschatological.

There is a special military usage of this instrumental sense, especially in the Septuagint, where it can signify first of all *who* is brought into battle with the combatants, that is, alongside whom the battle is waged,[68] and secondly *what* is used in battle.[69] In short, the sense of accom-

63. Cf. *Corp. Herm.* Poim., 32, where knowing is the equivalent to empowerment.

64. It appears seven times. Most often it is seen as synonymous with ἐν αὐτῷ (7x), ἐν ᾧ (7x), ἐν Χριστῷ Ἰησοῦ (7x), ἐν τῷ Χριστῷ (4x), ἐν Χριστῷ (2x), ἐν τῷ κυρίῳ (1x), ἐν τῷ Ἰησοῦ (1x).

65. BDF §219(4), cf. R. Bultmann, *Theology of the New Testament* (trans. K. Grobel; 2 vols.; New York: Charles Scribner's Sons, 1951, 1955), II, p. 177.

66. See here the commentaries, as well as W. Grundmann, 'δύναμαι, κτλ', *TDNT*, II, p. 313, *idem*, 'ἰσχύω', p. 399.

67. Cf. Houlden, *Paul's Letters*, p. 243.

68. BAGD, p. 259 (4.a); 1 Macc. 1.7; 3.3; 4.6, 29; 7.14, 28; Jdt. 16.3; the influence of the Hebrew preposition ב is more than likely; for examples see BDB, pp. 89-90; cf. also the important 1QM 11.5 discussed below.

69. Frequent in LXX; cf. Eph. 1.20—ἐν δεξιᾷ αὐτοῦ; Luke 1.17—ἐν πνεύματι καὶ δυνάμει.

paniment comes exceedingly close to an instrumental meaning. Eph. 6.10 becomes an order, then, to 'take up the Lord' in the sense of a warrior taking up armour, mustering troops, arranging for allies. The community is called upon to 'wield the Lord,' so to speak, a striking reversal of the usual Divine War tradition where the people function as one of the δύναμεις of the Divine Warrior.

This still leaves open the question as to whether God is in view here as the Lord who grants power, or whether God is the one who grants power 'through' the Lord Christ, where ἐν indicates the means and not so much the causal source. In nearly all cases in Ephesians κύριος refers either explicitly or implicitly to Christ. A clear distinction between God and κύριος appears to exist in 4.5, 6. A number of texts are ambiguous as to whether they refer to God or to Christ, perhaps intentionally so. The variant τῷ θεῷ for τῷ κυρίῳ in 5.10 suggests as much.[70] Further, 6.8 (δοῦλος...κομίσεται παρὰ κυρίου) may be ambiguous since reward and gift giving is generally the prerogative of God, who gives in and through Christ.[71] This ambiguity can also be seen, parenthetically, in the reworking of Ps. 67.19 LXX in Eph. 4.7-10. If 4.7 is translated in light of 1.17-23, where God's action in the resurrection of Christ is the measure for what God does in and for the church (vv. 20-23), then one should read: 'To each one of us was given the gift according to the measure of the gift of Christ'. God is the prime actor, the chief recipient is the church, and the measure of that gift is the gift of life and exaltation given to Christ. At the same time, the ambiguity of the genitive (τοῦ Χριστοῦ) and the following treatment of Ps. 67.19 LXX suggests a 'replacement' of God by Christ in which Christ is not only the recipient of the gift but the giver as well. The descent of the victor clearly evokes Christ (4.9, 10). And, unlike in the psalm, it is in the descent that the decisive action—the giving of gifts—takes place.

One can argue that in traditional *topoi* such as 5.10 and 6.8, where Ephesians' Jewish readers would be accustomed to hearing 'God' in κύριος, the author wants to have the readers see *both* God and Christ. It is the former which must be highlighted in 6.10, however, as the following catena of power terms suggests (ἐν τῷ κράτει τῆς ἰσχύος αὐτοῦ). In fact, the author of Ephesians is willing to push this blurring of

70. Cf. 1 Thess. 4.1; Rom. 8.8; 14.18 (12.2; cf. also 1 Cor. 7.32, where θεῷ is the variant reading), where God is explicitly the one who is to be pleased.

71. Cf. 1.1; 3.2, 3, 5, 7; cf. also 2 Cor. 5.9, where Christ is pictured as the judge who rewards.

identity directly into the relationship between God and the church. The phrase ἐν τῷ κράτει τῆς ἰσχύος αὐτοῦ echoes 1.19, where the focus is on the nature and effect of τὸ ὑπερβάλλον μέγεθος τῆς δυνάμεως of the πατὴρ τῆς δόξης (v. 17). This δύναμις is measured by its having effected the resurrection and exaltation of Christ and, proleptically, by Christ's vanquishing of all foes, by his achieving of headship (1.22; cf. 1.10).[72]

The strategy of the author requires that he not have invented this combination of terms, as much as it suits his pleonastic style and purpose.[73] His Colossian *Vorlage* also knows how to heap up power terminology (cf. Col. 1.11; ἐν πάσῃ δυνάμει δυναμούμενοι κατὰ τὸ κράτô τῆς δόξης αὐτοῦ[74]). While the author of Ephesians may in this instance be dependent on Colossians, the shaping of the wording also evokes several Old Testament texts. The most relevant are Deut. 3.24 and Isa. 40.26b, where δύναμις, ἰσχύς and κράτος (here as an adjective for the hand of God: ἡ χείρ ἡ κραταία) appear. This has the effect of identifying the power the readers are to take up as specifically *God's*.[75] An identical formulation to the one in Eph. 6.10 appears in Dan. 4.30 (Q), only now on Nebuchadnezzar's lips, referring to his own power in creating Babylon. While this text would seem to contradict the point made in Ephesians, the larger context indicates that Nebuchadnezzar's own pretensions to power are only that, and that ultimately the κράτος τῆς ἰσχύος belongs to God as the ὕψιστος τῆς βασιλείας τῶν ἀνθρώπων (4.32). In 1QM 10.5 the high priest[76] is giving the 'troops' final exhortation prior to battle in order to strengthen them with the courage

72. The wisdom emphasis on primacy of the ἄνθρωπος in creation (Ps. 8.7) is transformed into a text of victory and/or exaltation via combination with Ps. 110.1. At the same time it should be noted that creation and warfare are intimately related in cosmogonic myth, that is, at the wellsprings of Divine War traditions.

73. With Grundmann, 'ἰσχύω', p. 402, and *contra* Schnackenburg, *Brief*, p. 278.

74. It should be noted, however, that there is considerably less stress on power and empowerment in Colossians than in Ephesians, reasons for which are no doubt rooted in the quite different pastoral objective of Colossians.

75. Κράτος and ἰσχύς are not employed in the undisputed letters of Paul, ἰσχύς nowhere else in the Pauline corpus, and κράτος once in Colossians and once in 1 Timothy. Paul prefers δύναμις τοῦ θεοῦ or less often τοῦ Χριστοῦ, which in turn is used much more sparingly in the deutero-Pauline writings.

76. So E. Lohse, *Die Texte aus Qumran: Hebräisch und deutsch* (Munich: Kösel, 1964), p. 291 n. 28

or strength of God (בגבורת אל). However, the exhortation shifts to a prayer of praise in which power is ascribed to God as the warrior who in the end wages the battle. This is expressed both by the refrain לכה המלחמה (11.1, 2, 4) and by a series of power terms quite like those in Ephesians: בכוחכה ובעוז חילכה הגדול (11.5).[77]

The combination of power terminology in 6.10 is thus not unique to Ephesians, let alone a product of the author's style. Its matrix is the attribution of power to God. Even in such texts where the people are depicted as participants in warfare, this vocabulary is reserved for the purpose of ascribing power to God alone. A more wide ranging discussion of power in the biblical literature would confirm the basic conviction that power is God's, and God's to exercise.[78] Even in those texts where other δύναμεις are spoken of, they are generally identified as part of the arsenal of means at God's disposal, and it is assumed that these powers derive their power from God.[79] The introduction of negative δύναμεις into the cosmos does not challenge this view, since within the ultimate plan of God even evil powers exercise their power within the temporally limited tolerance of God.[80] What is not lost sight of is the ultimate source of power.

Ephesians 6.10 is a call to step into the role of the Divine Warrior by taking up his power. It is not thereby suggested that God disappears from the scene, or that he is replaced by a usurping community. God's grace is unquestionably the essential premise of the call to the community to become μιμηταὶ τοῦ θεοῦ, 'lest anyone should boast!' (2.8, 9). At the same time, the reversal of role, prepared for in the preceding chapters of Ephesians, is present. Christ disappears from the scene completely, or more accurately, the author of Ephesians applies Paul's ecclesiology radically by having the messianic warrior 'lose himself' in the corporate community that is now ordered to invest itself with the role and equipment of the Divine Warrior. The tone is thus set for the following elaboration of the Divine Warrior in armour. Whereas there are many similarities and likely points of contact with the thinking and language of Wisdom of Solomon, the author intends to take up the image of the Divine Warrior with the full radicalism anticipated in

77. Cf. also 1QS 11.19, 20; 1QH 4.32; 9.16, 17; 11.8; 18.8.

78. See Grundmann on δύναμαι and ἰσχύω (cited above) and W. Michaelis, 'κράτος, κτλ.', *TDNT*, III, pp. 905-915.

79. Δύναμεις is the usual LXX translation of צבאות.

80. Cf. Col. 1.16 and 2.15, and also 1QS 3.15-17.

1 Thessalonians with respect to democratization and, with its own twist, pacification. Once again there is not only appropriation but reinterpretation, now within the Pauline 'school'.

The call in v. 10 to be empowered with the strength of the might of God is now reiterated in v. 11: 'put on (ἐνδύσασθε) the πανοπλία τοῦ θεοῦ.' As the preceding discussion anticipated and the ensuing one will show, the genitive τοῦ θεοῦ should be read as indicating that the believers are called upon to put on God's own armour, and not simply one God supplies. It will be crucial to keep that in view in order to fully appreciate the status of the community and its task.[81] Kamlah is correct in recognizing the community's armour as God's, but he is quite mistaken in characterizing this identification as *unbekümmert*.[82] There are texts in which 'putting on' is related with little metaphorical significance to arming for battle.[83] But there are also others, including Isa. 59.17, Wis. 5.18, and 1 Thess. 5.8, in which 'putting on' or 'being clothed with' takes on metaphorical meaning within the context of battle.[84] There are other times when it is not battle but cultic performance which provides the context for seeing garb as metaphorically or symbolically significant.[85]

The allusiveness of this language increases within Pauline usage.

81. So also Barth, *Ephesians 4–6*, p. 784; Houlden, *Paul's Letters*, p. 338; Schlier, *Brief*, p. 290; R.A. Wild, SJ, 'The Warrior and the Prisoner: Some Reflections on Ephesians 6:10-20', *CBQ* 46 (1984), p. 287. For an explicit rejection of this interpretation see Gnilka, *Epheserbrief*, p. 305 n. 8. He reads Eph. 6.10-17 in light of the tradition of the fortified believer, already a distant moralization of the ancient mythological tradition of the warfare of the gods. Oepke ('ὅπλον', p. 301) refers to this as an 'elastic subjective genitive'. As indicated already in the study of 1 Thess. 5, I take the tradition dependent specifically on Isa. 59 as significantly different from that reflected in, for example, 2 Cor. 6 and 10.

82. Kamlah, *Form*, p. 191.

83. E.g. 1 Kgdms. 17.5, 38; Jer. 46 (LXX 26).4; Ezek. 38.4.

84. E.g. clothed with spirit: Judg. 6.34; 1 Chron. 12.18; 2 Chron. 24.20; Jerusalem arises and puts on ἰσχύς, Isa. 51.9 (of interest here is that in MT it is God who arises; cf. 52.1); the 'armed horse' in Job 39.19 has δύναμις, i.e. a πανοπλία is placed about it, its neck 'clothed' with φόβος; in 1 Macc. 3.2 Judas arises and all with him fight the wars of Israel with εὐφροσύνη; in v. 2 Judas as a γίγας 'puts on' a θώραξ, and girds himself with the σκεύη τὰ πολεμικά and wages (συνίστημι) wars; in the hymn to Simon in 1 Macc. 14.9 the youths 'put on' the δόξαι and the στολαὶ πολέμου.

85. 2 Chron. 6.41; Ps. 131.16 LXX (cf. Isa. 61.10); the high priest wears δήλωσις and ἀλήθεια, 1 Esdr. 5.40 (Heb.: *Urim* and *Tumim*); cf. Sir 45.8,13.

Important, in addition to 1 Thess. 5.8, is Rom. 13.12 and 14. 'Putting on' the weapons of light and the parallel 'putting on' of Christ suggest resonance with the combination of identification with Christ and the presenting of arms in Rom. 6.1-14. In Ephesians the 'taking off' of the old ἄνθρωπος and the 'putting on' of the new in 4.22-24 and its repetition in 6.11 alerts readers to the relationship between the experience of baptism and the call to take up arms, between identification with Christ and the call to inhabit the armour of God.

Familiarity with Wis. 5.17 is likely, even if not provable, in the use of πανοπλία in Eph. 6.11. It suggests that the author stands consciously in a tradition of interpretation. However, Ephesians and Wisdom of Solomon diverge sharply in their treatment of Isaiah 59. With the exception of 1 Thessalonians 5, in this tradition the Divine Warrior arises to defend his virtues or the δίκαιοι and to punish those who have been victimizing them. The divine judge attacks *human* offenders, however much or little they are depicted as being under the influence or in alliance with superhuman forces.[86] The divine warfare is not directed at the διάβολος or at θάνατος (e.g. Wis. 2.24), but rather at the ἀσεβεῖς or the ἄδικοι who have made their pact with death. 1 Thessalonians 5 alters that construct to the extent that it is the believers who are drawn into the divine assault against darkness. The darkness is not described, only alluded to by the imperial slogan Εἰρήνη καὶ ἀσφάλεια (5.3) and by the sleep and drunkenness of those who live there (5.7). This leaves the impression that in view is still the construct of human sinfulness and the divine judge's warfare in response to it, however ironically it is worked out in 1 Thessalonians 5.[87]

In Ephesians this species of warfare is turned aside. The conflict (πάλη[88]) is explicitly not against blood and flesh (v. 12). It is difficult not

86. Cf. here the 'party of death' in Wis. 2.24, where death has entered into the human sphere because of the jealousy of the διάβολος.

87. Unlike 2 Thess. 2.3-10, where Christ as Divine Warrior eliminates not only the wicked but also ὁ ἄνθρωπος τῆς ἀνομίας, the υἱὸς τῆς ἀπωλείας (whatever his identity is, his coming is clearly identified as κατ' ἐνέργειαν τοῦ Σατανᾶ; v. 9), 1 Thess. mentions Σατανᾶς only in connection with Paul's travel plans, and not at all within the context of divine warfare in ch. 5.

88. Πάλη is a *hapax legomenon* in the New Testament. Barth is mistaken in seeing in it chiefly an athletic term, and misguided in suggesting that it is employed here for pacifist reasons (*Ephesians*, II, p. 764). The warfare is after all with enemies of cosmic stature; this battle is in no way marked by kindness toward enemies. While Pfitzner (*Paul*, pp. 157-64) has shown the degree to which athletic and

to see in this a polemic against the understandings of divine warfare found, e.g., in Wisdom of Solomon and Qumran, where such warfare is repeatedly and specifically characterized as against 'flesh'.[89] In Ephesians the struggle is directly with the διάβολος and his allies or troops.[90]

The struggle is initially characterized as resistance (στῆναι πρός) to the μεθοδεία of the διάβολος. Μεθοδεία is a *hapax legomenon*, and should be interpreted as the strategies and tactics of the enemy, already anticipated in 4.14.[91] Μεθοδεία could refer to what Wisdom of Solomon warns about in 1.12-16, where the rulers or judges (in effect, the readers, 1.1) are enjoined not to seek or make a covenant with death, nor to give in to temptation. This would be a colourful way of warning people not to succumb to desires and enticements. Or, one might see the struggle not so much at the level of 'life style' but as defense against a threatening devil as pictured, for example, in 1 Pet. 5.6-11. It should be noted, however, that in 1 Peter it is *God* as Divine Warrior who will intervene to save and exalt those who are being warned to be careful.[92] In Ephesians, by contrast, exaltation is referred as a past and completed event (2.5, 6), however much that is understood proleptically.[93] Significantly, readers are not called upon to trust God but to put on God's

military imagery converges in Paul, its frequent meaning in Hellenistic usage as 'wrestling' in no way excludes the more general meaning of πάλη as 'struggle' or 'battle' (H. Greeven, 'πάλη', *TDNT*, V, p. 721). Moreover, whereas πάλη does not appear in LXX, παλαίω does several times, and in a number of instances refers to battle: of dragons in Est. 1.1e; of the sea (monster) in Job 38.8 (Aq.), indicating the term's presence within contexts of mythological battle. Abbott (*Epistles*, p. 181) supports the reading of the verse taken here, only he suggests that one take πάλη in its limited meaning of wrestling and restrict it to 'blood and flesh'. He thus sees πάλη as inappropriate for battle with cosmic powers, and suggests one supply μάχη or μαχετέον (so also Pfitzner, *Paul*, p. 159).

89. Cf. בשׂר in, for example, CD 1.2; 1QM 12.11, 12; 15.13; 19.4.

90. Given that διάβολος is a *hapax legomenon* in the Pauline corpus, this is probably a further indication of the author of Ephesians' familiarity with Wisdom of Solomon.

91. Cf. 1QH 2.16. See also W. Michaelis, 'μεθοδεία', *TDNT*, V, pp. 102-103.

92. The believers are characterized as wholly dependent on the Divine Warrior's intervention on their behalf. Liberation and exaltation are still in the future (v. 6). On the other hand, the vocabulary suggests some contact with the tradition with which Ephesians is working; notice especially the reference to resisting (ἀντίστητε) the διάβολος (v. 8), who is seeking to devour anyone he can find. Cf. also the call to be watchful and sober (v. 8).

93. Cf. Steinmetz, *Protologische Heilszuversicht*, pp. 39-44.

armour. Thus the call to resist the μεθοδεῖαι τοῦ διαβόλου means more here then a defensive stance of faithfulness. The call to seize divine power and to put on the armour of God implies a much wider horizon, which is why the author must now specify the precise nature of the πάλη.

After turning aside any misunderstanding that the battle is against blood and flesh, the real enemies are identified as ἀρχαί, ἐξουσίαι, κοσμοκράτορες τοῦ σκότους τούτου, τὰ πνευματικὰ τῆς πονηρίας ἐν τοῖς ἐπουρανίοις. The identity of these powers has been the subject of a great deal of scholarly attention.[94] Frequently they have been interpreted exclusively as hostile heavenly or astrological powers,[95] sometimes in gnostic terms.[96] Implied is a cosmology that locates these hostile powers 'in the heavenlies'[97] interposing themselves between the believer and God. Salvation thus requires the successful struggle with these powers. There is no question that this Ephesian *topos* lived on within this strand of interpretation.[98] Carr reads the text very much in this light,

94. In addition to the commentaries cited, see the studies by H. Berkhof, *Christ and the Powers* (trans. J.H. Yoder; Kitchener, ON: Herald Press, 1977), who is followed by J.H. Yoder, *The Politics of Jesus* (Kitchener, ON: Herald Press, 1972), pp. 135-62; G.B. Caird, *Principalities and Powers: A Study in Pauline Theology* (Oxford: Clarendon Press, 1956); W. Carr, *Angels and Principalities: The Background, Meaning, and Development of the Pauline Phrase hai archai kai hai exousiai* (SNTSMS, 42; Cambridge: Cambridge University Press, 1981); Heinrich Schlier, *Principalities and Powers in the New Testament* (ET; Freiburg: Herder; Edinburgh/London: Nelson, 1961); Wink, *Naming the Powers*, and more recently C.E. Arnold, *Ephesians: Power and Magic: The Concept of Power in Ephesians in Light of its Historical Setting* (SNTSMS, 63; Cambridge: Cambridge University Press, 1989).

95. Arnold's study (*Ephesians*, pp. 14-69) identifies the chief concern behind the preoccupation with power and powers in Ephesians as the pervasive practice of magic as means of manipulation of 'heavenly' powers. I agree with Arnold that power and the exercise of it is of central importance for the author of Ephesians, even if I am more willing than he is to follow Schlier and Wink in expanding the meaning of powers to include those 'heavenly' powers that have earthly manifestation. Further, his study is less interested than is mine in the issue of identification of the believing community with the Divine Warrior.

96. See relevant literature in Schlier, *Brief*, pp. 290-91.

97. See A.T. Lincoln, *Paradise Now and Not Yet: Studies in the Role of the Heavenly Dimension in Paul's Thought with Special Reference to his Eschatology* (Cambridge: Cambridge University Press, 1981); *idem*, 'A Reexamination of "the Heavenlies" in Ephesians', *NTS* 19 (1973), pp. 468-83.

98. E.g. Clement of Alexandria, *Exc. Theod.* 73.1–85.3; *Teach. Silv.* 84.15–85.1; 91.18-20; 114.2-15.

but suggests that as such it represents an anachronism in Ephesians, and must be seen as a Valentinian interpolation.[99] Carr's reading of 6.12 is necessitated chiefly by his thesis that in the New Testament 'the powers' are always benign; 6.12 represents an unambiguous counter-example and must therefore be an interpolation.[100]

Wink's comprehensive treatment of the vocabulary of the 'powers' indicates that in the majority of cases the nomenclature for 'powers' refers to human institutions or the persons inhabiting those positions or offices.[101] Nevertheless, the line between human and divine or demonic realms is not a clear one, most especially in the case of the 'powers'. Col. 1.16 illustrates this by explicitly mixing the categories of visible and invisible, heavenly and earthly. The specific pairing of ἀρχαὶ καὶ ἐξουσίαι which heads up the list of powers in Eph. 6.12 appears ten times in the New Testament. In only three instances does the pair clearly refer to human authorities or institutions (Lk. 12.11; 20.20; Tit. 3.1). The other instances appear in the Pauline corpus: 1 Cor. 15.24; Eph. 1.21; 3.10; 6.12; Col. 1.16; 2.10, 15. In 1 Cor. 15.24, the earliest of the texts, Christ exercises his βασιλεία by destroying (καταργέω) the powers, including finally θάνατος itself (himself?). Ephesians 6.12 draws its allusive power, then, not only from the common currency of its terminology within the larger biblical and socio-political contexts, but specifically also from the way it recalls Paul's use of the phrase within one of his most striking characterizations of cosmic battle. There can thus be no doubt that, in addition to human potencies and institutions, Eph. 6.12 intends to evoke the full range of demonic forces with which the saints have to do battle. The inclusion in the list of powers in v. 12 of κοσμοκράτορες τοῦ σκότους τούτου and τὰ πνευματικὰ τῆς πονηρίας ἐν τοῖς ἐπουρανίοις moves the imagination, first, back to v. 11 and thus to identify the powers with the hostile machinations of the διάβολος. Second, readers will recall 2.2, where ὁ αἰὼν τοῦ κόσμου τούτου is governed by the ἄρχων τῆς ἐξουσίας τοῦ ἀέρος, a πνεῦμα presently shaping the behaviour of the sons of disobedience. The author's objective in 6.12 is then to pit the community against all the powers, human,

99. Carr, *Angels and Principalities*, pp. 104-10.

100. See C.E. Arnold, 'The 'Exorcism' of Ephesians 6.12 in Recent Research: A Critique of Wesley Carr's View of the Role of Evil Powers in First-Century AD Belief', *JSNT* 30 (1987), pp. 71-87; Wild, 'Warrior', p. 285; Wink, *Naming the Powers*, pp. 23-26.

101. *Naming the Powers*, pp. 13-35.

supra- and sub-human, the height and depth, width and breadth of opposition to God. Wink's summary characterization in contemporary categories is apt when he identifies the powers as

> legitimations, seats of authority, hierarchical systems, ideological justifications, and punitive sanctions which their human incumbents exercise and which transcend these incumbents in both time and power.[102]

Even though Schlier's characterization understates the comprehensiveness of the author's vision by muting the socio-political dimension, he evokes the ominous nature of the powers well:

> The enemies are not this or that person, nor one's own self—they are not 'blood and flesh'. Naturally, blood and flesh can be found on the front lines of this battle (cf. 2.3). But the conflict runs much deeper. The struggle is finally against a myriad of tirelessly attacking opponents, too slippery to grasp, with no specific names, only collective designations. They are superior to humans from the outset through their superior position 'in the heavenlies', superior through their invisibility and their unassailability. After all, their position is an all-pervasive 'atmosphere' of existence which they themselves generate. They are all, in the end, inherently full of deadly evil (author's translation).[103]

This characterization of the powers prevents a choice between sociologically and politically identifiable 'powers' and those perceived as 'spiritual' and thus described mythologically. Both are intended. Better

102. *Naming the Powers*, p. 85. While Arnold (*Ephesians*, pp. 84-51) is right to warn against Wink's tendency to demythologize the powers, I believe Wink is correct in positing that, given the intentional comprehensiveness of the list of powers, Eph. 6.12 perforce also evokes the 'spirit of empire'. This text, in a fashion similar to the use of the slogan 'Peace and Security!' in 1 Thess. 5.3, has the potential of placing the church into a critical position *vis-à-vis* Rome. *Contra* A. Lindemann, *Der Epheserbrief* (Zürcher Bibelkommentare NT, 8; Zürich: Theologischer Verlag, 1985), p. 113, and Mußner, *Brief an die Epheser*, p. 167.

103. Schlier, *Brief*, p. 291. German original:

> Die Feinde sind nicht der oder jener, auch nicht ich selbst, sind nicht Blut und Fleisch. Auch Blut und Fleisch können natürlich in diesem Kampf vorgeschoben werden, vgl. 2, 3. Aber die Auseinandersetzung geht tiefer. Sie geht gegen eine Unzahl von unermüdlich angreifenden Gegnern, die nicht recht zu fassen sind, die keinen eigentlichen Namen haben, nur Kollektivbezeichnungen; die auch von vornherein dem Menschen überlegen sind, und zwar durch ihre überlegene Position, durch ihre Position 'in den Himmeln' des Daseins, überlegen auch durch die Undurchsichtigkeit ihrer Position und ihre Unangreifbarkeit—ihre Position ist ja die 'Atmosphäre' des Daseins, die sie selber in ihrem Sinn um sich verbreiten; die endlich alle voll wesenhafter, tödlicher Bosheit sind.

yet, the author of Ephesians would not have seen these as alternative categories, but as diverse manifestations of a seamless web of reality hostile to God. After all, as we are seeing, his understanding of the church participates as well in this mix of the human and the divine, the earthly and the heavenly. The church too is already ἐν τοῖς ἐπουρανίοις (2.6).[104]

It is more than likely that the author of Ephesians is quite aware of the close proximity of his depiction of the community in the armour of God fighting cosmic powers to the Pauline depiction of Christ fighting the cosmic enemies of God in 1 Cor. 15.24 (ὅταν καταργήσῃ πᾶσαν ἀρχὴν καὶ πᾶσαν ἐξουσίαν καὶ δύναμιν). More, he intends his depiction to be seen in critical interaction with the Corinthian text. In effect he replaces Christ the warrior with the saints as corporate warrior. Said more carefully, he exploits the implications of Paul's ecclesiology which identifies the church as σῶμα τοῦ Χριστοῦ by now moving the church into the battle Christ wages in 1 Corinthians 15. After all, the author has earlier already explicitly placed the believers with the victorious Christ (1.21, 22) on the heavenly throne (2.5, 6). It is important to observe that in 1 Corinthians 15 as in Ephesians 6 assurance of status precedes full engagement with the powers: Christ's resurrection precedes his reign, one marked by the battle with the powers, a reign which comes to an end only with the full defeat of the powers. Once he has subjected 'all things' (τὰ πάντα) to him,[105] Christ hands over his βασιλεία to God, so that God himself might be 'all in all' (ἵνα ᾖ ὁ θεὸς [τὰ] πάντα ἐν πᾶσιν; v. 28). Paul employs Pss. 110.1 and 8.6, which are significantly in the *past* tense, to show the certainty of the victorious outcome of Christ's *present* struggle with the powers. While the battle is real, so is the certainty of a victorious outcome. Psalm 8 is quoted in order to make precisely that point. This construct is faithful to the structure of

104. This does not contradict the statement that the battle is finally not against 'blood and flesh'. The full scope and level of struggle is not comprehended if understood as a battle against human beings. After all, ch. 2 in particular has indicated Christ's fundamentally friendly disposition, and thus implicitly also of his body, to blood and flesh. However, ch. 5 indicates that the battle against darkness and the forces of evil takes place within the conflicts and confrontations of social existence. It is in the realm of human interaction that the battle with the supra-human powers (also) takes place.

105. The closer one moves to Ps. 8.6 the clearer it is that it is *God* who subjects all things to Christ. However, given that Christ is the Divine Warrior in this text, the issue of agency in the citation of Ps. 8.6 is intentionally ambiguous.

holy war, where God is the guarantor of victory even before the battle ensues.

Ephesians goes further than that, however, by placing the community into the armour of God, in imitation directly of God.[106] Paul already laid the groundwork for that in 1 Thess. 5.8. Ephesians now pulls the strands of 1 Thessalonians 5 and 1 Corinthians 15 together and places the church into direct confrontation with the powers, and thus also into the eschatological location of final battle.[107] This is indicated by the fact that Eph. 1.20-23 takes up 1 Cor. 15.25, 27[108] in characterizing Christ's victory and status by citing and quoting Pss. 110.1 and 8.6.[109] If one reads

106. One might have expected Christ as κεφαλή to inhabit the role of the *vicarius Dei*. However, Christ as head is not present in this image. Little if anything that has been said of Christ has not already been said or intimated of his body in the previous chapters. H. Conzelmann's comments point in this direction: 'Der Zwischenraum zwischen Gott und uns ("die Himmel") ist der Sitz der Mächte. Der Mensch steht unter ihnen, im Leibe Christi aber ihnen gegenüber' (*Der Brief an die Epheser*, in H.W. Beyer *et al.* [eds.], *Die kleineren Briefe des Apostels Paulus* [NTD, 8; Göttingen: Vandenhoeck & Ruprecht, 1962], p. 89). Herein may well also lie the clue to the absence of any mention in Ephesians of the *parousia* of Christ. The church *is* the *parousia*, and as such, implicated in what that *parousia* means for the fate of the powers.

107. 'Final battle' does not mean that it cannot be conceived as a prolonged struggle. 1 Cor. 15 itself allows for Christ's reign to be a prolonged struggle with the powers. It is 'final' in that it is initiated by the arrival of the Christ, that it is waged against the ultimate enemies, and that it is waged from out of the certainty of final victory. It is that interpretive possibility which Ephesians exploits. It is a frame of reference which can account for present battles as well as the eschatological context of which they are a part. This has been observed to be already the case in each of the previous treatments of the Isaianic motif of the Divine Warrior. K.-M. Fischer (*Tendenz und Absicht des Epheserbriefs* [FRLANT, 3; Göttingen: Vandenhoeck & Ruprecht, 1973], p. 165) fails to recognize this by suggesting that there are two quite distinct eschatologies at work in Ephesians, and that the apocalyptic tradition has been contemporized.

108. Ps. 8.6 is quoted in Eph. 1.22 not from the LXX but in direct conformity to 1 Cor. 15.27. (Ps. 8.7 LXX reads: πάντα ὑπέταξας ὑποκάτω τῶν ποδῶν αὐτοῦ, whereas 1 Cor. 15.27 has πάντα γὰρ ὑπέταξεν ὑπὸ τοὺς πόδας αὐτοῦ.) Conscious interaction with 1 Cor. 15.24-28 may be illustrated also by the fact that Eph. 5.5 speaks rather anomalously of 'the kingdom of Christ and of God'. Notice that in 1 Cor. 15 Christ's βασιλεία becomes God's βασιλεία once Christ has vanquished the last foe, death.

109. For a discussion of the appropriation of Ps. 110 in early Christian reflection on Christ, see D.M. Hay, *Glory at the Right Hand: Psalm 110 in Early Christianity*

Eph. 1.20-23 in the light of 6.12, it is likely that the dative in τῇ ἐκκλησίᾳ should be read as an instrumental dative.[110]

Inasmuch as Colossians is the most immediate foil for Ephesians, 6.12 also represents a critique of the Colossian reading of the cosmic state of affairs. Colossians 1.16 describes Christ as the one who has created all θρόνοι, κυριότητες, ἀρχαί, and ἐξουσίαι. At the same time, Col. 2.15 depicts God as having already defeated the ἀρχαί and ἐξουσίαι and paraded them about in triumph. In both cases, the message to readers is clear: nothing in the cosmos is to be feared; there is no battle still to be fought, and no victory yet to be won. The powers have either been brought into line or been rendered impotent. If Ephesians represents one side of a debate within the Pauline school, it can be seen to want to reinvest the cosmos with a significant element of danger. While it shares with Colossians the confidence in the lordship and victory of God as expressed in Col. 2.15, it views the establishing of that lordship as still incomplete. The triumphal procession of Col. 2.15 is premature, as it were. Ephesians summons the church to take up the role of the Divine Warrior who has yet to finish the task of vanquishing the powers. Hence the author reads the present as filled with the noise of cosmic battle. 1 Corinthians 15, with its depiction of Christ's reign as marked by battle against the cosmic foes of God and thus the still incomplete work of reconciliation, is used by the author of Ephesians to disturb the Colossian calm.

In a sense the list of powers in Eph. 6.12 is hardly essential. The structural relationship between the church's identity and its task on the one hand, and between the church's empowerment and its place in the divine programme on the other, has already been set by the call to take up divine power, to put on the divine armour, and to engage in battle with the διάβολος. Nevertheless, adding the coterie of powers makes explicit that the church is not simply called with grandiose language to withstand the devil while it waits for final liberation (*à la* 1 Peter), but that it is called into the center of 'the battle of the gods', as it were. This list of powers should then not be seen as simply a particularly striking example of the author's love of pleonasm—unless of course pleonasm serves particularly well the intentions outlined above.

(SBLMS, 18; Nashville/New York: Abingdon Press, 1973), especially pp. 97-100.

110. Cf. here especially also 3.10 where the ἀρχαί and ἐξουσίαι ἐν τοῖς ἐπουρανίοις are informed or confronted with God's manifold wisdom διὰ τῆς ἐκκλησίας.

Lindemann is quite correct in observing that at least at the level of imagery the church does its struggling from the safety of the heavenly realm (2.6). But he is wrong in holding that there is thereby no longer any motivation for the battle announced in ch. 6.[111] Safety does not reside in the location of the church, since τὰ ἐπουράνια are, as v. 12 indicates, also the location of the enemies of God.[112] Safety resides solely in the certainty of victory that comes from the fact that in the end the saints are engaged in *God's* battle. In the scriptural tradition no war worthy of the characterization 'holy' or 'divine' is ever fought apart from the certainty of victory. The formula 'into your hands have I given them' is essential and thus also ubiquitous within the war narratives of the Hebrew Bible.[113] It does not suggest disengagement. On the contrary, the repeated and overloaded images and language of certainty find their necessary corollary in this final image of the church in battle with the cosmic powers.

The interpretive revolution started in 1 Thessalonians 5 is brought to completion, at least with respect to the matter of democratization.

111. *Epheserbrief*, pp. 111-16. Not surprisingly Lindemann gives 6.10-20 virtually no attention in his *Die Aufhebung der Zeit: Geschichtsverständnis und Eschatologie im Epheserbrief* (Gütersloh: Gerd Mohn, 1975); nor does he pay it any attention in *Paulus*, pp. 122-30, where he discusses parallels between Paul and Ephesians but provides no account of the relationship between Eph. 6 and 1 Thess. 5. That is largely the implication of Hay's comment as well: 'Consistent with his idea that salvation is by grace, the author feels he can affirm nothing less than that believers enjoy an essentially unimprovable situation' (*Glory at the Right Hand*, p. 98). Hay seems puzzled by the juxtaposition of 'session' (being seated at the right hand) and combat. He appears to forget that messianic exaltation is biblically an equivalent to empowerment for successful warfare. But then he also reads Ephesians to say that the church is forever subordinate to its head, Christ, who 'alone' is lord of the cosmos and the church. I read Ephesians as employing the language in considerably more 'democratized' terms, as has already become clear.

112. Inasmuch as the church is located with Christ on the heavenly throne, the heavenly realm only suggests the level of the battle—its gravity, not its triviality. Wink suggests that 'in the heavenlies' functions in Ephesians as a metaphor not for location but importance, a 'dimension of reality of which the believer becomes aware as a result of being "raised up" by God with Christ' (*Naming the Powers*, p. 92).

113. Given the importance of the warfare image for the Ephesian understanding of the church's task and identity, the certainty of victory provides at least in part the motive for the preponderance of 'already' language (cf. e.g. 2.5, 6). In fact, were it not for the presence of such assurance there would be no continuity with the biblical tradition of divine warfare.

Whereas in Isaiah 59 it is God who as mythologically coloured Divine Warrior fights punitively against a faithless human community, a structural relationship still very much present in Wisdom of Solomon, it is now a human community—albeit a community of holy ones by virtue of Christ's act of peace—that is thrust into the very role and action of the Divine Warrior. As such the community is directly at war with the peers of God, as it were—the devil and his principalities and powers.

Verse 13 must now be interpreted in this light. The author recapitulates the two previous verses as a bridge to the panoply itself. The call to take up the panoply is repeated, only now instead of ἐνδύσασθε the author employs ἀναλάβετε. This moves the language closer to Wisdom of Solomon's treatment of the motif (λήμψεται), where the armour includes not only the protective gear which the Divine Warrior wears, but the weapons with which he wages war. As vv. 14-17 will show, Ephesians in like manner expands the Isaianic motif explicitly to include weapons of combat. The call to resist in v. 11 is also taken up again, only now στῆναι πρός is replaced by the virtual synonym ἀντιστῆναι. The διάβολος is not mentioned again, but the context of battle is set 'in the evil day,' taking up the language of 5.16, although now in the singular. This increases the sense of identification of the struggle of the saints with the intervention of the Divine Warrior by evoking 'the day of the Lord'.[114]

No doubt the eschatological frame of reference out of which many within Pauline congregations will have read this document also contributes to the eschatological resonance of this language, not least under impact of 1 Thessalonians 5. However, as already pointed out in the case of 1 Thessalonians 5, 'the day' need not be understood in exclusively and singularly eschatological, let alone apocalyptic, terms. The 'evil day' in Eph. 6.13 can thus also be a reference to the day of battle without having its meaning exhausted by apocalyptic notions.

Of further importance is how κατεργάζομαι is translated. There can be no doubt that if Ephesians is read as I have read it, the usual Pauline meaning 'to complete' or 'to do or bring about' is wholly inadequate.[115] While that is admittedly the preponderant meaning of the term in the

114. Cf. the discussion of this in relation to 1 Thess. 5 above.

115. E.g., Rom. 2.9; 4.15; 7.15; 15.18; 1 Cor. 5.3; 2 Cor. 4.17; 5.5; 9.11; 12.12; Phil. 2.12. Gaugler (*Epheserbrief*, p. 225) suggests that the term be translated here to reflect preparations for battle or the 'doing' of warfare itself.

Septuagint, in 1 Esdr. 4.4 it means 'to defeat' or 'to destroy'.[116] Bauer is correct in seeing this as the appropriate translation for Eph. 6.13: 'proving victorious over.'[117] Κατεργάζομαι functions then virtually as a synonym of καταργέω in 1 Cor. 15.24 and 26, which is in turn an equivalent to the subjecting (ὑποτάσσω) of τὰ πάντα. This use of κατεργάζομαι places the saints in the position of cosmic Divine Warrior. Ἅπαντα must then refer to 'all' hostile powers.[118]

Στῆναι and its compounds are significant in this context. In v. 11 the readers are called to put on the armour so that they might be able to 'stand against' (στῆναι πρός) the machinations of the διάβολος; v. 13 replaces that with ἀντιστῆναι and ends the sentence with στῆναι; v. 14 begins with the imperative στῆτε, upon which the following participles related to the various pieces of armour and weaponry are dependent. Obviously, ἵστημι permits a significant range of meaning, even or especially when appearing within a theological or metaphorical context.[119] The specific context here is one of battle. In the discussion of Wis. 5.1 above I pointed out that the image of the δίκαοις standing (στήσεται) with παρρησία (5.1) is one of royal status and confidence. I suggested further that the stance of the δίκαιος presupposes the intervention of the Divine Warrior in 5.17, even if that intervention is described *after* the description of the 'standing' royal δίκαιος in 5.1. I also pointed out that there are intimations that the vindication and exaltation of the δίκαιοι imply or invite their participation in the judging activity of the Divine Warrior. Their 'standing' with confidence as the sons of God implies as much (5.5). The relation of 'standing' to militancy is dramatically reflected further in Wis. 18.16, where the λόγος 'stands' (στάς) filling (ἐπλήρωσεν) everything (τᾶ πάντα) with death, the precise inverse of what is presented in Ephesians. The λόγος *qua* ὀργή is resisted (ἀντέστη) in turn by the ἀνὴρ ἄμεμπτος (18.21), standing (στάς) in the

116. Cf. also Josh. 18.1, and Judg. 16.16. Cf. Barth, *Ephesians*, II, p. 765; see literature in n. 41. Barth nevertheless backs away from this interpretation out of what must be dogmatic reasons: 'In Eph. 6 far more emphasis is placed on readiness and firmness in the struggle than upon any actual human accomplishment during the battle' (p. 766).

117. BAGD, p. 421.b.4. See such usage also in Philo *Sacr.* 62; Jos. *Ant.* 2.44. G. Bertram ('κατεργάζομαι', *TDNT*, III, pp. 634-35) is unwilling to decide the matter, whereas W. Grundmann ('στήκω, ἵστημι', *TDNT*, VII, p. 652 n. 39) opts for 'having done all'.

118. Cf. 1QH 3.34-36.

119. Grundmann, 'ἵστημι', pp. 636-53.

midst of the corpses and cutting off the ὀργή (v. 23)—not unlike, interestingly, what in Ephesians the church is called upon to do as the body of Christ, as the corporate ἀνὴρ τέλειος (Eph. 4.13-16). Only now it is the whole array of powers which are the enemy, not the ὀργή of God.

Illuminating also is the use of the Hebrew equivalents of 'standing' (especially עמד and קום) in the literature of Qumran. 1QH 10(2) is striking for its similarities to Ephesians. The psalmist combines insight into and interpretation of mysteries (1QH 10.13) with outright conflict between himself as the contentious one (איש ריב; 10.14), a storm of zeal (רוח קנאה; 10.15; cf. Isa. 59.17) and the men of deceit (אנשי רמיה) whose thoughts are the schemes (μεθοδεία?) of Belial (מזמות בליעל; 10.16; cf. Eph. 4.14 and especially 6.11!). The psalmist's loins are strengthened with might so as to be able to stand in the realm of evil (ואמוץ כוח ותעמד פעמי בגבול רשעה, 10.8). And those who are of Belial's congregation did not know that his 'stand' is from the Lord (10.22; cf. Wis. 5.4, 5).[120] What must be noted in this psalm, as in Qumran generally, is that unlike in Ephesians it is ultimately God alone who is the protector, who strengthens, and who wins the battle of judgment against the sons of deceit. God permits their capacity to do battle precisely in order to show his glory in their judgment (cf. 1QH 12[4].20-38). This is no less true in 1QM (e.g. 14; 18.10-13).

This perspective is very similar to that found in the dynamics between the largely passive δίκαιοι and the oppressive ἀσεβεῖς in Wisdom of Solomon. Their mutual hostility prepares the ground for vindication at the hand of the Divine Warrior. As a result the δίκαιοι 'stand' victoriously (5.1). The roots of this usage rest in the ancient tradition of divine warfare in which, as Exod. 14.13 illustrates, the faithful are called upon not to fear but 'to stand' and courageously observe their liberation by Yahweh. This dependency on Yahweh is also present in the royal tradition, even though the participation of the monarch is not thereby denied, as Ps. 17 LXX illustrates. God girds the king with strength, and sets his feet on the heights (ὁ θεὸς ὁ περιζωννύων με δύναμιν [...] καὶ ἐπὶ τὰ ὑψηλὰ ἱστῶν με; vv. 33, 34). The king's enemies in turn will not be able to stand (οὐ μὴ δύνωνται στῆναι; v. 39), because the king will crush them, girded as he now is with power for war.

It is apparent from these examples that 'standing' implies more than

120. Cf. 1QH 10.25-29, which lists the weaponry of the enemies, including flaming arrows; cf. Eph. 6.16! Cf. also *Odes* 8.3-7, which combines standing in face of coming war with open mouth (cf. Eph. 6.19).

surviving the onslaughts of the enemy. The joining of that language to the identification of the community with the role of the Divine Warrior suggests 'standing' as the stance of victory at the end of the evil day.[121]

3. *The Armour of God*

A string of participles elaborates what it means to 'stand.' In the process the author introduces the armour of God familiar to the readers and announced in 6.11.[122] Much of the armour will have been familiar by virtue of the ubiquitousness of armed soldiers in first-century urban Asia Minor. More important, however, the readership will have had at least some familiarity with the scriptural image of God in armour as derived from Isaiah 59. 1 Thessalonians 5 shows that Paul introduced his congregations to precisely that image. Familiarity with 1 Thessalonians *per se* is possible but not certain for the general readership (or audience) of Ephesians. However, to the extent that the intended readership is the Pauline 'school', familiarity is likely with not only 1 Thessalonians and Isaiah 59, but quite possibly also with Wisdom of Solomon 5. However that may be, the critical interaction of this motif is not with the image of the Roman legionnaire[123] but with the image of the Divine Warrior in Isaiah 59.[124] The elements of armour are thus to be evaluated principally in light of their metaphorical and symbolic force within the tradition of the appropriation of the Isaianic motif. The force of the image in Ephesians derives from the recognition that the armour is God's. Nevertheless, the author does not simply reiterate Isa. 59.17-19 or 1 Thess. 5.8, but rather

121. So also Wink, *Naming the Powers*, p. 87.

122. στῆτε

περιζωσάμενοι	ἐν ἀληθείᾳ
ἐνδυσάμενοι	τὸν θώρακα τῆς δικαιοσύνης
ὑποδησάμενοι	ἐν ἑτοιμασίᾳ τοῦ εὐαγγελίου τῆς εἰρήνης
ἀναλαβόντες	τὸν θυρεὸν τῆς πίστεως
	δυνήσεσθε...σβέσαι ...
δέξασθε*	τὴν περικεφαλαίαν τοῦ σωτηρίου
	τὴν μάχαιραν τοῦ πνεύματος

*The imperative δέξασθε breaks the pattern.

123. So also Gnilka, *Epheserbrief*, p. 310, and Schlier, *Brief*, p. 294.

124. So also J. Ernst, *Die Briefe an die Philipper, an Philemon, an die Kolosser, und die Epheser* (Regensburg: Pustet, 1974), p. 399. Schnackenburg is quite wrong in saying that the image of God as holy warrior 'steht höchstens entfernt dahinter' (*Brief*, p. 283).

takes up the image and rearticulates it in a way that conforms to the intentions of the letter as a whole.[125]

Having discussed the treatments of the divine armour in Isaiah 59, Wisdom of Solomon 5, and 1 Thessalonians 5, it is useful here to place the specific sets of armour next to each other so as to observe the changes the Isaianic armour has undergone, but also to see how Ephesians has adapted it.

Isa. 59.17-19	*Wis. 5.17-23*	*1 Thess. 5.8*	*Eph 6.11-17*
	λήμψεται		ἐνδύσασθε/ἀναλάβετε
	πανοπλίαν		πανοπλίαν
	τὸν ζῆλον αὐτοῦ		τοῦ θεοῦ
	ὁπλοποιήσει		
	τὴν κτίσιν		
	(στήσεται 5.1)		στῆτε
			περιζωσάμενοι
			τὴν ὀσφὺν ὑμῶν
			ἐν ἀληθείᾳ
ἐνεδύσατο	ἐνδύσεται	ἐνδυσάμενοι	ἐνδυσάμενοι
δικαιοσύνην	θώρακα δικαιοσύνην	θώρακα πίστεω̂	θώρακα τῆς δικαιοσύνῆ
ὡς θώρακα		καὶ ἀγάπης	
			ὑποδησάμενοι
			τοὺς πόδας
			ἐν ἑτοιμασίᾳ
			τοῦ εὐαγγελίου
			τῆς εἰρήνης
			ἀναλαβόντες
			τὸν θυρεὸν
			τῆς πίστεως
περιέθετο	περιθήσεται	(ἐνδυσάμενοι)	δέξασθε
περικεφαλαίαν	κόρυθα	περικεφαλαίαν	περικεφαλαίαν
σωτηρίου	κρίσιν ἀνυπόκριτον	ἐλπίδα σωτηρίας	τοῦ σωτηρίου
ἐπὶ τῆς κεφαλῆς			
περιεβάλετο			
ἱμάτιον ἐκδικήσεως			
περιβόλαιον			
ὡς ἀνταπόδοσιν			
ὄνομα			
(φοβηθήσονται)			

125. See the rich literature on the image of the panoply, but also on the various elements of the armour listed in Ephesians 6, in Oepke and Kuhn, 'ὅπλον', pp. 292-315. In contrast to the position taken here, Oepke suggests that Paul (*sic*) has primarily the Roman legionary in mind, and elaborates on that motif with Old Testament images (p. 301).

	λήμψεται	
	ἀσπίδα	
	ἀκαταμάχητον	
	ὁσιότητα	
	ὀξυνεῖ	
ὀργη... ἥξει	ἀπότομον ὀργὴν	
	εἰς ῥομφαίαν	μάχαιραν τοῦ πνεύματος
		ὅ ἐστιν ῥῆμα θεοῦ
	συνεκπολεμήσει αὐτῷ	
	ὁ κόσμος	
	βολίδες ἀστραπῶν	τὰ βέλη (τὰ) πεπυρωμένα
		τοῦ πονηροῦ
	χάλαζαι θυμοῦ	
	πλήρεις	
	ὕδωρ θαλάσσης	
ὡς ποταμός	ποταμοί	
	ἀντιστήσεται	ἀντιστῆναι
	πνεῦμα δυνάμεως	
	ἐκλικμήσει..λαῖλαψ	
	ἐρημώσει...ἀνομία	
	κακοπραγία	
	περιτρέψει	

The Belt of Truth

At the head of the list of elements of armour in Ephesians is the girding of the loins with truth (περιζωσάμενοι τὴν ὀσφὺν ὑμῶν ἐν ἀληθείᾳ).[126] Ἀλήθεια enjoys considerable prominence in Ephesians. In 1.13 the author restates Col. 1.5 in making the λόγος τῆς ἀληθείας synonymous with τὸ εὐαγγέλιον τῆς σωτηρία. A verbal form of 'truth' rare in the Pauline corpus is ἀληθεύειν ('truthing', 4.15), serving to characterize mutual relations within the body of Christ. In v. 21 the author refers to the truth being in Jesus (ἀλήθεια ἐν τῷ Ἰησοῦ). The καινὸς ἄνθρωπος believers are asked to put on is created ἐν δικαιοσύνῃ and [ἐν] ὁσιότητι τῆς ἀληθείας (v. 24). The allusive quality of ἀλήθεια is matched by the following sentence: 'Therefore, since you have taken off the lie (τὸ ψεῦδος; v. 25[127]), speak truth to each other.'[128] This is followed in

126. For girdle see Oepke and Kuhn, 'ὅπλον', pp. 302-308.

127. Cf. the synonymous taking off the παλαιὸς ἄνθρωπος in 4.22.

128. The author quotes Zech. 8.16. Zechariah 8 as a whole has many notable points of contact with Ephesians: God introduces himself as one who will be God in ἀλήθεια and δικαιοσύνη (v. 8; cf. Eph. 4.24). Instead of judgment he will show εἰρήνη (v. 12; cf. Eph. 2.4, 11-22). The people are in turn to speak truth to their neighbours, to make peaceable judgments (κρὶμα εἰρηνικόν), not to plan (μὴ λογίζεσθε) evil against the neighbour, nor to love false oaths (ὅρκον ψευδῆ; vv. 16, 17); they are to 'love truth and peace' (v. 19; cf. Eph. 4.3, 15, 25-29, 32). Zechariah 8

v. 27, significantly, by the statement μηδὲ δίδοτε τόπον τῷ διαβόλῳ, clearly anticipating the struggle of 6.10-20, not least the role of ἀλήθεια in that battle. Truth is also implicated in the definition of light *vis-à-vis* darkness in 5.9.

The prominence of ἀλήθεια, including its proximity to τὸ εὐαγγέλιον τῆς σωτηρίας in 1.13 and to τὸ εὐαγγέλιον τῆς εἰρήνης in 6.15, suggests that its presence in 6.14 functions as a recapitulation of a note sounded repeatedly in Ephesians. This conforms to the function of this image of the church in the divine armour as a *peroratio*. To place ἀλήθεια at the head of the list of items of armour serves two purposes: first, in imitation of God who puts on his virtues or attributes for battle, the community takes up a central virtue which describes not only its mode of relating but its very character; thereby, second, is also signalled if not exactly explained what it means for the community to be active as the Divine Warrior. 'Truthing' is the mode of the church's divine warfare.

'Αλήθεια is present also in Isaiah 59 in the drama of divine intervention, where 'she' is driven from the roads and destroyed along with the other virtues (vv. 14, 15), on whose behalf the Divine Warrior then intervenes. It will be recalled that the taking up of the virtues into the armour symbolizes Yahweh's act of vindication, symbolic then also of the nature of divine intervention. 'Αλήθεια does not, however, appear in the armour in Isaiah 59. But it is taken up in into the armour in Eph. 6.14 as girdle.[129] The importance the author accords ἀλήθεια is indicated not least by the fact that this is a new addition to the image of the armed Divine Warrior, but also by the fact that it is given first mention in the description of the armour. The author has not departed from the image of the Divine Warrior with this image. In Ps. 64.7 LXX God is said to have 'girded' himself with power (περιεζωσμένος ἐν δυναστείᾳ;

ends with a prediction that the Gentiles (λαοὶ πολλοὶ καὶ ἔθνη πολλά) will seek to join Jews because it is obvious that God is with them (vv. 20-23; cf. Eph. 2.11-13, 19!). It is difficult to resist the conclusion that the brief citation of Zech. 8.16 in Eph. 4.25 is but the tip of the iceberg in terms of the role Zech. 8 plays in the thought of the author of Ephesians.

129. With prompting from D.N. Freedman, Barth (*Ephesians*, II, p. 768 n. 60) correctly draws the connection between ἀλήθεια here and the personified attendant of God in the Old Testament, quite possibly connected to the Divine Council. Cf. also Gaugler, *Epheserbrief*, p. 225, who refers to ἀλήθεια as 'ein göttliches Wesen'. Neither makes the connection to the role of these virtues in the drama of Isa. 59, however.

cf. 92.1). Close to the way the image functions in Ephesians is that God girds the royal psalmist with power for battle (Ps. 17.33, 40 LXX; cf. 44.4).[130] Similar, and likely directly affecting the treatment in Ephesians, is Isa. 11.5 LXX, where the king is girded with justice and truth (καὶ ἔσται δικαιοσύνῃ ἐζωσμένος τὴν ὀσφὺν αὐτοῦ καὶ ἀληθείᾳ εἰλημένος τὰς πλευράς). Ephesians imitates the author of Isaiah 59 in taking up the important virtues into the image of the intervening deity, suggesting that God's ways of being present will not be thwarted, suggesting also the manner of the intervention of the Divine Warrior—the exercise of truth.

The Breastplate of Justice

The breastplate of justice or righteousness is taken virtually without alteration from the armour of Isa. 59.17 (θώραξ τῆς δικαιοσύνης; cf. Isa. 59.17 LXX, δικαιοσύνη ὡς θώραξ), evidence that the author explicitly takes up a tradition already familiar to him and his readers as scriptural. Insofar as Ephesians is intended to be read in relation to a growing collection of Paul's letters, including 1 Thessalonians, the author intends to signal that he is following Paul in interpreting Isaiah 59, and not simply reappropriating 1 Thess. 5.8. There, as indicated in the last chapter, Paul 'translates' δικαιοσύνη as πίστις καὶ ἀγάπη. The author of Ephesians wishes readers and hearers to place his treatment of the motif of the Divine Warrior in armour in juxtaposition to scriptural precedent. This strengthens the thesis argued here, namely that with impetus from Paul, the author of Ephesians intends to place the image of the ἐκκλησία in the divine armour in direct contact with the Isaianic precedent where it is *God himself* who inhabits the armour over against his errant people.

In comparison with the importance it enjoys in the undisputed letters of Paul, δικαιοσύνη plays a less prominent role than does ἀλήθεια in Ephesians up to this point, appearing alongside it on two occasions. It is God who creates the new ἄνθρωπος with δικαιοσύνη and ὁσιότης τῆς ἀληθείας (holiness of truth; 4.24). Appropriately, along with ἀλήθεια, δικαιοσύνη represents ὁ καρπὸς τοῦ φωτὸς (the fruit of light; 5.9). It

130. Note also the importance of 'standing on the heights' (17.34), and the lending of the 'shield of salvation' (v. 36). This psalm differs from Ephesians not so much in the specific imagery but in that it is strictly God who is the helper. As such it is closer to 1 Peter, where arming in 4.1 clearly goes hand in hand with the need for divine intervention in 5.6-11.

appears then that its presence in 6.14 serves more to identify the community with God than to say much about the nature of conduct. Conduct is implied, to be sure, in that the δικαιοσύνη of God implies the active practice of justice. Even so, δικαιοσύνη is not itself the object of reflection, but serves largely as an allusion to divine presence and action. That becomes highly significant, however, when δικαιοσύνη becomes the armour and as such the task of the community which inhabits it.[131]

The Shoes of Peace

Verse 15 introduces a new item into the armour—shoes with which to be ready to announce peace (ὑποδησάμενοι τοὺς πόδας ἐν ἑτοιμασίᾳ τοῦ εὐαγγελίου τῆς εἰρήνης). Attention to feet no doubt echoes the depiction of the messenger of peace in Isa. 52.6-7 (cf. Eph. 2.13, 17).[132] It is significant that whereas the Masoretic Text suggests it is God's messenger who announces the good news of God's coming, the Septuagint leaves no doubt that the feet belong to God. In keeping with the overall intentions of Ephesians, the community is once again identified with God the warrior, only now, in anticipation, with God the victorious warrior who brings news of his own victory.

Εἰρήνη has already received considerable attention in Eph. 2.11-22, again with obvious allusions to Deutero Isaiah (vv. 13, 17; cf. Isa. 52.7; 59.19). In that pericope Christ is εἰρήνη personified, overcoming through his own death the enmity between τὰ ἀμφότερα (v. 14) and οἱ ἀμφότεροι (v. 16), and announcing the good news of peace to the far (Gentiles) and the near (Jews), making the two into one body, reconciling

131. *Contra* Oepke, who suggests that this is 'deliberately presented as a defensive piece of equipment. The reference is not, *of course*, to the divine attribute, as in Is. 59.17' (italics mine; Oepke and Kuhn, 'ὅπλον', p. 310). Further, given his understanding that these verses emerge from Paul, he then also links the meaning of δικαιοσύνη with Paul's use of it elsewhere, in particular Rom. 3.22. I agree that it is impossible for a Paulinist like the author of Ephesians and his readership not to see δικαιοσύνη as centrally related to God's saving initiatives. It is precisely that conviction, however, which provides the foil in this instance.

132. Here again Oepke ('ὅπλον', p. 312) understands Paul to be filling out the image of the Roman legionary, and to be only secondarily dependent on Isa. 52.7. Obviously the image of a warrior with sandals is not an outlandish one for author or readers, but the connection to the εὐαγγέλιον τῆς εἰρήνης will push readers in another direction, perhaps even highlighting the irony of the image. Oepke himself recognizes that there is repeated dependency on Isaiah in the preceding verses ('ὅπλον', p. 312 n. 9).

them to God. Εἰρήνη is thus essentially the content of the μυστήριον (ch. 3).

The presence of εἰρήνη in 6.15 suggests that a significant dimension of the struggle of the saints in the role of the Divine Warrior is to seize every opportunity to get the news of peace out to those who are still 'far off'. Those who are here summoned to announce peace are themselves those who were once far off (οἵ ποτε ὄντες μακράν; 2.13; cf. 2.3). For them, εἰρήνη is in large measure an already established reality. From this viewpoint von Harnack fittingly characterizes the irony of identifying the warrior with the mission of peace as *eine erhabene Paradoxie*.[133]

In my view, another, more fitting interpretation is possible, however. The rare term ἑτοιμασία,[134] best translated here as 'preparedness' or 'readiness', alerts the reader to the degree to which the battle places the full realization of εἰρήνη on hold pending the successful outcome of the battle with the powers. So while the author is willing to celebrate the reconciliation effected in the coming and death of Christ, the announcement of full εἰρήνη[135] must await full victory. Ἑτοιμασία thus reflects a certain eschatological reserve. That victory is assured, that εἰρήνη has been tasted, changes nothing about the gravity of the present struggle.

Ἑτοιμασία does not simply function as an injection of realism, however. In its more frequent verbal form it often serves in the Septuagint to depict the divine activity of creation, salvation, or judgment.[136] A

133. A. von Harnack, *Militia Christi: Die christliche Religion und der Soldatenstand in den ersten drei Jahrhunderten* (Darmstadt: Wissenschaftliche Buchgesellschaft, 1963 [Tübingen: Mohr, 1905]), p. 13. Cf. also Oepke's identical characterization ('fine paradox', 'ὅπλον', p. 312). Harnack's characterization is repeated by many commentators.

134. In the New Testament only here, and seldom in LXX. The verbal form ἑτοιμάζειν is more common, although also rare in the Pauline corpus (1 Cor. 2.9; Phlm. 22; cf. 2 Tim. 2.21).

135. Here to be read in the full sense of the Hebrew שלום. For full discussion of the meaning of εἰρήνη and in particular the hymn in 2.11-18, see, e.g. Gnilka, *Epheserbrief*, pp. 138-52; P. Stuhlmacher, '"Er ist unser Friede" (Eph. 2,14). Zur Exegese und Bedeutung von Eph. 2,14-18', in *idem*, *Versöhnung, Gesetz und Gerechtigkeit: Aufsätze zur biblischen Theologie* (Göttingen: Vandenhoeck & Ruprecht, 1981); E. Brandenburger, *Frieden im Neuen Testament: Grundlinien urchristlichen Friedensverständnisses* (Gütersloh: Gütersloher Verlagshaus/Gerd Mohn, 1973), pp. 66, 67; E. Dinkler, *Eirene: Der urchristliche Friedensgedanke* (Heidelberg: Carl Winter/Universitätsverlag, 1973), pp. 24-32.

136. W. Grundmann, 'ἕτοιμος, κτλ.', *TDNT*, II, pp. 704-706, and texts cited there.

particularly striking and relevant example is Ps. 67.11, 12 LXX: God in his kindness has taken care of the poor (ἡτοίμασας ἐν τῇ χρηστότητί σου τῷ πτωχῷ, ὁ θεός). The Lord will then give a word (ῥῆμα) to those who announce good news with great power (κύριος δώσει ῥῆμα τοῖς εὐαγγελιζομένοις δυνάμει πολλῇ). The Masoretic Text preserves the content of the news as 'The kings of the armies flee!' which is then followed by the women dividing the spoils. The context is unambiguously one of announcing victory. We already know that the author is familiar with this psalm and has subjected it to considerable reflection and interpretation.[137] So, even though ἑτοιμασία refers here to preparedness of the saints in the role of the Divine Warrior to announce the arrival of εἰρήνη, the relationship of that term to the creating, saving, and judging[138] activity of God strengthens the impression that this term too serves to solidify the identification of the church with God as intervener.

I suggested earlier that 1 Thessalonians 5 can be read as an exercise in irony, in which the fearsome language of invasion of the day becomes in fact the invasion of saving light, reversing the initial irony of Amos. Examples have been given of the way Ephesians continues that revaluation of confrontation and judgment. However, this particular phrase regarding the announcement of peace does not represent irony at all. In Ephesians, unlike in the other texts studied so far, the enemy is the common enemy of humankind, of blood and flesh, namely, διάβολος and his δυνάμεις. This is not an enemy to whom peace is announced. Nor is the battle with them over, even if victory is certain. Ἑτοιμασία must then refer to the anticipation of victory and the announcement of victory once it has been achieved. As such it serves as encouragement to the troops, as it were. Εἰρήνη is then more than what has been achieved in the past by and through Christ, but must also refer to the state which follows cessation of warfare once the powers have been vanquished (cf. v. 13). The injection of the note of peace at this point serves not to undo the militancy but to indicate what is at stake in the battle with the powers. To see the injection of peace at this point as 'paradox' is to misunderstand the image. There is no irony or paradox in being ready to announce peace once enemies have been vanquished. What would have been shocking to early readers familiar with the construct of divine

137. Cf. the discussion above regarding 4.8 and surrounding verses. Cf. also the ῥῆμα θεοῦ in 6.17, and the request on the part of 'Paul' in v. 19 that he might be given a λόγος to make known the μυστήριον τοῦ εὐαγγελίου.

138. E.g. Isa. 14.21 and 30.33.

warfare is that it is the saints who inhabit the armour and thus the role of victor over the powers, and that, as victors, it is they who are to announce victory.

The Shield of Faith(fulness)

A further item unique to the armour in Ephesians is the θυρεὸς τῆς πίστεως (v. 16).[139] 1 Thess. 5.8 identifies πίστις along with ἀγάπη as the περικεφαλαία. Here it merits a separate item in the armour. Πίστις does not carry the theological freight in Ephesians that it does in the undisputed letters of Paul. There is a formulaic use of πίστις in 1.15; 2.8 and 3.17, dependent on traditional Pauline usage. 4.5 and perhaps 4.13 suggest πίστις is also an objective and quantifiable reality, reflective of the growing maturation of 'the faith'. Πίστις as 'faithful performance' in 3.12, where Christ's πίστις[140] becomes the basis of 'our' royal status reflected in the exercise of παρρησία and προσαγωγή, comes closest to the identification of πίστις as part of the arsenal of the Divine Warrior in 6.16. If one accords importance to the defensive dimension of the image of the shield then it is possible to see ἡ πίστις as the means of protection. But that is to misread the meaning of the armour, as the previous study of Isaiah 59 has shown. It is the armour of the Divine Warrior which is in view, and defence is precisely not the point, or at least not the first point. Πίστις is part of the arsenal of attack.

That warfare includes defence is, of course, obvious. That is suggested by the elaboration on the function of the shield, namely, the quenching

139. For discussion of θυρεός and literature see Oepke and Kuhn, 'ὅπλον', pp. 312-13.

140. 'διὰ τῆς πίστεως αὐτοῦ [Χριστοῦ]' suggests that 'faithfulness' might be the most appropriate translation of πίστις in 6.16 (as is also generally the case in LXX). This means that it is quite misguided to see in this item of the armour an indication that this cannot possibly be God's own armour on the grounds that God obviously cannot believe (Gaugler, *Epheserbrief*, p. 221). R. Bultmann and A. Weiser ('πιστεύω, κτλ.', *TDNT*, VI, pp. 174-228) treat πίστις as chiefly a human disposition of trust toward God. However, within a reciprocal covenantal relationship πίστις means trust, truthfulness, and fidelity, and thus is quite properly practised or possessed by God. Πίστις is thus identified as one of God's virtues, frequently rendering אמת or אמונה in the LXX. In Isa. 59.14 and 15 אמת is translated as ἀλήθεια. Πίστις would have served just as well (cf. Jer. 7.28!). Cf., e.g., Ps. 32.4 LXX; Hos. 2.20 LXX (πίστις as God's means of reconciliation; cf. Jer. 39.41; 40.6 LXX), Hab. 2.4 LXX (the δίκαιος will live by 'my' [God's!] πίστις); Lam. 3.23 LXX, Sir. 49.10 (where πίστις is a means of liberation).

of the flaming arrows of (the) evil (one). However, even this image is not unambiguously an image of believers under siege, as most commentators tend to see it.[141] The connotations run just as easily in the direction of seeing the saints as Divine Warrior placing the powers under siege. This can be illustrated by ancient images and discussions of siege warfare (cf. Isa. 37.33).[142] Furthermore, this language already possesses a mythological dimension identifying it with 'the wars of the gods.' God himself as Divine Warrior employs arrows in his attacks.[143] Of interest are the closely related βολίδες ἀστραπῶν of Wis. 5.21. Here, however, it is 'the evil one' who sends his arrows.[144] But Ps. 34.2 LXX describes God as being called upon to rise as Divine Warrior and take up weapon and shield (ὅπλον καὶ θυρεός) to intervene on behalf of the afflicted.[145] The implication is clear. The saints are engaged in the warfare of the gods, as it were. Only now the image is not so much one of God shooting from above as it is of the powers shooting from their heavenly fortress under siege by attacking saints in the form and armour of the Divine Warrior.[146]

141. So, e.g., repeatedly, Schlier, *Brief*, pp. 297, 299.

142. Cf. relief of the Siege of Lachish in *ANET*. Cf. also Aeneas Tacticus, 'On the Defense of Fortified Positions', §33 (*Aeneas Tacticus, Asclepiodotus, Onasander* [LCL; London: Heinemann/New York: Putnam's Sons, 1923]), and P. Ducrey, *Warfare in Ancient Greece* (trans. J. Lloyd; New York: Schocken, 1985), p. 169. Cf. Barth, *Ephesians*, II, p. 772, especially n. 86 for literature; Wink, *Naming the Powers*, pp. 86-87.

143. In Deut. 32.23 LXX it is God who will gather evil (κακά) against his faithless people, sending his arrows (τὰ βέλη μοῦ) against them. Cf. Job 6.4; 20.25; Ps. 7.14 LXX (where they are among God's σκεύη θανάτου); 17.15; 37.3; 63.8; 76.18 (a mythological way of describing the Exodus as the victory over the sea monster). In Ps. 10.2 LXX it is the ἁμαρτωλοί who shoot the arrow against the faithful, cf. 56.5; 90.5. In Isa. 5.28 the arrows of the Assyrians are *God's* means of warfare (cf. 7.24); in Isa. 49.2 God's servant is an arrow. Cf. finally, Josephus, *Ant.* 1.203, where God is said to have burned up Sodom with a fiery arrow.

144. Cf. 1QH 2.26; 3.16, 27.

145. In contrast to his habit of exegeting the image as a whole as fundamentally defensive, Oepke suggests that Ps. 34.2 LXX is essentially carried over from God to the believers in Eph. 6.16 ('ὅπλον', p. 313). Cf. also the closely related ὑπερασπιστής in Pss. 32.20, 58.12 and 113.17-19 LXX, where God is described as Israel's shield, i.e., its protector and liberator.

146. In a real sense Ephesians participates in the dislocation of space and time we observed also in Wisdom of Solomon, in that the saints are *already* seated with Christ in the heavenlies, from where it can also be said that they fight the powers.

The Helmet of Salvation

Verse 17 returns to an item of armour familiar from Isaiah 59. Up to this point participles have elaborated what it means 'to stand' (vv. 13, 14). Now the saints are to grasp or seize (δέξασθε[147]) the helmet of salvation (περικεφαλαία τοῦ σωτηρίου). Dependency on Isaiah is illustrated by the fact that in 1.13 the feminine noun σωτηρία is used. Further, 1 Thess. 5.8 identifies the helmet with the ἐλπὶς σωτηρίας. Thus the helmet of salvation functions perhaps less as recapitulation of a previous emphasis on salvation than as a signal that the author intends to make it obvious that 6.14-17 represents a new appropriation of the Isaianic image, going back behind both 1 Thessalonians and Wisdom of Solomon for the precise wording of the metaphor.[148] This does not imply attention to the feature of the helmet so much as it calls attention to Isaiah 59 and its focus on the Divine Warrior in his role as cosmic intervener and judge. As such the defensive element is clearly pushed into the background.[149] In fact, in the ancient world the helmet serves not only defensive needs, but in its more elaborate forms serves to intimidate the enemy.[150] In keeping with the overall strategies of the author of Ephesians, the call on the community to take up the helmet of salvation worn by God in Isaiah 59 thus clearly implicates the community in the act of saving.[151] The author infers this from the way Paul uses the helmet for

The *Haustafel* has seen to it, however, that we imagine the saints ἐπὶ τῆς γῆς.

147. Barth (*Ephesians*, II, p. 775 n. 106) suggests that one should read this as 'receive', presumably in keeping with the nature of salvation. Wild ('Warrior', pp. 286 n. 5, 297) agrees, depending strangely on Gnilka (*Epheserbrief*, p. 313) who rightly sees it as little more than as stylistic variation. It should be translated here as 'to take up' or 'grasp'.

148. Isa. 59.17: περικεφαλαία σωτηρίου; Wis. 5.18: κόρυς κρίσις ἀνυπόκριτος; 1 Thess. 5.8: περικεφαλαία ἐλπὶς σωτηρίας.

149. *Contra* Oepke, who after indicating the direct reliance on Isaiah 59 nevertheless can say: 'Salvation is given the passive and fully New Testament sense of σωθῆναις ('ὅπλον', p. 315).

150. Cf. Homer, *Iliad* 3.11; Polybius, *Hist.* 6.23.8.

151. Barth characterizes this as an act of 'democratizing': 'God's victory is passed down to all of the saints, and the saints are treated as people worthy to be elevated to God and to share in his victory' (*Ephesians*, II, p. 775). Both the democratizing potential as well as the connection of this motif with that of announcing peace or salvation (cf. v. 15) is illustrated by *Beth ha-Midr* 3.73.17, which identifies the Messiah on whose head God places a crown and the helmet of salvation as the one who announces salvation to Israel from the mountaintop (in P. Billerbeck, *Die Briefe des Neuen Testaments und der Offenbarung Johannis* [H.L. Strack and

the community in 1 Thess. 5.8. He now radicalizes Paul by also dropping the reference to 'hope', rendering salvation not only something already experienced by the saints (cf. 2.8), but a divine initiative in which they participate.[152]

The Sword of the Spirit

The aggressive interventionist tone is strengthened by the fact that the helmet of salvation is attached via the imperative δέξασθε to the μάχαιρα τοῦ πνεύματος. There is a widespread tendency to interpret this image, in keeping with its view of the rest of the panoply, as essentially defensive. The sword is, after all, 'only' the μάχαιρα, a dagger distinguished from the larger battle sword, the ῥομφαία.[153] However, to translate μάχαιρα as dagger and thus to signify no more than defensive armour represents a misreading of the origin of this language.[154] It is important to note, for example, that with one exception (66.16) the Septuagint of Isaiah always renders חרב as μάχαιρα. This is the case also in divine warfare texts such as Lev. 26.8, 25, 32; Deut. 20.13; 32.41-42; 33.29; Jer. 25.17 LXX and the 'Song of the Sword' in Jer. 27.35-38 LXX.[155] Given Ephesians' clear dependency on the biblical tradition,

P. Billerbeck, *Kommentar zum Neuen Testament aus Talmud und Midrasch* (Munich: Beck, 1954), III], p. 618).

152. *Contra* Schlier, *Brief*, p. 297, who conflates 1 Thess. 5.8 with Eph. 6.17. Therewith is not denied that hope has a place in Ephesians (cf. 1.18; 4.4). The rhetorical strategy here calls for maximum identification with the divine initiative. To introduce hope here would be to render the saints too passive with respect to the dynamic of salvation.

153. See W. Michaelis, 'μάχαιρα', *TDNT*, IV, pp. 524-25. He largely undercuts his own discussion by admitting that 'in the light of the Hebrew חרב there is no set distinction between μάχαιρα and ῥομφαία' (p. 525). It should be noted that even in Rom. 13.4, where μάχαιρα is sometimes understood to signify in a ceremonial way the authority of the state, it also clearly represents the arsenal of ἐξουσία as the διάκονος of (God's) ὀργή; cf. the citing of Deut. 32.35 in the immediately preceding Rom. 12.19.

154. Polybius identifies the sword which is part of the πανοπλία of the *hastati* as a μάχαιρα (*Hist.* 4.23). Cf. also Barth, *Ephesians*, II, p. 776; Wink, *Naming the Powers*, p. 86.

155. The LXX does not allow the inference that μάχαιρα refers to a small defensive sword. Ezekiel can use four different terms for sword to translate חרב (μάχαιρα, ῥομφαία, ξίφος, ἐγχειρίδιον) with no discernible pattern or reason for the choice of one over the other (e.g., μάχαιρα 5.2, 12; 26.6; 28.7; 30.4; 31.17; ῥομφαία 12.14; 21.9, 14-17; 29.8; ξίφος 16.40; 23.47; ἐγχειρίδιον 21.3). One can also point to

especially for this particular *topos*, the choice of word for sword must be seen as governed by biblical usage, most particularly by those texts which speak of God as Divine Warrior.

An offensive or aggressive reading of the presence of μάχαιρα is supported by the fact that the sword is identified as the sword of the spirit. The proximity of πνεῦμα/רוח to the 'winds of war' employed by the Divine Warrior is shown in Isa. 59.19. The Septuagint replaces the Masoretic Text's 'driven by he wind/spirit of Yahweh', or translates its own *Vorlage* with μετὰ θυμοῦ. But nothing prevents the author of Ephesians from alluding, although in highly altered form, to the wind or spirit of the Divine Warrior present in Isaiah 59. Wisdom of Solomon 5.23 sets the πνεῦμα δυνάμεως next to the violent λαῖλαψ as an example of armed creation. Wind/spirit is a frequent part of the arsenal of the Divine Warrior beyond the immediate tradition with which the author of Ephesians is working. The Septuagint translates Exod. 15.8 (cf. v. 10) as God driving a wedge into the sea with his πνεῦμα τοῦ θυμοῦ. Psalm 17 LXX celebrates creation itself as a divine war in which the Lord lays bare the foundations of the world (οἰκουμένη) with the wind or spirit of his wrath (πνεῦμα ὀργῆς σου; v. 16).[156] Isaiah refers several times to the Divine Warrior's spirit or wind, in 11.15 to his πνεῦμα βιαίος, and in 27.8 to his πνεῦμα θυμοῦ. In short, the combination of μάχαιρα and πνεῦμα should be read within the context of the motif of the Divine Warrior, and be seen as conjuring the exercise of fierce power against the enemies of God.

It is of course impossible that πνεῦμα would not also have evoked the rich texture of meaning it has taken on within the Pauline tradition. Its availability to the believers as part of the divine armour dovetails with the Pauline conviction that spirit represents the inbreaking of the eschaton. To possess it also constitutes evidence of royal status, that is, participation now already in the exalted status of the sons (and daughters) of God, that is, the status of monarchs. That Paul was quite capable of understanding that in militant terms has already been shown above in discussing Romans 6 and 13.

Wis. 5.20 where ὀργή is fashioned into a ῥομφαία, and to Wis. 18.15, where the warrior λόγος wields his ξίφος, which illustrates that one is hard pressed to be able to make a case for a particular term for sword indicating levels of warfare.

156. Cf. here the πνεῦμα κυρίου in Wis. 1.7 which, as the discussion of Wisdom of Solomon earlier pointed out, is implicated in divine warfare by functioning essentially as the Divine Warrior's secret service in the οἰκουμένη.

The μάχαιρα τοῦ πνεύματος is further specified as the ῥῆμα θεοῦ. In one sense this deliberately restricts the allusive capacity of the motif. At the same time, it suggests that the church as the divine warrior is called upon to 'wield' the word of God, which is more than the 'quoting' of known ῥήματα θεοῦ. It suggests rather the full force of uttering the divine word as a means of assault on the powers. Relatedly, Wisdom of Solomon 18 illustrates forcefully that λόγος can be both the Divine Warrior's surrogate (vv. 14-16) and also the means of fighting its ὀργή (v. 22). It may be that Isa. 11.4 LXX may be the closest parallel to Eph. 6.17, in which the king smites the earth with the λόγος τοῦ στόματος, and will destroy the ἀσεβεῖς with the πνεῦμα διὰ χειλέων (cf. *Pss. Sol.* 17.24). Isa. 49.2 LXX does not mention the 'word', but comes close with a characterization of the mouth as a sharp sword (τὸ στόμα μου ὡσεὶ μάχαιραν ὀξεῖαν).[157] Psalm 67.12 LXX, a text repeatedly referred to in this discussion and evidently important to the author of Ephesians, speaks of the Lord giving a ῥῆμα to the carriers of good news, presumably to bring the news of the demise of the kings. There follows immediately a discussion of the women dividing the spoils of victory. In the potentially contemporaneous *Odes* 15.9; 29.9, 10, and 39.9 'word' is a means of divine conquest, wielded at times by the people, at others by God. It is difficult to suggest any more here than that the defining of the μάχαιρα τοῦ πνεύματος as the ῥῆμα θεοῦ should be read in the light of the tradition of implicating the word of God in his divine warfare. It should not be interpreted here in connection with the 'washing with the word' in Eph 5.23, but strictly within the image of divine warfare.

But why ῥήμα rather than λόγος? It is possible that the author uses the two terms interchangably. On the other hand, we may see in the choice of vocabulary the influence of Isaiah 59. Both πνεῦμα and ῥήμα appear in Isa. 59.21 as the content of the διαθήκη the Lord will establish with the recipient and his seed. It is quite possible that in addition to the varied background identified above, the specific impetus behind the introduction of the spirit and the word of God into the armour is the integration of Isa. 59.21 into the image of the Divine Warrior, especially since the christological and eschatological perspective of the Ephesian author is shaped by the conviction that the covenant hoped for in Isa. 59.21 is being realized. The reconciliation brought about by the irenic Christ in ch. 2, which is specifically talked about as constituting the

157. Cf. Rev. 1.16; 2.12. For an example of enemies' tongues as swords see 1QH 5.14, 15.

integration of those who were once strangers to the covenants of Israel, is here recapitulated by integrating the vocabulary of the promise of covenant into the image of the divine warrior. Further, the unfinished nature of that task, both in relation to extending the body of Christ as in ch. 4 and here the overcoming of the hostile powers, is thus also signalled. So, on the one hand, ῥῆμα and λόγος can be seen as virtual synonyms (vv. 17, 19), suggesting that the 'wielding' of the word of God is to be regarded as the announcing of the mystery of the gospel of peace (cf. vv. 15 and 19; cf. also 2.13, 17). On the other hand, the distinction in vocabulary allows for the possibility that ῥῆμα be seen more exclusively as a means of confrontation and judgment, related to ἐλέγχειν in 5.11.[158]

4. *Paul's Relationship to the Saints as Divine Warrior*

In 6.18-20 the author reintroduces the tone of mutual solidarity which introduced the *Haustafel*. He also introduces Paul as paradigmatic or 'typological prisoner'.[159] Importantly, this serves to extend or elaborate the Divine Warrior image. First of all, the call to prayer is in the form of a participle, dependent on the imperative calling for the taking up of the helmet and the sword.[160] Secondly, the weapon of the spirit is immediately employed, so to speak, within the prayerful stance of mutual solidarity. The focus has shifted slightly from the corporate community in armour to the community looking to the needs of its members engaged in battle. It should not be missed, however, that the author fully intends to emphasize that this work of solidarity is nothing less than the activity of the Divine Warrior. The believers are called to pray always ἐν πνεύματι through every prayer and entreaty, to be alert (ἀγρυπνοῦντες) for this with all readiness and prayer.

The special emphasis Ephesians brings to this is illustrated when this

158. See the discussion earlier regarding 5.11, and note that even that act of confrontation is seen as an act of transformation, faithful to its use by Paul himself (1 Cor. 14.24). This would bring the meaning of ῥῆμα τοῦ θεοῦ close to the way the λόγος τοῦ θεοῦ is characterized in Heb. 4.12 as μάχαιρα δίστομος. Much later and in a very different way the *Gospel of Philip* will illustrate the power of the word when it speaks of the powers as not being able to endure the name 'Christian' (NHC II, 3.62.26-35).

159. Wild, 'Warrior', p. 288. Wild is quite correct in saying that Ephesians represents a veritable 'Paulology' (p. 289), as I have intimated earlier in this chapter.

160. Cf. Wink, *Naming the Powers*, p. 88.

verse is compared with the related 1 Pet. 4.7; 5.8 and Col. 4.2-4. The relationship between prayer and alertness within the context of struggle is present in 1 Peter. However, as indicated earlier, 1 Peter does not go as far as Ephesians in identifying believers with the Divine Warrior. They are passive dependents on God's intervention. That dependency sets the context of prayer (vv. 6, 7). In Col. 4.2-4, doubtless the immediate *Vorlage* for Eph. 6.18,[161] watchfulness and readiness do not relate to a context of battle with evil. Whatever the origin of the vocabulary, it is interpreted in Colossians in light of the task of evangelism. In contrast, Ephesians succeeds in reorienting the meaning of prayer as understood within the Pauline 'school' by relating it to the status and task of the community as the Divine Warrior.[162] It becomes part of the arsenal of the Divine Warrior. The prayers of the community are to be offered for all the saints, suggesting a primary focus not on the one(s) praying, but on those prayed for. If it is kept in mind that this verse extends the image of the community as the Divine Warrior in vv. 14-17, then prayer itself becomes a way in which the community intervenes on behalf of all the saints. Prayer is then not only an entreaty for God to see to the needs of the saints, but is itself a response to those needs.[163]

Prayer is to be undertaken, first, for all the saints, and only then for Paul. A comparison with Col. 4.2 brings to light yet again the Ephesian strategy of pushing the saints into the front lines of struggle. Col. 4.3 is thus picked up again only after the saints have been given first billing.

161. Col. 4.2-4: Τῇ προσευχῇ προσκαρτερεῖτε, γρηγοροῦντες ἐν αὐτῇ ἐν εὐχαριστίᾳ, προσευχόμενοι ἅμα καὶ περὶ ἡμῶν, ἵνα ὁ θεὸς ἀνοίξῃ ἡμῖν θύραν τοῦ λόγου λαλῆσαι τὸ μυστήριον τοῦ Χριστοῦ, δἰ ὃ καὶ δέδεμαι, ἵνα φανερώσω αὐτὸ ὡς δεῖ με λαλῆσαι.

162. *Contra* Barth, *Ephesians*, II, p. 779. One should recall that the ἀνὴρ ἄμεμπτος in Wis. 18.21-22 utilizes προσευχή as one of his weapons.

163. Cf. the striking words in *Teach. Silv.* 117.5-24 (cf. 106.30-33) which appears to know Eph. 6 (as well as Isa. 59 and Wisdom of Solomon) and which may indicate that the implication I have drawn became the basis of theological reflection:

> *Open the door for yourself* that you many know what is. *Knock on yourself that the Word may open for you.* For he is the Ruler of Faith and the *Sharp Sword*, having become all for every one because he wishes to have mercy on every one. My son, prepare yourself to escape from the world-rulers of darkness and of this sort of air which is full of powers. But if you have Christ, you will conquer this entire world. That which you will open for yourself, you will open. That which you will knock upon for yourself, you will knock upon, benefiting yourself. Help yourself, my son.' (trans. M.L. Peel and J. Zandee in *The Nag Hammadi Library in English*, pp. 360-61; italics mine).

'Paul' requests now that he[164] too be remembered. This conforms to the strategy observed in Eph. 3.8, where Paul is placed in an inferior position relative to the readers of the letter. As prototypical 'warrior' (cf. Wisdom of Solomon's πρόμαχος in 18.21) Paul puts the needs of all the saints before his own.[165]

The saints are to wage prayer that 'Paul' might be given a λόγος with (ἐν) openness of mouth so as to make known the mystery of the good news with παρρησία.[166] We find here a typical Pauline mix of vulnerability and dependency on the one hand, and power and confidence on the other. One is tempted to see this presentation of Paul as a deliberate parallel to the ἀνήρ ἄμεμπτος in Wis. 18.21-22, who also requires προσευχή and λόγος to fight not the powers of evil but God's ὀργή, God's λόγος. A number of examples were cited earlier which illustrate how widely in the scriptural tradition 'word' is understood as a weapon. The difference is, of course, that Paul is not in the position of the ἀνὴρ ἄμεμπτος who must fight for a helpless people, except to the extent that his warfare and that of the saints is on behalf of those still under oppression of the evil prince of the air (ch. 2). Here 'Paul' appeals to the people to support him, a clear expression of vulnerability. For strategic reasons identified earlier, the author of Ephesians no doubt wants to evoke precisely that image of Paul. Note that the open mouth is an image of vulnerability for Paul in 2 Cor. 6.11.

Vulnerability is not, in the view of Paul or that of his student, weakness. 2 Corinthians illustrates that for Paul openness and vulnerability (6.11) go hand and hand with παρρησία (3.12), an attribute of power and royal confidence (cf. the discussion of Wisdom of Solomon 5 earlier).

164. Whereas in Col. 4.3 one finds initially the first person plural, in Eph. 6.19 Paul is alone after the saints.

165. The strategy of the student agrees to a significant extent with that of the teacher Paul, who mixed vulnerability, to a degree which exposed him to ridicule (2 Cor. 10-13), with the call to imitate him (1 Thess. 1.6; 1 Cor. 11.1). Normally, the need for pseudepigraphy illustrates the necessity of having to 'hide' behind the star in order to get a hearing. In the case of Ephesians the pseudepigrapher shows himself to be a true Paulinist, however, when he makes the star take a back seat to the saints. The criticism of hero worship implicit in this would grow in strategic importance if the readers knew or suspected that this is not the 'historical' Paul, but the dead/'risen' Paul who continues to speak with open mouth through his 'school'.

166. Ideas and vocabulary present in 2 Corinthians appear to be playing a significant role here, as the following discussion shows. Πρεσβεύω appears only here and in 2 Cor. 5.20 in relation to the διακονία τῆς καταλλαγῆς (2 Cor. 5.18).

It connotes the status enjoyed by those who have access to the presence of God, and who utter there the words of and about God (2.17). In Ephesians the context of proclamation has been identified as a cosmos filled with hostile powers (3.10). For that task, fleshed out with the motif of the Divine Warrior in armour in 6.10-20, παρρησία signifies status, power, and the confidence of monarchs (3.12; cf. Wis. 5.1[167]). A comparison with Col. 2.15 shows this clearly, where God is said to have vanquished the powers, paraded them in victory, making an example of them ἐν παρρησία.[168] The stress in Ephesians on παρρησία suggests, then, that Paul and, inasmuch as Paul is exemplar for the community, the community also, are placed into the role of defeater of the powers (cf. κατεργάζομαι in v. 13).

However, in the present text 'Paul' appears not as victorious warrior but as δέσμιος (cf. 3.1), as an emissary in chains (πρεσβεύω ἐν ἁλύσει). In and of itself this does not mitigate the image of Paul as warrior.[169] Indeed, it is this irony which pervades virtually every facet of the appropriation of the warfare motif in Ephesians, as it already did in 1 Thessalonians 5. That this suffering is central to the image of Paul is suggested by his having been 'sent' in chains. He is, after all, a δέσμιος τοῦ Χριστοῦ (3.1; cf. 2 Cor. 2.14). Paul is evoked in a way appropriate to his official memory, one he had to argue for when alive, but one which became the mark of hero after his death. Thus, inasmuch as Paul functions in Ephesians not so much as an imprisoned warrior, but rather as one whose bondage sets the context of his warfare (no doubt a legacy of Paul's own identification of his suffering with that of Christ, whose suffering was the ironical expression of the power of God; cf. 1 Cor. 1.18), the author of Ephesians is reasserting the *imitatio Pauli* as the *imitatio Christi.* [170]

167. Wild ('Warrior', p. 293) believes as I do that the author of Ephesians is in conscious dialogue with Wis. 5.

168. Cf. Lev. 26.13, where God takes the people out of slavery μετὰ παρρησίας. Barth's translation of παρρησία as 'high spirits' thus appears silly (*Ephesians*, II, p. 781). He returns to translating παρρησιάζομαι as being 'frank' and 'bold' on p. 783.

169. Cf. especially Paul's own characterization of himself as warrior in 2 Cor. 6.7 within the context of vulnerable suffering (vv. 8-9); cf. also 2 Cor. 10.3-6, again within the context of accusations of weakness (v. 10); 2 Cor. 2.14 evokes the image of Paul as participant in the victory procession both (perhaps quite intentionally) as victor and as vanquished.

170. See the discussion of the relationship between oppression and παρρησία in

Suffering is, perhaps surprisingly, not a major emphasis in Ephesians. The contrast to 1 Thessalonians should be observed, where the theme of suffering in ch. 2 might lead to a largely defensive reading of the armour motif in ch. 5, one I did not follow in my exegesis of that passage. In Ephesians the rhetorical momentum is from the outset in the direction of the image of the empowered community, called, finally, to take up the armour and thus also the role of the Divine Warrior. That suffering does and will play a role in the battle with the powers is not denied by the author; it is simply not an important part of the picture of the community of saints as Divine Warrior.

The recalling of the dimension of suffering in the image of Paul as prisoner must thus serve a different purpose than setting a model. The placing of Paul in chains, who then requests the community *qua* Divine Warrior to see to it that he receive the openness of mouth to say what he has to say with boldness (παρρησιάσωμαι ὡς δεῖ με λαλῆσαι) once again places the community in a relationship of superiority *vis-à-vis* Paul.[171] The saints are thus both themselves recipients *and* deliverers of help. It would go too far to say that the community replaces God. But its function and its location ἐν τοῖς ἐπουρανίοις (2.6) put it in a very good position to play the role of heavenly ἀντιλαμβανόμενος. Thus the relationship between Paul and the saints that has been redactionally controlled throughout Ephesians is retained here. The means of that control introduce a note of irony in that Paul is an ambassador with good news who nevertheless appears in chains—a messenger with (ostensibly) restricted movement; the saints, on the other hand, are free as the Divine Warrior to wage war at the highest level, indeed to see to it that their hero Paul be given the mouth and the confidence to announce the mystery.

The strategy of the author of Ephesians is clearly to inflate the sense of power with which the saints enter the fray of battle. Whereas in 2 Cor. 6.7 and 10.4 Paul describes himself as warrior, he reserves the image of

Wild, 'Warrior', pp. 289-94. What is inexplicably lacking is any appreciation by Wild of παρρησία as stance and behaviour of the conqueror or liberator. It would have served his argument well.

171. Cf. Wis. 10.21 where σοφία as ῥυόμενη (v. 15) opens the mouths of the dumb so that they can sing praises and hymns to God's defending hand. Note that the holy and blameless ones sing as those who are dependent on God's and/or wisdom's deliverance. Paul is precisely in this position in Ephesians; the community of saints, however, is not.

the Divine Warrior for the community in 1 Thessalonians 5, illustrating that in his mind this motif has considerably different connotations than that of the 'fortified philosopher'. Faithful to Paul's precedent, in Ephesians the image of Paul as warrior is muted. He serves rather as the δίκαιος who confronts, encourages, reveals the mystery to the church, but who in the end is dependent on the help of the Divine Warrior to get him through. The community as Divine Warrior is summoned to participate in delivering that help.

5. *Observations*

The Ephesian picture of the armour is intended to convey completeness, not least by its characterization as 'πανοπλία' in 6.11 and 13. The community of saints is clothed and armed with an impressive list of divine virtues, attributes, and covenant dynamics which render it capable of fighting the battle of and with the 'gods': ἀλήθεια, δικαιοσύνη, ἑτοιμασία, εἰρήνη, πίστις, σωτηρία, πνεῦμα, and ῥῆμα. These are symbolically represented by belt, breastplate, footware, shield, helmet, and sword. To suggest that this is not a full armour, and that there are several items missing, such as lance and bow, fails to recognize the degree to which the sword functions as representative of divine warfare against enemies in traditional divine war texts, the tradition in relation to which the author of Ephesians desires the motif here to be read.[172] More important, the image of God as the Divine Warrior itself suggests that there is no interest in downplaying any aggressive or at least initiatory elements in the image, most especially given who the enemies are, namely, the full array of powers. Were the enemy simply 'blood and flesh', then everything that is known about the disposition of Ephesians toward the human community would call for the 'taking off' of the armour; the cross (2.16) would have taken on greater relief, as would images of inclusion and transformation. Inasmuch as 1 Thessalonians 5 would have functioned as precedent, the ironical nature of this battle would have been exploited more fully. The panoply might have included then also ἀγάπη, as Paul does in 1 Thess. 5.8. Here, however, the struggle *on behalf of* blood and flesh is identified as battle with the διάβολος and his powers, and the author is interested in conjuring a picture of the complete Divine Warrior who is up to the challenge, as well as in

172. Whereas Yahweh is described on a few occasions as carrying a spear (חנית, Ps. 35.3 and Hab. 3.11), the LXX translates it as ὅπλον.

stressing those values or virtues that can be seen as confrontations with the hostile powers.

That the image could have been further expanded and elaborated is shown by its appropriation in Wisdom of Solomon and 1 Thessalonians, as well as by the symbolic elaboration of dress and armour of the divine militia in Qumran's War Scroll. But the image of the Divine Warrior in armour is itself already shorthand, as in Isaiah 59 and most especially 1 Thessalonians 5, for the overwhelming greatness of effective power that sees to it that justice, truth, and peace are 'waged' and finally prevail. In the end, that is a disposition friendly to victims, who in Ephesians are the human community as such at the hands of the prince of the power(s) of the air (2.1, 2). The most startling dimension of the Ephesian picture is the degree to which the author is prepared not simply to reiterate in parenetic fashion the precedent of 1 Thessalonians, but to take from Paul permission to reinterpret Scripture (Isaiah 59) afresh by placing the community quite deliberately into the role of the Divine Warrior at war with the 'gods' of the air.

If one asks what this transfer of the armour of the Divine Warrior to the community of saints means in Ephesians, a rather wide range of answers suggests itself. First of all, the fact that the armour is made up of largely ethically identifiable virtues ties the image closely to the performance of 'good works' (2.10). Those 'works' should in turn be seen in relation to building up the body of Christ (4.11-13), and thus to participation in the ἀνακεφαλαίωσις of the cosmos (1.10). The image of the warrior serves thus to recapitulate the parenetic interests of the letter as a whole. But to implicate the community of saints in the ἀνακεφαλαίωσις of the cosmos by means of the image of the saints in the divine armour suggests that that process is best described not only by imagery of growth and evolution (2.21-22; 4.13), but as a battle at the very frontlines of cosmic hostility to God's economy of grace (ἡ οἰκονομία τῆς χάριτος τοῦ θεοῦ, 3.2).

Insofar as the saints perform this role not only 'in the heavenlies' but on the earth, the Divine Warrior is here interpreted as democratized and functioning within the *Alltag*.[173] The image is not thereby simply ethicized, however. The confrontation with darkness in the everyday is precisely engagement in battle with the διάβολος and his δύναμεις. To that extent the 'virtues' are not simply the virtues familiar within the performance of ethical responsibilities, but nothing less than the dynamics of

173. So also Wild, 'Warrior', p. 298.

divine engagement in human affairs. It is thus not appropriate, against virtually all commentators who speak always of 'the [individual] Christian', to exegete this image in individualistic terms of the Christian taking strength from God for a faithful and moral life marked by resistance to temptations.[174] But neither is it in keeping with the intentions of the author to see in this a mythologized image of the fortified soul engaged in struggle with hostile powers.[175] Rather, the author of Ephesians combines in a radical way the Pauline ecclesiology of Christ, or, vice versa, his Christology of the church, with the messianic task of overcoming the powers *à la* 1 Corinthians 15. And since the relationship between God and his surrogate regarding agency has always been intentionally fuzzy,[176] the author of Ephesians exploits exactly that ambiguity by placing the church in the role of God in the struggle of reconciliation, one profound facet of which is the subjugation of the powers.

The image of the Divine Warrior as treated in Ephesians lends itself to a mythologizing of the role of the church or of the place of believers in the cosmos.[177] But it can also invite a certain demythologization or at least 'immanentization' of the powers, and, for that matter, of the heavenlies, and thus finally also of the process of how the powers are vanquished.[178] As the earlier discussion of Ephesians has indicated, the lines between earth and heaven, between mythologically painted realities and ethically and socially lived reality, are not clearly drawn—or better, they are deliberately smudged. The effect is, however, that the interpretive possibilities multiply and that a final definitive interpretation which is persuasive to everyone becomes impossible. The diversity of interpretations in the *Wirkungsgeschichte* of Eph. 6.10-20 illustrates that.[179] This

174. E.g. Ign. *Pol.* 6.2, Clem. Alex. *Protrept.* 11.116.2.

175. E.g. Clem. Alex. *Exc. Theod.* 72.1-85.3.

176. See here especially the way Ps. 110.1 was applied to a victorious Christ in 1 Corinthians 15 and the rearticulation of Ps. 68 in Eph. 4. This is endemic to the whole tradition of royal ideology as it applies to the question of agency in warfare.

177. This is illustrated by later gnostic appropriations of this motif of conflict with the powers, e.g. *Hyp. Arch.* NHC 2.4.20-27, and especially also *Teach. Silv.* NHC 7.84.15-118.9, and *Ep. Pet. Phil.* NHC 8.2.135-38. See discussion in Wild, 'Warrior', pp. 294-97.

178. Correctly perceived by Wink, *Naming the Powers*, pp. 89-96.

179. 'Die Paraklese geht in immer neue geschichtliche Kontexte ein, reflektiert das römische Militärwesen, setzt sich vom gnostischen Dualismus ab, wird zur Ermunterung für das Martyrium, erfaßt das Mönchtum, beeinflußt den Humanismus und bewegt wieder anders die Mystik' (Schnackenburg, *Brief*, p. 349). See literature

is also shown by the history of recent scholarship. The approach taken here has been to explore what interpretive possibilities suggest themselves when the text is read as the youngest in a series of attempts to elucidate the meaning of the Isaianic image of the Divine Warrior in armour, with the consciousness of standing in a stream of interpretation.

there on the *Wirkungsgeschichte* on pp. 349-55. For a broader discussion cf. also von Harnack, *Militia Christi*, pp. 12-31.

CONCLUSION

Several important features have emerged in the study of the texts which stand in the shared tradition of the Divine Warrior in full armour, often in great relief. Polarities of light and darkness, of impiousness and righteousness, of judgment and salvation constitute the frame of reference for the treatment of the Divine Warrior in Isaiah 59, Wisdom of Solomon 5, 1 Thessalonians 5, and Ephesians 6, the last representing the culmination of this tradition within the biblical literature. The mythological image of the Divine Warrior—the arming and dressing of the warrior deity for battle—is recognized by all the authors of these texts as a forceful expression of the power and inevitability of divine intervention both in judgment and salvation. Each author recognizes and exploits the metaphorical possibilities of the motif. Divine intervention is interpreted as the presence and exercise of divine qualities, virtues, and actions in each of these texts, not least in Ephesians.

Third Isaiah takes the familiar motif of Yahweh as Divine Warrior and fashions it into a highly usable and reusable one. The author of the Wisdom of Solomon refashions the motif in relation to the fate of Second Isaiah's servant. In 1 Thessalonians 5 Paul takes the breathtaking step of placing the confused and even fearful Thessalonians into God's armour, thereby implicating them in the invasion of the Divine Warrior. Moreover, the surprise element of that divine intrusion is heightened by the nature of that participation—the militant exercise of faith, love, and the hope of salvation. In important ways Ephesians builds on the groundwork of 1 Thessalonians 5, most particularly in the turning upside down of the scenario of retaliation and agency: the fearsome intervention of God the warrior in Isaiah 59 and Wisdom of Solomon 5 comes now in the form of a community of children of light, eager and ready to announce peace, but only after being victorious over the enemies of blood and flesh.

Paul's innovation in democratizing Isaiah's Divine Warrior in 1 Thessalonians 5 is thus reasserted and subjected to further reflection and elaboration in Ephesians. However, whereas one can speak of a certain pacification of the Divine Warrior in 1 Thessalonians 5, Ephesians provides yet another twist. In all the previous treatments of the scenario of divine warfare within this trajectory, the enemies are the human community. The ironical element in 1 Thessalonians consists of the fact that the human enemies, living in darkness, are being surprised by the Divine Warrior who, in the form of the 'sons of day'—themselves recruited from the ranks of those who sit in darkness—exercises the warfare of faith, love, and the hope of salvation. While peace, love, and reconciliation are crucially important in Ephesians (see especially ch. 2), the image of the warrior is intentionally painted in aggressive and confrontative colours. That is because the enemies are the hostile powers 'in the heavenlies,' not the people who sit under their dominion. There is thus something quite traditional and unironic about the image of the warrior in Ephesians—reaching back to the tradition prior to 1 Thessalonians—in that this Divine Warrior really is out to conquer hostile enemies, the powers. The objectives of the irony in 1 Thessalonians are retained, however, in that the battle is fought not *against* human beings, but *on their behalf*, ultimately on behalf of the reconciling intentions of God, namely, to gather up all things in Christ (Eph. 1.10).

The 'pacification' one can observe in 1 Thessalonians 5, implied in the ironical warfare of love, gives way in Ephesians to the hostile confrontation with the equally hostile powers of the διάβολος. The image of the confrontation of the Divine Warrior with his enemies has been turned on its head: whereas in Isaiah 59 and Wisdom of Solomon 5 it was the heavenly Divine Warrior who warred against human earthly enemies, in Ephesians 6 it is the earthly human (at the same time heavenly) community of saints which now confronts heavenly powers.The 'experiment in transcendence', to use Georgi's felicitous phrase, observed in 1 Thessalonians 5 and anticipated in the Wisdom of Solomon, comes to full flower in Ephesians. The saints participate in God's activity as cosmic warrior.

In conclusion, the particular trajectory of the larger tradition of the Divine Warrior—Isaiah 59, Wisdom of Solomon 5, 1 Thessalonians 5, and finally Ephesians 6—has proven to be a rich and creative sapiential tradition of appropriation, reformulation, and transformation of the motif of the Divine Warrior. Each of the texts, including Isaiah 59, gives ample evidence of conscious rearticulation and reinterpretation of known traditions. Each of these texts can also be assumed to grow out of not the solitary imagination of an individual author, but out of the inspired give and take of communal reflection on inheritance and tradition. The *traditum* has controlled the *traditio*; *traditio* has in turn shaped the *traditum*. In no way does that mitigate the creative and even radical participation in the divine task of prophecy. Ephesians is a splendid culmination of that process within the biblical canon.

BIBLIOGRAPHY

Abbott, T.K., *Epistles to the Ephesians and to the Colossians* (ICC; Edinburgh: T. & T. Clark, 1897).

Achtemeier, E., *The Community and Message of Isaiah 56–66* (Minneapolis: Augsburg, 1982).

Ackroyd, P.R., *Exile and Restoration: A Study of Hebrew thought of the Sixth Century BC* (London: SCM Press, 1968).

Aejmelaeus, L., *Wachen vor dem Ende: Die traditionsgeschichtliche Wurzeln von 1. Thess 5.1-11 und Luk 21.34-36* (Suomen Eksegeettisen Seuran Julkaisuja, 44; Helsinki, 1985).

Aeneas Tacticus, 'On the Defense of Fortified Positions', in *Aeneas Tacticus, Asclepiodotus, Onasander* (LCL; London: Heinemann; New York: Putnam's Sons, 1923).

Albrektson, B., *History and the Gods: An Essay on the Idea of Historical Events as Divine Manifestations in the Ancient Near East and in Israel* (Lund: Gleerup, 1967).

Anderson, A.A., *The Book of Psalms* (NCBC; 2 vols.; Grand Rapids: Eerdmans, 1972).

Arnold, C.E., *Ephesians: Power and Magic: The Concept of Power in Ephesians in Light of its Historical Setting* (SNTSMS, 63; Cambridge: Cambridge University Press, 1989).

—'The "Exorcism" of Ephesians 6.12 in Recent Research: A Critique of Wesley Carr's View of the Role of Evil Powers in First-Century AD Belief', *JSNT* 30 (1987), pp. 71-87.

Bach, R., *Die Aufforderungen zur Flucht und zum Kampf im alttestamentlichen Prophetenspruch* (WMANT, 9; Neukirchen–Vluyn: Neukirchner Verlag, 1962).

Balch, D.J., *Let Wives be Submissive: The Domestic Code in 1 Peter* (SBLMS, 26; Chico, CA: Scholars Press, 1981).

Barth, M., *Ephesians: Introduction, Translation, and Commentary* (AB, 34, 34A; Garden City, NY: Doubleday, 1974).

—'Traditions in Ephesians', *NTS* 30 (1984), pp. 3-25.

Barton, J., *Oracles of God: Perceptions of Ancient Prophecy in Israel after the Exile* (London: Darton, Longman and Todd, 1986).

Berkhof, H., *Christ and the Powers* (trans. J.H. Yoder; Kitchener, ON: Herald Press, 1977).

Bertram, G., 'κατεργάζομαι', *TDNT*, III, pp. 634-35.

Best, E., *A Commentary on the First and Second Epistles to the Thessalonians* (BNTC; London: A. & C. Black, 1972).

Betz, H.D., *Nachfolge und Nachahmung Jesu Christi im Neuen Testament* (BHT, 37; Tübingen: Mohr [Siebeck], 1967).

Bickermann, E., *Studies in Jewish and Christian History, Part 1* (AGJU, 9; Leiden: Brill, 1976).
Billerbeck, P., *Die Briefe des Neuen Testaments und der Offenbarung Johannis* (H.L. Strack and P. Billerbeck, *Kommentar zum Neuen Testament aus Talmud und Midrasch* [München: Beck, 1954], III).
Blenkinsopp, J., *A History of Prophecy in Israel* (Philadelphia: Westminster Press, 1983).
—'Interpretation and the Tendency to Sectarianism: An Aspect of the Second Temple History', in E.P. Sanders, A.I. Baumgarten, and A. Mendelson (eds.), *Jewish and Christian Self-Definition*. II. *Aspects of Judaism in the Graeco-Roman Period* (Philadelphia: Fortress Press, 1981), pp. 1-26.
Brandenburger, E., *Frieden im Neuen Testament: Grundlinien urchristlichen Friedensverständnisses* (Gütersloh: Gütersloher Verlagshaus/Gerd Mohn, 1973).
Brown, F., Driver, S.R., and C. Briggs, *A Hebrew and English Lexicon of the Old Testament* (Oxford: Clarendon Press, 1907 [abbrev. BDB]).
Brown, J.P., 'Peace Symbolism in Ancient Military Vocabulary', *VT* 21 (1971), pp. 1-23.
Bruce, F.F., *1 & 2 Thessalonians* (WBC, 45; Waco, TX: Word Books, 1982).
Brueggemann, W., 'Unity and Dynamic in the Isaiah Tradition', *JSOT* 29 (1984), pp. 89-107.
Bultmann, R., *Theology of the New Testament* (trans. K. Grobel; 2 vols.; New York: Charles Scribner's Sons, 1951, 1955).
Bultmann, R., and A. Weiser, 'πιστεύω, κτλ', *TDNT*, VI, pp. 174-228.
Caird, G.B., *Principalities and Powers: A Study in Pauline Theology* (Oxford: Clarendon Press, 1956).
Carr, W., *Angels and Principalities: The Background, Meaning, and Development of the Pauline Phrase hai archai kai hai exousiai* (SNTSMS, 42; Cambridge: Cambridge University Press, 1981).
Carrington, P., *The Primitive Christian Catechism* (Cambridge: Cambridge University Press, 1940).
Carroll, R.P., 'Second Isaiah and the Failure of Prophecy', *ST* 32 (1978), pp. 119-31.
—*When Prophecy Failed: Reactions and Responses to Failure in the Old Testament Prophetic Traditions* (London: SCM Press, 1979).
Charlesworth, J.H. (ed.), *The Old Testament Pseudepigrapha*. I. *Apocalyptic Literature and Testaments* (Garden City, NY: Doubleday, 1983).
—(ed.), *The Old Testament Pseudepigrapha*. II. *Expansions of the 'Old Testament' and Legends, Wisdom and Philosophical Literature, Prayers, Psalms, and Odes, Fragments of Lost Judeo-Hellenistic Works* (Garden City, NY: Doubleday, 1985).
Childs, B.S., 'The Canonical Shape of the Prophetic Literature', *Int* 32 (1978), pp. 46-55.
Clements, R.E., *Isaiah 1–39* (NCBC; Grand Rapids: Eerdmans, 1980).
Coggins, R., A. Phillips and M. Knibb (eds.), *Israel's Prophetic Tradition: Essays in Honour of Peter R. Ackroyd* (Cambridge: Cambridge University Press, 1982).
Collins, J.J., *Between Athens and Jerusalem: Jewish Identity in the Hellenistic Diaspora* (New York: Crossroad, 1983).
—'Cosmos and Salvation: Jewish Wisdom and Apocalyptic in the Hellenistic Age', *HR* 17 (1977), pp. 121-42.
Conzelmann, H., *Der Brief and die Epheser*, in H.W. Beyer *et al.*, *Die kleineren Briefe*

des Apostels Paulus (NTD, 8; Göttingen: Vandenhoeck & Ruprecht, 1962), pp. 56-91.

Crenshaw, J.L., 'Popular Questioning of the Justice of God in Ancient Israel', *ZAW* 82 (1970), pp. 380-95; reprinted in J.L. Crenshaw (ed.), *Studies in Ancient Israelite Wisdom* (LBS; New York: Ktav, 1976), pp. 289-304.

— (ed.), *Studies in Ancient Israelite Wisdom* (LBS; New York: Ktav, 1976).

Cross, F.M., *Canaanite Myth and Hebrew Epic: Essays in the History of the Religion of Israel* (Cambridge, MA: Harvard University Press, 1973).

—'The Council of Yahweh in Second Isaiah', *JNES* 12 (1953), pp. 274-77.

—'The Divine Warrior in Israel's Early Cult', in A. Altmann (ed.), *Biblical Motifs: Origins and Transformations* (Studies and Texts, 3; Cambridge, MA: Harvard University Press, 1966), pp. 11-30; now in Cross, *Canaanite Myth,* pp. 79-111.

—'The Song of the Sea and Canaanite Myth', *JTC* 5 (1968), pp. 1-25.

Crouch, J.E., *The Origin and Intention of the Colossian Haustafel* (FRLANT, 109; Göttingen: Vandenhoeck & Ruprecht, 1971).

Dahood, M., SJ, *Psalms Vols. I–III* (AB 16-17A; Garden City, NY: Doubleday, 1966–70).

Dassmann, E., *Der Stachel im Fleisch: Paulus in der frühchristlichen Literatur bis Irenäus* (Münster: Aschendorff, 1979).

Day, J., *God's Conflict with the Dragon and the Sea: Echoes of a Canaanite Myth in the Old Testament* (Cambridge: Cambridge University Press, 1985).

De Vries, S.J., 'Observations on Quantitative and Qualitative Time in Wisdom and Apocalyptic', in J.G. Gammie *et al.* (eds.), *Israelite Wisdom: Theological and Literary Essays in Honor of Samuel Terrien* (Missoula, MT: Scholars Press, 1978), pp. 263-76.

Delling, G., 'ἡμέρα', *TDNT*, II, pp. 943-53.

Dibelius, M., and H. Greeven, *An die Kolosser, Epheser, an Philemon* (HNT, 12; Tübingen: Mohr [Siebeck], 3rd edn, 1953).

Dinkler, E., *Eirene: Der urchristliche Friedensgedanke* (Heidelberg: Carl Winter/ Universitätsverlag, 1973).

Dobschütz, E. von, *Die Thessalonicher-Briefe* (ed. F. Hahn; Göttingen: Vandenhoeck & Ruprecht, 1974 [1909]).

Ducrey, P., *Warfare in Ancient Greece* (trans. J. Lloyd; New York: Schocken Books, 1985).

Duhm, B., *Das Buch Jesaia* (4th edn; HAT; Göttingen: Vandenhoeck & Ruprecht, 1968 [1892]).

Eaton, J., 'The Isaiah Tradition', in Coggins, *et al* (eds.), *Israel's Prophetic Tradition*, pp. 58-76.

Edgar, T.R., 'The Meaning of Sleep in I Thessalonians 5.10', *JETS* 22 (1979), pp. 344-49.

Eissfeldt, O., *The Old Testament: An Introduction* (trans. P.R. Ackroyd; New York: Harper & Row, 1965).

Elliger, K., *Die Einheit des Tritojesaja* (BWANT, 45; Stuttgart: Kohlhammer, 1928).

—'Der Prophet Tritojesaja', *ZAW* 49 (1931), pp. 112-41.

Elliott, J.H., *A Home for the Homeless: A Sociological Exegesis of 1 Peter, its Situation and Strategy* (Philadelphia: Fortress Press, 1981).

Emonds, H., OSB, 'Geistlicher Kriegsdienst: Der Topos der militia spiritualis in der antiken Philosphie', in *Heilige Überlieferung: Ausschnitte aus der Geschichte des*

Mönchtums und des heiligen Kultes (Münster: Aschendorff, 1938), pp. 21-50; reprinted in Harnack, *Militia Christi* (1963), pp. 133-62.

Ernst, J., *Die Briefe an die Philipper, an Philemon, and die Kolosser, und die Epheser* (Regensburg: Pustet, 1974).

Fichtner, J., 'Der Alttestamentliche Text der Sapientia Salomonis', *ZAW* 16 (1939), pp. 155-92.

—'Jesaja unter den Weisen', *ThLZ* 74 (1949), pp. 75-80; reprinted as 'Isaiah among the Wise', trans. B.W. Kovacs, in Crenshaw (ed.), *Studies in Ancient Israelite Wisdom*, pp. 429-38.

Fischer, J., *Das Buch Isaias* (Bonn: Peter Hanstein, 1939).

Fischer, K.-M., *Tendenz und Absicht des Epheserbriefs* (FRLANT, 3; Göttingen: Vandenhoeck & Ruprecht, 1973).

Fishbane, M., *Biblical Interpretation in Ancient Israel* (Oxford: Clarendon Press, 1985).

Fohrer, G., *Das Buch Jesaja III* (Zürcher Bibelkommentar; Zürich: Zwingli Verlag, 1964).

Fredriksson, H., *Jahwe als Krieger: Studien zum alttestamentlichen Gottesbild* (Lund: Gleerup, 1945).

Frend, W.H.C., *Martyrdom and Persecution in the Early Church: A study of a Conflict from the Maccabees to Donatus* (Oxford: Basil Blackwell, 1965).

Friedrich, G., '1 Thessalonicher 5.1-11: Der apologetische Einschub eines Späteren', *ZTK* 10 (1993), pp. 288-315.

Gammie, J.G. *et al.* (eds.), *Israelite Wisdom: Theological and Literary Essays in Honor of Samuel Terrien* (Missoula, MT: Scholars Press, 1978).

Gaugler, E., *Der Epheserbrief* (Auslegung Neutestamentlicher Schriften, 6; Zürich: EVZ, 1966).

Georgi, D.,'Gott auf den Kopf stellen: Überlegungen zu Tendenz und Kontext des Theokratiegedankens in paulinischer Praxis und Theologie', in J. Taubes (ed.), *Theokratie* (Religionstheorie und Politische Theologie, 3; Munich: Fink; Paderborn: Schöningh, 1987), pp. 148-205.

—*The Opponents of Paul in Second Corinthians* (trans. and rev. edn; *Die Gegner des Paulus im 2. Korintherbrief: Studien zur Religiösen Propaganda in der Spätantike* [1964] with 1984 'Epilogue' [Philadelphia: Fortress Press, 1984]).

—'Der Vorpaulinische Hymnus, Phil 2,6-11', in E. Dinkler (ed.), *Zeit und Geschichte: Dankesgabe an Rudolf Bultmann zum 80. Geburtstag* (Tübingen: Mohr, 1964).

—*Weisheit Salomos: Unterweisung in lehrhafter Form.* III. *Jüdische Schriften aus hellenistisch-römischer Zeit* (Gütersloh: Gütersloher Verlagshaus/Gerd Mohn, 1980).

—'Das Wesen der Weisheit nach der "Weisheit Salomos"', in J. Taubes (ed.), *Gnosis und Politik* (Religionstheorie und Politische Theologie, 2; Munich: Fink; Paderborn: Schöningh, 1984), pp. 66-81.

Gilbert, M., ''Wisdom Literature', in M.E. Stone (ed.), *Jewish Writings of the Second Temple Period* (Philadelphia: Fortress Press, 1984), pp. 301-13.

Gnilka, J., *Der Epheserbrief* (Freiburg: Herder, 1971).

Good, R.M., 'The Just War in Ancient Israel', *JBL* 104 (1985), pp. 385-400.

Goodspeed, E.J., *The Meaning of Ephesians* (Chicago: University of Chicago Press, 1956).

Gottwald, N.K., *The Hebrew Bible: A Socio-Literary Introduction* (Philadelphia: Fortress Press, 1985).

—'"Holy War" in Deuteronomy: Analysis and Critique', *RevExp* 61 (1964), pp. 269-310.

—*The Tribes of Yahweh: A Sociology of the Religion of Liberated Israel 1250–1050 BCE* (Maryknoll, NY: Orbis Books, 1979).

—'War, Holy', *IDBSup* (1976), pp. 942-44.

Greeven, H., 'πάλη', *TDNT*, V (1967), p. 721.

Greßmann, H., *Der Ursprung der israelitisch-jüdischen Eschatologie* (FRLANT, 6; Göttingen: Vandenhoeck & Ruprecht, 1905).

Grundmann, W., 'δύναμαι, κτλ', *TDNT*, II (1964), pp. 284-317.

—'ἕτοιμος, κτλ', *TDNT*, II (1964), pp. 704-6.

—'ἰσχύω, κτλ', *TDNT*, III (1965), pp. 397-402.

—'στήκω, ἵστημι', *TDNT*, VII (1971), pp. 636-53.

Hanson, P.D., *The Dawn of Apocalyptic* (Philadelphia: Fortress Press, 1975).

—'Isaiah 52.7-10', *Int* 33 (1979), pp. 389-94.

—'Jewish Apocalyptic Against its Near Eastern Environment', *RB* 78 (1971), pp. 31-58.

—'Old Testament Apocalyptic Reexamined', *Int* 25 (1971), pp. 454-79; reprinted in Hanson (ed.), *Visionaries and Their Apocalypses*, pp. 37-60.

—*The People Called: The Growth of Community in the Bible* (San Francisco: Harper & Row, 1986).

Hanson, P.D. (ed.), *Visionaries and Their Apocalypses* (IRT, 4; Philadelphia: Fortress Press; London: SPCK, 1983).

Harnack, A. von., *Militia Christi: Die christliche Religion und der Soldatenstand in den ersten drei Jahrhunderten* (Darmstadt: Wissenschaftliche Buchgesellschaft, 1963 [Tübingen: Mohr, 1905]).

Harnisch, W., *Eschatologische Existenz: Ein exegetischer Beitrag zum Sachanliegen von I. Thessalonicher 4,13–5,11* (Göttingen: Vandenhoeck & Ruprecht, 1973).

Hay, D.M., *Glory at the Right Hand: Psalm 110 in Early Christianity* (SBLMS, 18; Nashville/New York: Abingdon Press, 1973).

Helfmeyer, F.J., *Die Nachfolge Gottes im Alten Testament* (BBB, 29; Bonn: Peter Hanstein, 1968).

Hendrix, H.L., 'Thessalonicans Honor Romans' (PhD dissertation, Harvard University, 1984).

—Review of P. Jewett, *The Thessalonian Correspondence: Pauline Rhetoric and Millenarian Piety* (Philadelphia: Fortress Press, 1986; *JBL* 107 [1988]), pp. 763-66.

Hiebert, T., *God of My Victory: The Ancient Hymn in Habakkuk 3* (HSM, 38; Atlanta: Scholars Press, 1986).

Hoppe, L.J., 'The School of Isaiah', *TBT* 23 (1985), pp. 85-89.

Houlden, J.L., *Paul's Letters From Prison: Philippians, Colossians, Philemon, and Ephesians* (Westminster Pelican Commentaries; Philadelphia: Westminster Press, 1977).

Jaubert, A., 'Les Sources de la Conception Militaire de L'Eglise en 1 Clément 37', *VC* 18 (1964), pp. 74-84.

Jensen, J., OSB, *Isaiah 1–39* (OTM, 8; Wilmington, DE: Glazier, 1984).

—*The Use of tôrâ by Isaiah: His Debate with the Wisdom Tradition* (CBQMS, 3; Washington, DC: Catholic Biblical Association, 1973).

Jeremias, Joachim, 'παῖς θεοῦ', *TDNT*, V (1967), pp. 654-717.

Jeremias, Jörg, *Theophanie: Die Geschichte einer alttestamentlichen Gattung* (Neukirchen–Vluyn: Neukirchener Verlag, 2nd edn, 1977).
Jewett, P., *The Thessalonian Correspondence: Pauline Rhetoric and Millenarian Piety* (Philadelphia: Fortress Press, 1986).
Jones, G.H., '"Holy War" or "Yahweh War"?', *VT* 25 (1975), pp. 642-58.
Kaiser, O., *Isaiah 1–12: A Commentary* (trans. R.A. Wilson; Philadelphia: Westminster Press, 1972).
—*Isaiah 13–39: A Commentary* (trans. R.A. Wilson; Philadelphia: Westminster Press, 1974).
Kamlah, E., *Die Form der katalogischen Paränese im Neuen Testament* (Tübingen: Mohr [Siebeck], 1964).
Käsemann, E., 'Das Interpretationsproblem des Epheserbriefes', *ThLZ* 86 (1961), pp. 1-8.
Kendall, D., SJ, 'The Use of Mispat in Isaiah 59', *ZAW* 96 (1984), pp. 391-405.
Kennedy, G.A., *New Testament Interpretation Through Rhetorical Criticism* (Chapel Hill: University of North Carolina Press, 1984).
Kirby, J.C., *Ephesians, Baptism and Pentecost: An Inquiry into the Structure and Purpose of the Epistle to the Ephesians* (London: SPCK, 1968).
Knight, G.A.F., *Isaiah 56–66* (ITC; Grand Rapids: Eerdmans, 1985).
Koch, K., *The Growth of the Biblical Tradition: The Form-Critical Method* (trans. S.M. Cupitt; New York: Charles Scribner's Sons, 1969).
—*The Prophets*. II. *The Babylonian and Persian Periods* (trans. M. Kohl; Philadelphia: Fortress Press, 1982).
Koester, H., '1 Thessalonians—Experiment in Christian Writing', in F.F. Church and T. George (eds.), *Continuity and Discontinuity in Church History: Essays Presented to George Huntston Williams* (SHCT, 19; Leiden: Brill, 1979), pp. 33-44.
—'Apostel und Gemeinde in den Briefen an die Thessalonicher', in D. Lührmann and G.Strecker (eds.), *Kirche: Festschrift für Günther Bornkamm* (Tübingen: Mohr [Siebeck], 1980), pp. 287-98.
—*Introduction to the New Testament*. II. *History and Literature of Early Christianity* (Philadelphia: Fortress Press, 1982).
Kuhn, K.G., 'The Epistle to the Ephesians in the Light of the Qumran Texts', in J. Murphy-O'Connor (ed.), *Paul and Qumran* (Chicago: Priory, 1968), pp. 111-18.
Kümmel, W.G., *Introduction to the New Testament* (trans. H.C. Kee; Nashville: Abingdon Press, 17th rev. edn, 1975).
Larcher, C., OP, *Études sur le Livre de la Sagesse* (Paris: Librairie Lecoffre, 1969).
—*Le Livre de la Sagesse ou la Sagesse de Salomon* (3 vols.; Paris: Librairie Lecoffre, 1984).
Lash, S.J.A.,'Where Do Devils Live? A Problem in the Textual Criticism of Eph 6.12', *VC* 20 (1976), pp. 161-74.
Laub, F., *Eschatologische Verkündigung und Lebensgestaltung nach Paulus: Eine Untersuchung zum Wirken des Apostels beim Aufbau der Gemeinde in Thessalonike* (Münchner Universitätsschriften; Regensburg: Friedrich Pustet, 1973).
Lincoln, A.T., *Paradise Now and Not Yet: Studies in the Role of the Heavenly Dimension in Paul's Thought with Special Reference to his Eschatology* (Cambridge: Cambridge University Press, 1981).
—'A Reexamination of "the Heavenlies" in Ephesians', *NTS* 19 (1973), pp. 468-83.

—'The Use of the Old Testament in Ephesians', *JSNT* 14 (1982), pp. 16-57.
Lind, M.C., *Yahweh is a Warrior: The Theology of Warfare in Ancient Israel* (Scottdale, PA/Kitchener, ON: Herald Press, 1980).
Lindblom, J., *Prophecy in Ancient Israel* (Oxford: Basil Blackwell, 1973).
Lindemann, A., *Die Aufhebung der Zeit: Geschichtsverständnis und Eschatologie im Epheserbrief* (Gütersloh: Gerd Mohn, 1975).
—*Der Epheserbrief* (Zürcher Bibelkommentare NT 8; Zürich: Theologischer Verlag, 1985).
—*Paulus im ältesten Christentum: Das Bild des Apostels in der frühchristlichen Literatur bis Marcion* (BHT, 58; Tübingen: Mohr, 1979).
Lohse, E., *Die Texte aus Qumran: Hebräisch und deutsch* (Munich: Kösel, 1964).
Lona, H.E., *Die Eschatologie im Kolosser- und Epheserbrief* (Würzburg: Echter Verlag, 1984).
Long, B.O., 'The Social World of Ancient Israel', *Int* 36 (1982), pp. 243-55.
Lüdemann, G., *Paul, Apostle to the Gentiles: Studies in Chronology* (trans. F.S. Jones; Philadelphia: Fortress Press, 1984).
Lührmann, D., 'Neutestamentliche Haustafeln und antike Ökonomie', *NTS* 27 (1980), pp. 83-97.
Macgregor, G.H.C., 'Principalities and Powers: The Cosmic Background of Saint Paul's Thought', *NTS* 1 (1954), pp. 17-28.
Malherbe, A.J., 'Antisthenes and Odysseus, and Paul at War', *HTR* 76 (1983), pp. 143-73.
—'"Gentle as a Nurse." The Cynic Background to I Thess ii', *NovT* 12 (1970), pp. 203-17.
—*Paul and the Thessalonians: The Philosophic Tradition of Pastoral Care* (Philadelphia: Fortress Press, 1987).
Mann, T.W., *Divine Presence and Guidance in Israelite Traditions: The Typology of Exaltation* (Baltimore/ London: The Johns Hopkins University Press, 1977).
Marshall, I.H., *1 and 2 Thessalonians* (NCBC; Grand Rapids: Eerdmans 1983).
Mason, R., 'The prophets of the restoration', in Coggins, *et al.* (eds.), *Israel's Prophetic Tradition*, pp. 137-54.
McKane, W., *Prophets and Wise Men* (SBT, 44; London: SCM Press, 1965).
McKenzie, J.L., *Second Isaiah* (AB 20; Garden City, NY: Doubleday, 1968).
Meade, D.G., *Pseudonymity and Canon: An Investigation into the Relationship of Authorship and Authority in Jewish and Earliest Christian Tradition* (WUNT, 39; Tübingen: Mohr, 1986).
Meeks, W.A., *The First Urban Christians: The Social World of the Apostle Paul* (New Haven: Yale University Press, 1983).
Melugin, R.F., 'Isaiah 52.7-10', *Int* 36 (1982), pp. 176-81.
Mendenhall, G.E., *The Tenth Generation: The Origins of the Biblical Tradition* (Baltimore/London: The Johns Hopkins University Press, 1973).
Mgogo, E.K.M., 'The Democratization of the Royal Ideology in the New Testament and Related Literature' (ThD dissertation, Harvard University Divinity School, 1975).
Michaelis, W., 'κράτος, κτλ', *TDNT*, III (1965), pp. 905-915.
—'μάχαιρα', *TDNT*, IV (1967), pp. 524-27.
—'μεθοδεία', *TDNT*, V (1967), pp. 102-3.

Miletic, S.F., *'One Flesh': Eph. 5.22-24, 5.31: Marriage and the New Creation* (AnBib, 115; Rome: Biblical Institute Press, 1988).
Miller, P.J., 'The Divine Council and the Prophetic Call to War', *VT* 18 (1968), pp. 100-107.
—*The Divine Warrior in Early Israel* (HSM, 5; Cambridge, MA: Harvard University Press, 1973).
—'El the Warrior', *HTR* 60 (1967), pp. 411-31.
—'God the Warrior: A Problem in Biblical Interpretation and Apologetics', *Int* 19 (1965), pp. 39-46.
Mitton, C.L., *The Epistle to the Ephesians: Its Authorship, Origin and Purpose* (Oxford: Clarendon Press, 1951).
Mowinckel, S., *The Psalms in Israel's Worship* (trans. D.R. Ap-Thomas; 2 vols.; New York/Nashville: Abingdon Press, 1962).
Muilenburg, J., 'The Book of Isaiah, Chapters 40–66', in G.A. Buttrick (ed.), *The Interpreter's Bible* (New York/Nashville: Abingdon Press, 1956), V, pp. 381-773.
Munro, W., *Authority in Paul and Peter: The Identification of a Pastoral Stratum in the Pauline Corpus and 1 Peter* (Cambridge: Cambridge University Press, 1983).
Murphy, R.E., 'Wisdom—Theses and Hypotheses', in J.G. Gammie, *et al.* (eds.), *Israelite Wisdom*, pp. 35-42.
Mußner, F., *Der Brief an die Epheser* (Ökumenischer Taschenbuchkommentar zum Neuen Testament, 10; Gütersloh: Gerd Mohn, Echter Verlag, 1982).
—*Christus, das All und die Kirche* (Trier: Paulus, 1955).
Nickelsburg, G.W.E., *Jewish Literature Between the Bible and the Mishnah: A Historical and Literary Introduction* (Philadelphia: Fortress Press, 1981).
—*Resurrection, Immortality, and Eternal Life in Intertestamental Judaism* (HTS, 26; Cambridge: Harvard University Press, 1972).
Odeberg, H., *Trito-Isaiah: A Literary and Linguistic Analysis* (Uppsala: Lundeqvist, 1931).
Oepke, A., *Die Briefe an die Thessalonicher* (NTD, 8; *Die kleineren Briefe des Apostels Paulus;* Göttingen: Vandenhoeck & Ruprecht, 1970 [1933]), pp. 122-52.
—and K.G. Kuhn, 'ὅπλον, κτλ', *TDNT*, V (1967), pp. 292-315.
Ollenburger, B.C., *Zion, the City of the Great King: A Theological Symbol of the Jerusalem Cult* (JSOTSup, 41; Sheffield: JSOT Press, 1987).
Orlinsky, H.M., *Essays in Biblical Culture and Bible Translation* (New York: Ktav, 1974).
Pauritsch, K., *Die neue Gemeinde: Gott sammelt Ausgestoßene und Arme (Jesaia 56–66)* (AnBib, 47; Rome: Biblical Institute Press, 1971).
Pearson, B., '1 Thessalonians 2.13-16: A Deutero-Pauline Interpolation', *HTR* 64 (1971), pp. 79-94.
Pedersen, J., *Israel: Its Life and Culture* (3 vols.; London: Geoffrey Cumberlege, Oxford University Press, 1926-40).
Peel, M.L., and J. Zandee, 'The Teachings of Silvanus', in *The Nag Hammadi Library in English* (intr. and trans. M.L. Peel and J. Zandee, ed. F. Wisse; New York: Harper & Row, 1977).
Percy, E., *Die Probleme der Kolosser- und Epheserbriefe* (Lund: Gleerup, 1946).
Petersen, D.L., *Late Israelite Prophecy: Studies in Deutero-Prophetic Literature and in Chronicles* (SBLMS, 23; Missoula, MT: Scholars Press, 1977).

Petersen, D.L. (ed.), *Prophecy in Israel: Search for an Identity* (IRT, 10; Philadelphia: Fortress Press; London: SPCK, 1987).
Pfammatter, J., *Epheserbrief/Kolosserbrief* (Die Neue Echterbibel: Neues Testament; Würzburg: Echter Verlag, 1987).
Pfitzner, V.G., *Paul and the Agon Motif: Traditional Athletic Imagery in the Pauline Literature* (NovTSup, 16; Leiden: Brill, 1967).
Pietersma, A., and C. Cox (eds.), *De Septuaginta: Studies in Honour of John William Wevers* (Mississauga, ON: Benben, 1984).
Plevnik, J., '1 Thess. 5.1-11: Its Authenticity, Intention and Message', *Bib* 60 (1979), pp. 71-90.
Plöger, O., *Theocracy and Eschatology* (trans. S. Rudman; Oxford: Basil Blackwell, 1968).
Pokorny, P., *Der Epheserbrief und die Gnosis: Die Bedeutung des Haupt- Gliedergedankens in der entstehenden Kirche* (Berlin: Evangelische Verlagsanstalt, 1965).
Polan, G.J., OSB, 'Salvation in the midst of Struggle', *TBT* 23 (1985), pp. 90-97.
Priest, J.F., 'Where is Wisdom To Be Placed?', *JAAR* 31 (1963), pp. 275-82; reprinted in Crenshaw (ed.), *Studies in Ancient Israelite Wisdom*, pp. 281-88.
Pritchard, J.B. (ed.), *The Ancient Near East: An Anthology of Texts and Pictures* (Princeton: Princeton University Press, 1958).
Rad, G. von, *Der Heilige Krieg im alten Israel* (Göttingen: Vandenhoeck & Ruprecht, 5th edn, 1969 [1951]).
—*Deuteronomy: A Commentary* (OTL; trans. D. Barton; Philadelphia: Westminster Press, 1966).
—*Old Testament Theology*. I. *The Theology of Israel's Historical Traditions* (trans. D.M.G. Stalker; New York: Harper & Row, 1962).
—*Old Testament Theology*. II. *The Theology of Israel's Prophetic Traditions* (trans. D.M.G. Stalker; New York: Harper & Row, 1965).
Reese, J.M., OSFS, *1 and 2 Thessalonians* (Wilmington, DE: Michael Glazier, 1979).
—*Hellenistic Influence on the Book of Wisdom and its Consequences* (Rome: Biblical Institute Press, 1970).
Rigaux, B., OFM, *Saint Paul: Les épîtres aux Thessaloniciens* (EBib; Paris: Gabalda, 1956).
—'Tradition et rédaction dans 1 Th. 5.1-10', *NTS* 21 (1974–75), pp. 318-40.
Ringgren, H., *Word and Wisdom: Studies in the Hypostatization of Divine Qualities and Functions in the Ancient Near East* (Lund: Hakan Ohlssons, 1947).
Robinson, J.M. (director), *The Nag Hammadi Library in English* (trans. members of the Coptic Gnostic Library Project of the Institute for Antiquity and Christianity; New York/San Francisco: Harper & Row, 1977).
Robinson, J.M., and H. Koester, *Trajectories through Early Christianity* (Philadelphia: Fortress Press, 1971).
Roon, A. van, *The Authenticity of Ephesians* (Leiden: Brill, 1974).
Rowland, C., *The Open Heaven: A Study of Apocalyptic in Judaism and Early Christianity* (London: SPCK, 1982).
Rubinkiewicz, R., 'Ps LXVIII 19 (=Eph IV 8). Another Textual Tradition or Targum?' *NovT* 17 (1975), pp. 219-24.
Schenke, H.-M., and K.M. Fischer, *Einleitung in die Schriften des Neuen Testaments*. I. *Die Briefe des Paulus und Schriften des Paulinismus* (Gütersloh: Gütersloher Verlagshaus/Gerd Mohn, 1978).

Schlier, H., *Der Brief an die Epheser: Ein Kommentar* (Düsseldorf: Patmos, 7th edn, 1971).
—*Christus und die Kirche im Epheserbrief* (BHT, 6, 1930; repr. 1966).
—*Principalities and Powers in the New Testament* (trans. from German; Freiburg: Herder; Edinburgh/London: Nelson, 1961).
Schmid, H.H., 'Heiliger Krieg und Gottesfrieden im Alten Testament', in *idem*, *Altorientalische Welt in der alttestamentlichen Theologie: Sechs Aufsätze* (Zürich: Theologischer Verlag, 1974).
—*Salôm: Frieden im Alten Orient und im Alten Testament* (SBS, 51; Stuttgart: Katholisches Bibelwerk, 1971).
—*Wesen und Geschichte der Weisheit: Eine Untersuchung zur altorientalischen und israelitischen Weisheitsliteratur* (Berlin: Töpelmann, 1966).
Schmithals, W., *Paul and the Gnostics* (trans. J.E. Steely; Nashville: Abingdon Press, 1972).
Schmitt, A., *Das Buch der Weisheit: Ein Kommentar* (Würzburg: Echter Verlag, 1986).
Schnackenburg, R., *Der Brief an die Epheser* (EKKNT, 10; Zürich: Benziger; Neukirchen–Vluyn: Neukirchener Verlag, 1982).
Schneider, J.,'ἔρχομαι, κτλ', *TDNT*, II, pp. 666-75.
Schnelle, U., 'Der erste Thessalonicherbrief und die Entstehung der paulinischen Anthropologie', *NTS* 32 (1986), pp. 207-24.
Schrage, W., 'Zur Ethik der neutestamentlichen Haustafeln', *NTS* 21 (1974/75), pp. 1-22.
Schroeder, D., 'Die Haustafeln des Neuen Testaments: Ihre Herkunft und ihr theologischer Sinn' (DTheol dissertation, Hamburg University, 1959).
Schüssler Fiorenza, E., *In Memory of Her: A Feminist Theological Reconstruction of Christian Origins* (New York: Crossroad, 1983).
Schwally, F., *Semitische Kriegsaltertümer, Erstes Heft: Der heilige Krieg im alten Israel* (Leipzig: Dieterich'sche Verlagsbuchhandlung, Theodor Weicher, 1901).
Schweizer, E., 'Die Kirche als Leib Christi in den paulinischen Antilegomena.', *TLZ* 86 (1961), pp. 241-56.
Scott, R.B.Y., 'The Book of Isaiah, Chapters 1–39', in G.A. Buttrick (ed.), *The Interpreter's Bible* (New York/Nashville: Abingdon, 1956), V, pp. 151-381.
—*The Way of Wisdom in the Old Testament* (New York: Macmillan, 1971).
Scullion, J., SJ, *Isaiah 40–66* (OTM, 12; Wilmington, DW: Michael Glazier, 1982).
Shaberg, J., 'Major Midrashic Traditions in Wisdom 1.1-6, 25', *JSJ* 13 (1982), pp. 75-101.
Skehan, P.W., 'Isaias and the Teaching of the Book of Wisdom', *CBQ* 2 (1940), pp. 89-99.
Smart, J.D., *History and Theology in Second Isaiah: A Commentary on Isaiah 35, 40–66* (Philadelphia: Westminster Press, 1965).
Smend, R., *Jahwekrieg und Stämmebund: Erwägungen zur ältesten Geschichte Israels* (Göttingen: Vandenhoeck & Ruprecht, 1963).
Smith, M., *Palestinian Parties and Politics That Shaped the Old Testament* (New York: Columbia University Press, 1971).
Smyth, H.W., *Greek Grammar* (rev. G.M. Messing; Cambridge, MA: Harvard University Press, 1920/1956 [abbrev. Smyth]).
Snaith, N.H., 'Isaiah 40–66: A Study of the Teaching of the Second Isaiah and its Consequences', in H.M. Orlinsky and N.H. Snaith, *Studies on the Second Part of*

the Book of Isaiah (VTSup, 14; Leiden: Brill, 1977), pp. 135-264.

Soggin, A.J., 'Der prophetische Gedanke über den heiligen Krieg, als Gericht gegen Israel', *VT* 10 (1960), pp. 79-83.

Steck, O.H., 'Der Rachetag in Jesaja LXI 2: Ein Kapitel redaktionsgeschichtlicher Kleinarbeit', *VT* 36 (1986), pp. 323-38.

Steinmetz, F.-J., *Protologische Heilszuversicht: Die Strukturen des soteriologischen und christologischen Denkens im Kolosser- und Epheserbrief* (Frankfurter Theologische Studien, 2; Frankfurt am Main: Josef Knecht, 1969).

Stolz, F., *Jahwes und Israels Kriege: Kriegstheorien und Kriegserfahrungen im Glauben des alten Israels* (Zürich: Theologischer Verlag, 1972).

Stone, M.E., 'Three Transformations in Judaism: Scripture, History, and Redemption', *Numen* 32 (1985), pp. 218-35.

Stuhlmacher, P., '"Er ist unser Friede" (Eph 2,14). Zur Exegese und Bedeutung von Eph 2,14-18', in Stuhlmacher, *Versöhnung, Gesetz und Gerechtigkeit: Aufsätze zur biblischen Theologie* (Göttingen: Vandenhoeck & Ruprecht, 1981).

Stuhlmueller, C., *Psalms*, I *(Psalms 71–72)* (OTM, 21; Wilmington, DE: Glazier, 1983).

—*Psalms*, II *(Psalms 73–150)* (OTM, 22; Wilmington, DE: Glazier, 1983).

Suggs, M.J., 'Wisdom of Solomon 2.10-5: A Homily on the Fourth Servant Song', *JBL* 76 (1957), pp. 26-33.

Taylor, W., 'Ephesians 6.10-24 and the Genre of Ephesians', (Pauline Epistles Section, SBL, 1985).

Toombs, L.E., 'War, ideas of', *IDB* 4 (1962), pp. 796-801.

Torrey, C.C., *The Second Isaiah* (New York: Charles Scribner's Sons, 1928).

Volz, P., *Jesaia II: Kommentar zum Alten Testament* (Leipzig: Scholl, 1932; Hildesheim/New York: Georg Olms, 1974).

Walter, N., '"Hellenistische Eschatologie" im Neuen Testament', in E. Grässer and O. Merk (eds.), *Glaube und Eschatologie* (Festschrift Werner Georg Kümmel; Tübingen: Mohr [Siebeck], 1985), pp. 335-56.

Ward, J.M., 'The Servant's Knowledge in Isaiah 40–50', in Gammie, *et al.* (eds.), *Israelite Wisdom*, pp. 121-36.

Weinfeld, M., 'Ancient Near Eastern Patterns in Prophetic Literature', *VT* 27 (1977), pp. 178-95.

—'Divine Intervention in War in Ancient Israel and in the Ancient Near East', in H. Tadmor and M. Weinfeld (eds.), *History, Historiography and Interpretation: Studies in Biblical and Cuneiform Literatures* (Jerusalem: Magus, 1983), pp. 121-47.

Weippert, M., '"Heiliger Krieg" in Israel und Assyrien: Kritische Anmerkungen zu Gerhard von Rads Konzept des "Heiligen Krieges im alten Israel"', *ZAW* 84 (1972), pp. 460-93.

Weiser, A. *The Psalms: A Commentary* (OTL; Philadelphia: Westminster Press, 1962).

Wengst, K., *Pax Romana, Anspruch und Wirklichkeit: Erfahrungen und Wahrnehmungen des Friedens bei Jesus und im Urchristentum* (Munich: Chr. Kaiser Verlag, 1986).

Westermann, C., *Basic Forms of Prophetic Speech* (trans. H.C. White; Philadelphia: Westminster Press, 1967).

—*Isaiah 40–66: A Commentary* (trans. D.M.G. Stalker; Philadelphia: Westminster Press, 1969).

Whedbee, J.W., *Isaiah and Wisdom* (Nashville/New York: Abingdon Press, 1971).

Whybray, R.N., *Isaiah 40–66* (NCBC; Grand Rapids: Eerdmans, 1981 [1975]).

—'Prophecy and Wisdom', in Coggins *et al.* (eds.), *Israel's Prophetic Tradition*, pp. 181-99.

Wild, R.A., SJ,'"Be Imitators of God": Discipleship in the Letter to the Ephesians', in F.F. Segovia (ed.), *Discipleship in the New Testament* (Philadelphia: Fortress Press, 1985), pp. 127-43.

—'The Warrior and the Prisoner: Some Reflections on Ephesians 6.10-20', *CBQ* 46 (1984), pp. 284-98.

Wilson, R.R., *Prophecy and Society in Ancient Israel* (Philadelphia: Fortress Press, 1980).

Wink, W., *Naming the Powers: The Language of Power in the New Testament* (The Powers, 1; Philadelphia: Fortress Press, 1984).

Winston, D., *The Wisdom of Solomon: A New Translation with Introduction and Commentary* (AB, 43; Garden City, NY: Doubleday, 1979).

Yarbro Collins, A., *The Combat Myth in the Book of Revelation* (Missoula, MT: Scholars, 1976).

Yoder, J.H., *The Politics of Jesus* (Kitchener, ON: Herald Press, 1972).

Ziegler, J. (ed.), *Isaias–Septuaginta* (Vetus Testamentum Graecum Auctoritate Academiae Litterarum Gottingensis editum, 14; Göttingen: Vandenhoeck & Ruprecht, 1967).

—*Sapientia Salomonis. Septuaginta* (Vetus Testamentum Graecum Auctoritate Academiae Litterarum Gottingensis editum, 12.1; Göttingen: Vandenhoeck & Ruprecht, 1962).

Indexes

Index of References

Old Testament

INDEX OF AUTHORS

JOURNAL FOR THE STUDY OF THE NEW TESTAMENT
SUPPLEMENT SERIES

1 W.R. Telford, *The Barren Temple and the Withered Tree: A Redaction-Critical Analysis of the Cursing of the Fig-Tree Pericope in Mark's Gospel and its Relation to the Cleansing of the Temple Tradition*
2 E.A. Livingstone (ed.), *Studia Biblica 1978, II: Papers on the Gospels (Sixth International Congress on Biblical Studies, Oxford, 1978)*
3 E.A. Livingstone (ed.), *Studia Biblica 1978, III: Papers on Paul and Other New Testament Authors (Sixth International Congress on Biblical Studies, Oxford, 1978)*
4 E. Best, *Following Jesus: Discipleship in the Gospel of Mark*
5 M. Barth, *The People of God*
6 J.S. Pobee, *Persecution and Martyrdom in the Theology of Paul*
7 C.M. Tuckett (ed.), *Synoptic Studies: The Ampleforth Conferences of 1982 and 1983*
8 T.L. Donaldson, *Jesus on the Mountain: A Study in Matthean Theology*
9 S. Farris, *The Hymns of Luke's Infancy Narratives: Their Origin, Meaning and Significance*
10 R. Badenas, *Christ the End of the Law: Romans 10.4 in Pauline Perspective*
11 C.J. Hemer, *The Letters to the Seven Churches of Asia in their Local Setting*
12 D.L. Bock, *Proclamation from Prophecy and Pattern: Lucan Old Testament Christology*
13 R.P. Booth, *Jesus and the Laws of Purity: Tradition History and Legal History in Mark 7*
14 M.L. Soards, *The Passion According to Luke: The Special Material of Luke 22*
15 T.E. Schmidt, *Hostility to Wealth in the Synoptic Gospels*
16 S.H. Brooks, *Matthew's Community: The Evidence of his Special Sayings Material*
17 A.T. Hanson, *The Paradox of the Cross in the Thought of St Paul*
18 C. Deutsch, *Hidden Wisdom and the Easy Yoke: Wisdom, Torah and Discipleship in Matthew 11.25-30*
19 L.J. Kreitzer, *Jesus and God in Paul's Eschatology*
20 M.D. Goulder, *Luke: A New Paradigm*
21 M.C. Parsons, *The Departure of Jesus in Luke–Acts: The Ascension Narratives in Context*
22 M.C. de Boer, *The Defeat of Death: Apocalyptic Eschatology in 1 Corinthians 15 and Romans 5*
23 M. Prior, *Paul the Letter-Writer and the Second Letter to Timothy*
24 J. Marcus & M.L. Soards (eds.), *Apocalyptic and the New Testament: Essays in Honor of J. Louis Martyn*
25 D.E. Orton, *The Understanding Scribe: Matthew and the Apocalyptic Ideal*
26 T.J. Geddert, *Watchwords: Mark 13 in Markan Eschatology*

27 C.C. Black, *The Disciples according to Mark: Markan Redaction in Current Debate*
28 D. Seeley, *The Noble Death: Graeco-Roman Martyrology and Paul's Concept of Salvation*
29 G.W. Hansen, *Abraham in Galatians: Epistolary and Rhetorical Contexts*
30 F.W. Hughes, *Early Christian Rhetoric and 2 Thessalonians*
31 D.R. Bauer, *The Structure of Matthew's Gospel: A Study in Literary Design*
32 K. Quast, *Peter and the Beloved Disciple: Figures for a Community in Crisis*
33 M.A. Beavis, *Mark's Audience: The Literary and Social Setting of Mark 4.11-12*
34 P.H. Towner, *The Goal of our Instruction: The Structure of Theology and Ethics in the Pastoral Epistles*
35 A.P. Winton, *The Proverbs of Jesus: Issues of History and Rhetoric*
36 S.E. Fowl, *The Story of Christ in the Ethics of Paul: An Analysis of the Function of the Hymnic Material in the Pauline Corpus*
37 A.J.M. Wedderburn (ed.), *Paul and Jesus: Collected Essays*
38 D.J. Weaver, *Matthew's Missionary Discourse: A Literary Critical Analysis*
39 G.N. Davies, *Faith and Obedience in Romans: A Study in Romans 1–4*
40 J.L. Sumney, *Identifying Paul's Opponents: The Question of Method in 2 Corinthians*
41 M.E. Mills, *Human Agents of Cosmic Power in Hellenistic Judaism and the Synoptic Tradition*
42 D.B. Howell, *Matthew's Inclusive Story: A Study in the Narrative Rhetoric of the First Gospel*
43 H. Räisänen, *Jesus, Paul and Torah: Collected Essays* (trans. D.E. Orton)
44 S. Lehne, *The New Covenant in Hebrews*
45 N. Elliott, *The Rhetoric of Romans: Argumentative Constraint and Strategy and Paul's Dialogue with Judaism*
46 J.O. York, *The Last Shall Be First: The Rhetoric of Reversal in Luke*
47 P.J. Hartin, *James and the Q Sayings of Jesus*
48 W. Horbury (ed.), *Templum Amicitiae: Essays on the Second Temple Presented to Ernst Bammel*
49 J.M. Scholer, *Proleptic Priests: Priesthood in the Epistle to the Hebrews*
50 D.F. Watson (ed.), *Persuasive Artistry: Studies in New Testament Rhetoric in Honor of George A. Kennedy*
51 J.A. Crafton, *The Agency of the Apostle: A Dramatistic Analysis of Paul's Responses to Conflict in 2 Corinthians*
52 L.L. Belleville, *Reflections of Glory: Paul's Polemical Use of the Moses–Doxa Tradition in 2 Corinthians 3.1-18*
53 T.J. Sappington, *Revelation and Redemption at Colossae*
54 R.P. Menzies, *The Development of Early Christian Pneumatology, with Special Reference to Luke–Acts*
55 L.A. Jervis, *The Purpose of Romans: A Comparative Letter Structure Investigation*

56 D. Burkett, *The Son of the Man in the Gospel of John*
57 B.W. Longenecker, *Eschatology and the Covenant: A Comparison of 4 Ezra and Romans 1–11*
58 D.A. Neale, *None but the Sinners: Religious Categories in the Gospel of Luke*
59 M. Thompson, *Clothed with Christ: The Example and Teaching of Jesus in Romans 12.1–15.13*
60 S.E. Porter (ed.), *The Language of the New Testament: Classic Essays*
61 J.C. Thomas, *Footwashing in John 13 and the Johannine Community*
62 R.L. Webb, *John the Baptizer and Prophet: A Socio-Historical Study*
63 J.S. McLaren, *Power and Politics in Palestine: The Jews and the Governing of their Land, 100 BC–AD 70*
64 H. Wansbrough (ed.), *Jesus and the Oral Gospel Tradition*
65 D.A. Campbell, *The Rhetoric of Righteousness in Romans 3.21-26*
66 N. Taylor, *Paul, Antioch and Jerusalem: A Study in Relationships and Authority in Earliest Christianity*
67 F.S. Spencer, *The Portrait of Philip in Acts: A Study of Roles and Relations*
68 M. Knowles, *Jeremiah in Matthew's Gospel: The Rejected-Prophet Motif in Matthaean Redaction*
69 M. Davies, *Rhetoric and Reference in the Fourth Gospel*
70 J.W. Mealy, *After the Thousand Years: Resurrection and Judgment in Revelation 20*
71 M. Scott, *Sophia and the Johannine Jesus*
72 S.M. Sheeley, *Narrative Asides in Luke–Acts*
73 M.E. Isaacs, *Sacred Space: An Approach to the Theology of the Epistle to the Hebrews*
74 E.K. Broadhead, *Teaching with Authority: Miracles and Christology in the Gospel of Mark*
75 J. Kin-Man Chow, *Patronage and Power: A Study of Social Networks in Corinth*
76 R.W. Wall & E.E. Lemcio, *The New Testament as Canon: A Reader in Canonical Criticism*
77 R. Garrison, *Redemptive Almsgiving in Early Christianity*
78 L.G. Bloomquist, *The Function of Suffering in Philippians*
79 B. Charette, *The Theme of Recompense in Matthew's Gospel*
80 S.E. Porter & D.A. Carson (eds.), *Biblical Greek Language and Linguistics: Open Questions in Current Research*
81 In-Gyu Hong, *The Law in Galatians*
82 B.W. Henaut, *Oral Tradition and the Gospels: The Problem of Mark 4*
83 C.A. Evans & J.A. Sanders (eds.), *Paul and the Scriptures of Israel*
84 M.C. de Boer (ed.), *From Jesus to John: Essays on Jesus and New Testament Christology in Honour of Marinus de Jonge*
85 W.J. Webb, *Returning Home: New Covenant and Second Exodus as the Context for 2 Corinthians 6.14–7.1*

86 B.H. McLean (ed.), *Origins of Method: Towards a New Understanding of Judaism and Christianity—Essays in Honour of John C. Hurd*
87 M.J. Wilkins & T. Paige (eds.), *Worship, Theology and Ministry in the Early Church: Essays in Honour of Ralph P. Martin*
88 M. Coleridge, *The Birth of the Lukan Narrative: Narrative as Christology in Luke 1–2*
89 C.A. Evans, *Word and Glory: On the Exegetical and Theological Background of John's Prologue*
90 S.E. Porter & T.H. Olbricht (eds.), *Rhetoric and the New Testament: Essays from the 1992 Heidelberg Conference*
91 J.C. Anderson, *Matthew's Narrative Web: Over, and Over, and Over Again*
92 E. Franklin, *Luke: Interpreter of Paul, Critic of Matthew*
93 J. Fekkes, *Isaiah and Prophetic Traditions in the Book of Revelation: Visionary Antecedents and their Development*
94 C.A. Kimball, *Jesus' Exposition of the Old Testament in Luke's Gospel*
95 D.A. Lee, *The Symbolic Narratives of the Fourth Gospel: The Interplay of Form and Meaning*
96 R.E. DeMaris, *The Colossian Controversy: Wisdom in Dispute at Colossae*
97 E.K. Broadhead, *Prophet, Son, Messiah: Narrative Form and Function in Mark 14–16*
98 C.J. Schlueter, *Filling up the Measure: Polemical Hyperbole in 1 Thessalonians 2.14-16*
99 N. Richardson, *Paul's Language about God*
100 T.E. Schmidt & M. Silva (eds.), *To Tell the Mystery: Essays on New Testament Eschatology in Honor of Robert H. Gundry*
101 J.A.D. Weima, *Neglected Endings: The Significance of the Pauline Letter Closings*
102 J.F. Williams, *Other Followers of Jesus: Minor Characters as Major Figures in Mark's Gospel*
103 W. Carter, *Households and Discipleship: A Study of Matthew 19–20*
104 C.A. Evans & W.R. Stegner (eds.), *The Gospels and the Scriptures of Israel*
105 W.P. Stephens (ed.), *The Bible, the Reformation and the Church: Essays in Honour of James Atkinson*
106 J.A. Weatherly, *Jewish Responsibility for the Death of Jesus in Luke–Acts*
107 E. Harris, *Prologue and Gospel: The Theology of the Fourth Evangelist*
108 L.A. Jervis & P. Richardson (eds.), *Gospel in Paul: Studies on Corinthians, Galatians and Romans for R.N. Longenecker*
109 E.S. Malbon & E.V. McKnight (eds.), *The New Literary Criticism and the New Testament*
110 M.L. Strauss, *The Davidic Messiah in Luke–Acts: The Promise and its Fulfillment in Lukan Christology*
111 I.H. Thomson, *Chiasmus in the Pauline Letters*
112 J.B. Gibson, *The Temptations of Jesus in Early Christianity*
113 S.E. Porter & D.A. Carson (eds.), *Discourse Analysis and Other Topics in Biblical Greek*

114 L. Thurén, *Argument and Theology in 1 Peter: The Origins of Christian Paraenesis*
115 S. Moyise, *The Old Testament in the Book of Revelation*
116 C.M. Tuckett (ed.), *Luke's Literary Achievement: Collected Essays*
117 K.G.C. Newport, *The Sources and Sitz im Leben of Matthew 23*
118 T.W. Martin, *By Philosophy and Empty Deceit: Colossians as Response to a Cynic Critique*
119 D. Ravens, *Luke and the Restoration of Israel*
120 S.E. Porter & D. Tombs (eds.), *Approaches to New Testament Study*
121 T.C. Penner, *The Epistle of James and Eschatology: Re-reading an Ancient Christian Letter*
122 A.D.A. Moses, *Matthew's Transfiguration Story in Jewish-Christian Controversy*
123 D.L. Matson, *Household Conversion Narratives in Acts: Pattern and Interpretation*
124 D.M. Ball, *'I Am' in John's Gospel: Literary Function, Background and Theological Implications*
125 R.G. Maccini, *Her Testimony is True: Women as Witnesses According to John*
126 B.H. Mclean, *The Cursed Christ: Mediterranean Expulsion Rituals and Pauline Soteriology*
127 R.B. Matlock, *Unveiling the Apocalyptic Paul: Paul's Interpreters and the Rhetoric of Criticism*
128 T. Dwyer, *The Motif of Wonder in the Gospel of Mark*
129 C.J. Davis, *The Names and Way of the Lord: Old Testament Themes, New Testament Christology*
130 C.S. Wansink, *Chained in Christ: The Experience and Rhetoric of Paul's Imprisonments*
131 S.E. Porter & T.H. Olbricht (eds.), *Rhetoric, Scripture and Theology: Essays from the 1994 Pretoria Conference*
132 J.N. Kraybill, *Imperial Cult and Commerce in John's Apocalypse*
133 M.S. Goodacre, *Goulder and the Gospels: An Examination of a New Paradigm*
134 L.J. Kreitzer, *Striking New Images: Studies on Roman Imperial Coinage and the New Testament World*
135 C. Landon, *A Text-Critical Study of the Epistle of Jude*
136 J.T. Reed, *A Discourse Analysis of Philippians: Method and Rhetoric in the Debate over Lierary Integrity*
137 R. Garrison, *The Graeco-Roman Contexts of Early Christian Literature*
138 K. Clarke, *Textual Optimism: The United Bible Societies' Greek New Testament and its Evaluation of Evidence Letter-Ratings*
139 Y.-E. Yang, *Jesus and the Sabbath in Matthew's Gospel: The Background, Significance and Implication*
140 T.R. Yoder Neufeld, *'Put on the Armour of God': The Divine Warrior from Isaiah to Ephesians*